Sara Douglass is one of Australia's leading fantasy writers. Author of the award-winning Axis Trilogy (*BattleAxe, Enchanter* and *StarMan*), *Threshold* and now the Wayfarer Redemption Trilogy (*Sinner, Pilgrim* and *Crusader*), she has also worked her way through three degrees at the University of Adelaide, culminating in a PhD in early modern English history.

Sara has had a number of careers – her most recent as an academic in the Arts Department at La Trobe University, Bendigo. *The Betrayal of Arthur* is her first book with Pan Macmillan.

The BETRAYAL OF ARTHUR

SARA DOUGLASS

PAN
Pan Macmillan Australia

First published 1999 in Macmillan by Pan Macmillan Australia Pty Limited
This edition published 2000 in Pan by Pan Macmillan Australia Pty Limited
St Martins Tower, 31 Market Street, Sydney

Copyright © Sara Douglass Enterprises 1999

Internal illustrations by Shaun Tan

National Library of Australia
cataloguing-in-publication data:

Douglass, Sara.
The betrayal of Arthur.

ISBN 0 330 36219 4.

1. Arthur, King. 2. Arthur, King – Legends. 3. Arthurian
romances – History and criticism. 4. Knights and
knighthood – Legends. I. Title.

809.93351

Typeset by Post Pre-press Group, Brisbane
Printed in Australia by McPherson's Printing Group

Contents

Part IV: The Quest for Arthur

Acknowledgements

This book could not have been written without the help of a number of people: my research assistant on this project, Dr Frances Gladwin, who tracked down some obscure texts in the aisles of the State Library of Victoria; the marvellous Bob Hoffman, of the Australian Online Bookshop (http://www.bookworm.com.au), who procured me some even more obscure texts from dusty corners of the globe; Diana Harrison, for accompanying me through a twenty-four hour Arthurian film fest; my agent, Lyn Tranter, for all her aid over the past five years; and Cate Paterson of Pan Macmillan for being enthused enough by this project to take the risk of paying me some money for it.

Permissions

Many publishers and copyright holders have given me permission to quote from their texts. Thanks to:

- Alan Lupack, Curator of the Robbins Library and co-designer of the Camelot Project (http://www.lib.rochester.edu/camelot/mainmenu.htm), for granting me permission to quote from the Arthurian material available at the web site.
- David Seaman, Director of the Electronic Text Centre (http://etext.lib.virginia.edu/), Alderman Library, University of Virginia, for granting me permission to quote from their etext of Sir Thomas Malory's *Morte Darthur*.
- The editors of *This England* magazine, for granting me permission to quote the opening verse from *Stand Up For England*.
- Charles Burroughs, director of the Centre for Medieval and Early Renaissance Studies, for granting me permission to quote from Donald G. Bzdyl's *Layamon's Brut*.

- E.J. Brill, for granting me permission to quote from Peter Korrel's *An Arthurian Triangle*.
- Harper Collins, UK, for granting me permission to quote from T.H. White's, *The Once and Future King*.
- Hodder and Stoughton Limited for permission to quote from Mary Stewart's, *The Last Enchantment*.
- Hodder and Stoughton Limited for permission to quote from Mary Stewart's *The Crystal Cave* and *The Hollow Hills*.
- William Heinemann Limited for granting me permission to quote from Mary Stewart's *The Crystal Cave* and *The Hollow Hills*.
- Penguin Books Limited for permission to quote from the following books: *The Death of King Arthur* translated by James Cable; *The History of the Kings of Britain* by Geoffrey of Monmouth, translated by Lewis Thorpe; *The Journey Through Wales* and the *Description of Wales* translated by Lewis Thorpe; *King Arthur's Death* translated by Brian Stone; *A History of the English Church and People* by Bede, translated by Leo Sherley-Price.
- All reasonable efforts have been made by myself and the publisher to contact the copyright holders of the quotations contained in this book. In the event that any of the copyright holders or their publishers comes forward after the publication of this edition, the publisher and I will endeavour to rectify the situation accordingly.

Sara Douglass
Bendigo, 1999

Conventions

A thousand years of Arthurian legend contain a myriad variant spellings of names. To avoid confusion I have spelt each name in one way throughout this book, even if the particular text I discuss spells it a different way. However, when I quote from an original medieval manuscript or early modern source I have preserved the pre-modern spelling, but have expanded contractions and replaced antiquated letters with their modern equivalents. For example, 'vnlawfull' becomes 'unlawfull', 'lauifh luft' becomes 'lavish lust'. Below, I list the ways I choose to spell names, some followed by a sample of the variant spellings (or variant names) that have appeared in the past.

ARTHUR: Artos
BEDWYR: Bedevere
GUENEVERE: Gwenevere, Guinevere, Gwenhwyfar, Guenhumara
LANCELOT: Launcelot
MORDRED: Medraut, Medrawt, Medrawd, Medrod
UTHER
YGERNA: Igerne, Igraine, Ygraine
MELIAGAUNT: Meliagaunce
MORGAN LE FAY
MORGAUSE
NIMUE: Vivien

Preface

This is not a factual account of a historic King Arthur – no such account does, or can, exist. Neither is this book meant to be a dry scholarly work more concerned with references than narrative, or a handbook of anything and everything to do with King Arthur and his world. Instead, this is a study of Arthur in his transition from the original medieval accounts to the hero of twentieth-century film and fiction, particularly focussing on the recurring betrayal theme which underpins the entire legend. Our modern image of Arthur is an odd one: while the events of Arthur's life have come down to us relatively unscathed from the medieval legends, popular perceptions of the man have been altered drastically from the original medieval character. The Arthur we see today – in countless films, coffee table books, neo-pagan revivals and even Las Vegas casino re-enactments, complete with fireworks – is an inspirational hero, an almost Christ-like figure from our past who we can believe in and yearn for. But our belief is a misconception – this hero exists neither in fact nor in legend. This modern, sanitised Arthur is a nineteenth-century creation, a medieval character emasculated in order to placate Victorian middle class parlour morality. Consequently, little of the Arthurian legend we have inherited now makes sense to us: how could this great and glorious king have failed? How was it that wife, friend and son could have let him down so badly?

We don't understand the betrayal of Arthur because our modern version of the Arthurian legend has lost most of its original medieval meaning. To truly understand the legendary Arthur (and I make a clear distinction between the legendary Arthur and a possible historic one) we need to understand the crucible from which Arthur emerged: the twelfth to fifteenth centuries. The medieval legend of Arthur depicts a man horribly betrayed from within his own household, but it also makes clear that Arthur's personal failings were the predominant cause of his fate. The medieval Arthur was at first a great and glorious king, true, but he was also a sinner, and it was his sin that brought him crashing down from the heights of glory to utter ruin. In fact, the medieval legends of Arthur depict a man who was ultimately a failure as a king: he began his reign with distinction, but pride, ambition, cruelty and the crippling sins of Eve eventually, inevitably, brought Arthur to personal misfortune and his realm to civil war and destruction. The story of Arthur can be seen as a tragedy – the betrayal of a king by his parents, wife, son and best friend. It is also a moral tale – if one succumbs to sin, even unintentionally, then one necessarily embraces disaster.

Undoubtedly this view of Arthur will be unpopular. Contemporary culture venerates Arthur as a secular Christ figure. In a world which we may feel is increasingly beyond our control, governed by corrupt politicians and bureaucrats, we reach out to the heroes from the past to find something, or someone, worth believing in. In this quest to find a hero – or a saviour we have seized the 'events' of the medieval Arthurian tale, but not the moral. We understand Arthur as a hero who was betrayed by others – a Christ betrayed by a Judas (whether Lancelot, Guenevere or Mordred). We don't want to believe that Arthur himself was so flawed that often in medieval legend he existed only as a foil to reflect the virtues of the characters who surrounded him. And yet this *is* the Arthur of medieval legend – an ordinary man thrust into extraordinary circumstances who tries his best, but whose failings (and the failings of those about him) inevitably lead to disaster.

The Betrayal of Arthur is a study of the man and the household that medieval legend bequeathed us, warts and all, morals and all. It is not a sop to popular culture, nor to popular need. Rather, it is the tale of a man so crippled by the burden of sin bequeathed to him by the medieval mind that he has never escaped, and will never escape, the frightful betrayal that killed him and destroyed his realm.

Because of the immense popularity of the Arthurian legend, and the length of time since its inception, the task of examining its development would prove impossible if the source material were not limited to some extent. Rather than trying to read and refer to everything ever written on Arthur, I have chosen instead to use what I call 'key texts', although these are not my *only* texts: I make extensive use of other materials (I discuss the key texts in Appendix B). I selected the key texts because they were either instrumental in aiding the development of the legend, or are indicative of the legend in any particular age (or both). The source must also concern itself only with the core legend: thus, I could not consider as a key text a modern fantasy novel that relates the adventures of an Arthur reborn into modern society – or some futuristic world – or a medieval romance that concerned itself primarily with the life and adventures of one of Arthur's knights. These key texts necessarily concentrate on Arthur's household, and on the theme of impending doom that characterises all Arthurian stories: the story of Arthur is, after all, a tragedy. Many of the texts come from the medieval period, 1136 to 1485 (Monmouth to Malory) as this was the key development period in the legend. From the period 1485 to 1859 I use only two key texts, the almost unknown Elizabethan drama *The Misfortunes of Arthur* and the mid- to late-nineteenth-century cycle of poems by Alfred Lord Tennyson, *The Idylls of the King*. Why no more from some 400 years of our cultural history? Because during this time the Arthurian legend lay largely quiescent, even the nineteenth-century Arthurian mania contributing little to the legend save a great deal of moralising and even more hype. But in our century the Arthurian legend has undergone renewed transformation, without losing any elements of the core legend, and so to demonstrate this process of this transformation I use seven novels that most readers will be familiar with. All of the key texts, save for Hughes, are easily available and, in the case of the medieval texts, they exist in good modern English translations so that readers of this book can follow their interest if they so choose.[1]

---

1 Virtually all of the medieval texts are available from the Camelot Project, an
   initiative of the University of Rochester, on the WWW at
   http://www.lib.rochester.edu/camelot/mainmenu.htm

I did consider using one or more films as core sources, but in the end I chose not to (although I will discuss the recent television series *Merlin* in my chapter on the wizard). Just as the printing press did in the fifteenth century, film is crippling and destroying the Arthurian legend in our century. Film directors know they can pack only so much into 90 or 120 minutes, and prefer sword-clashing action and horse-back chases to an accurate rendering of the Arthurian legend. Some of the films produced during the 1950s to the 1970s are a curious hash of scenes that produce only bland and silly treatments of the Arthurian legend: *Knights of the Round Table* (1953), *The Black Knight* (1954), *Siege of the Saxons* (1963) and *King Arthur, The Young Warlord* (1975), for example.[2] Those produced in the last twenty years ignore the larger part of the Arthurian legend to concentrate on the Guenevere, Lancelot, and Arthur love triangle (although sword-clashing action remains as a director's favourite). The film *First Knight* is a perfect example of this; it is a trivial, misleading and irrelevant depiction of the Arthurian legend. Its sets are baffling (a mix of Renaissance, Dark Age and nineteenth-century neo-gothic architecture), and its plot inane. The film's only grace is its depiction of Arthur as an aging 'do-nothing' king, preferring to sit in his castle chapel and pray as Lancelot rescues Guenevere from whatever scrape she has got herself into. Other films do manage to explore other aspects of the Arthurian legend – *Excalibur* depicts Lancelot's madness – but because of their restricted space and thus plots, none achieve the depth of the written word. They illuminate only a pitifully tiny part of the Arthurian legend; if western culture must rely on film to carry the legend forward, then we will lose most of our knowledge of Arthur's tragic life. Fortunately, many contemporary novelists are

---

2 Kevin J. Harty, 'Film Treatments of the Legend of King Arthur', in Valerie M. Lagorio and Mildred Leake Day, eds., *King Arthur Through the Ages* (New York, 1990), II, pp. 278–90. Norris J. Lacey, Geoffrey Ashe and Debra N. Mancoff also examine twentieth-century film treatments of the Arthurian legend in *The Arthurian Handbook* (Garland, second edition, 1997), which is particularly good for discussing some of the better European Arthurian films.

still interested in the core legend and are thus far more useful than film script writers in examining the Arthurian legend. It is the wordsmiths who will carry Arthur through into the next millennium.

KEY TEXTS

c. 1136: Geoffrey of Monmouth, *The History of the Kings of Britain*

c. 1250–1280: Layamon, *Brut*

c. 1350s: the Stanzaic *Le Morte Arthur*

c. 1440s: the Alliterative *Morte Arthure*

c. 1450s–1480s: Sir Thomas Malory, *Morte Darthur*

1588: Thomas Hughes, *The Misfortunes of Arthur*

1859–1885: Alfred Lord Tennyson, *The Idylls of the King*

c. 1938–1945: T.H. White, *The Once and Future King*

1963: Rosemary Sutcliff, *Sword at Sunset*

1970–1983: Mary Stewart, *The Crystal Cave, The Hollow Hills, The Last Enchantment, The Wicked Day*

1983: Marion Zimmer Bradley, *The Mists of Avalon*

SUPPORTING TEXTS

c. 540: Gildas, *The Ruin of Britain*

c. 731: Bede, *A History of the English Church and People*

c. 800s: (Nennius) *History of the Britons*

c. 900s: *Annales Cambriae*

c. 1125: William of Malmesbury, *Chronicle of the Kings of England*

c. 1135: Henry of Huntingdon, *Chronicle*

c. 1150–1175: Chretien de Troyes' romances

c. 1188: Gerald of Wales, *Journey Through Wales & Description of Wales*

c. 1230s: *La Mort le Roi Artu*

c. 1330s: Robert Mannyng of Brunne, *The Chronicle*

1534: Polydore Vergil's *History*

1544: John Leland, *The Assertion of King Arthure*

1584: Richard Lloyd, *A Brief Discourse . . . of the Nine Worthies*

I also use two editions of Tennyson: the 1913 edition which has the four original *Idylls* and the 1898 edition which has the twelve updated ones.

The House of Arthur

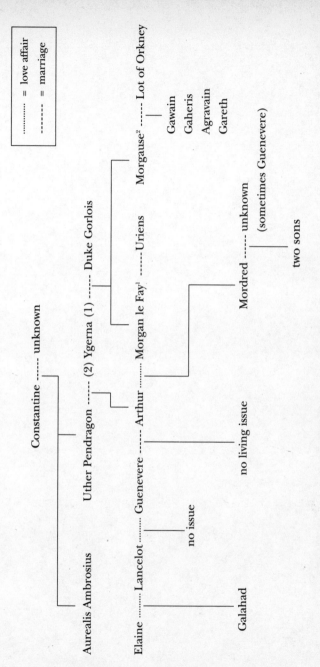

| | = love affair |
| | = marriage |

1 On this family tree I have made Morgan the mother of Arthur's incestuous son, Mordred. In other versions of the tale Morgause is the mother, and in yet other versions Mordred is the nephew of Arthur from an unnamed sister.

2 Sometimes the daughter of Uther and Ygerna.

The Core Arthurian Legend

At the heart of all the variations of Arthur's story is the core Arthurian legend as we know it now. This derives from the medieval *period rather than the Dark Ages (when a historical Arthur would have lived), and contains only tantalising glimmers of historical fact. It is also not exclusively British. By the twelfth century tales of Arthur were widely known in western Europe, especially in Brittany, and French, German and even Spanish and Italian authors and troubadours all contributed to the development of the legend. About Arthur gathered other traditional figures: Lancelot, Tristram and various knights of the Round Table; as well some shadowy reincarnations of the old goddesses of pagan Europe. But in all the variations and permutations of the Arthurian story, there remains the core, the legend that is most widely known and that most explicitly refers to the life of the man who for a few brief, golden years kept the Saxons from his patch of Britain.*

This is the legend to which I refer in the course of this book. It is reasonably lengthy, and contains episodes and characters that many people – familiar only with Arthur and his immediate household – may not be well acquainted with. In the core legend some of the better known characters and situations may also appear subtly different. This can cause some confusion. For example, Morgan le Fay and Morgause are both sisters of Arthur, and both appear at certain times and in certain variations of the legend as the mother of Arthur's son, Mordred. I have chosen to depict Morgan as Mordred's mother, as did most medieval authors (although many modern authors portray Morgause as Arthur's evil-intentioned seductress).

Yet, despite the occasional differences in this core legend to some modern versions, the basic patterns remain. Within all the permutations of plot, and about all the characters, time and legend have woven a tight web of betrayal about Arthur. This king was doomed from conception.

1

In the aftermath of the Roman withdrawal from Britain during the early fifth century, the island descended into chaos. British chieftains and petty kings elected from among themselves a king in an effort to weld together a unified force to repel the Picts, invaders from the north. Eventually a noble named Vortigern gained the throne by murdering the previous incumbent, Constantine. Constantine's two sons, Aurealis Ambrosius and Uther Pendragon, fled to Brittany to avoid being murdered themselves.

As a leader Vortigern was no better and no worse than most, but he made a fatal error. In trying to cope with the increasing threat from the Picts, he invited Saxon mercenaries from Northern Europe to aid his own troops. It was a mistake and allowing the Saxons in by the back door increased, rather than decreased, the rate of invasion.

Driven into his mountain fortress in Wales, Vortigern turned to his magicians, asking them what could be done. The magicians told him to build a high fortress from which he could sally forth to repel the Saxons (or to hide in, if all else failed). Vortigern's masons and engineers attempted to build this fortress, but every attempt ended with the collapse of the fortress walls. Vortigern again consulted the magicians, and they told him that to secure the building, he must find a boy without a father, kill him, then sprinkle his blood over the foundation stones.

Vortigern's men searched until they found a boy named Merlin. Supposedly the son of a demon-incubi and a British princess, Merlin escaped his fate by informing Vortigern that the reason the walls of his fortress fell down was because the foundations lay above a pool in which two dragons slept. The pool subsequently being exposed, Merlin prophesied the return of Aurealis Ambrosius and Uther Pendragon, as well as the rise of a great king named Arthur. This king, Merlin foretold, would weld the British into such an effective force that they would rout the Saxons completely, leading Britain into an era of unprecedented peace and prosperity.

Merlin's initial prophesy quickly came to pass. Within a short time Ambrosius invaded from Brittany, toppling Vortigern and taking the throne of high king for himself. With Ambrosius came his younger brother, Uther. For some years Ambrosius, with Uther as his war-captain, fought against the Saxons. Eventually Ambrosius died, and Uther succeeded him as high king. During the first weeks of his reign, Uther summoned all his war-captains and nobles to a council. Among them came the Duke of Cornwall, Gorlois, with his beautiful and much younger wife, Ygerna, and their small daughter, Morgan. Gorlois also brought with him his son by an earlier marriage, Cador.

Uther had eyes for no-one but Ygerna. He was a man possessed, lusting for the woman, but knowing that he could not wrest her from Gorlois without causing a fatal civil war. Merlin, ever prowling about in darkened corners, offered Uther a solution. He, Merlin, would ensure that Gorlois would take Ygerna back to his cliff top stronghold of Tintagel in Cornwall. Thinking Ygerna safe behind its walls, Gorlois would then ride forth with his troops to keep Uther at bay. Merlin would subsequently arrange matters so that Uther could enter the castle and take Ygerna at his leisure while Gorlois was away.

This also came to pass. Insulted by Uther's obvious lust for his wife, Gorlois took his family back to Tintagel and locked Ygerna and Morgan safely, as he thought, behind its walls while he sallied forth with his soldiers to meet Uther in battle. Late that evening Merlin, Uther and Uther's body-servant slipped away from their camp and rode for Tintagel, some miles away. Using his magical arts, Merlin altered Uther's appearance so that he looked like Gorlois. As a result, Uther was able to ride directly into the stronghold of Tintagel, stride the stairs to Ygerna's chamber and sate his lust even as Ygerna thought she lay with her husband.

On that night, in that bed of deception, Arthur was conceived.

While Ygerna was being unwittingly ravished, Uther's men made a night attack on Gorlois' camp, in which the Duke was killed.[1] His men-at-arms carried their leader's cooling corpse back to Tintagel,

1 In almost every medieval version of the Arthurian legend, the actual time of death of Gorlois – whether it was before Uther entered Ygerna's body and engendered Arthur, or after – has been the pivotal point upon which the entire doom-raddled legend has turned.

only to meet Uther striding down the stairs, Ygerna behind him. Face-to-face with the body of Gorlois (and his own treachery), Uther decided to 'make amends'. He sent for a priest, married Ygerna and installed her as his queen.

Within nine months Ygerna was delivered of a son who she and Uther named Arthur. While he was pleased that he had a son, Uther was only too well aware of the controversy that surrounded the boy's birth. Many among the British whispered that Arthur was the son of Gorlois, not Uther. Amid such rumour Uther would not name the boy his heir. Ygerna could bear him another heir . . . surely. So Uther handed the infant to Merlin who took Arthur into the northern wilds of Britain and fostered him with a trustworthy nobel called Sir Ector, his wife, and their son, Kay.

For fifteen years Uther reigned as high king over the British, constantly fighting to keep the Saxons at bay. Many times Ygerna fell pregnant to her husband, but she bore him no more living sons. Some she miscarried, some died at birth, others were daughters, for which the king had no use. Arthur remained Uther's only son and, as the fighting against the Saxons became more desperate, the aging and sick monarch asked Merlin to bring Arthur back to the court so Uther could name the boy his heir.

Arthur arrived at Uther's court just as the high king died: no-one knows what words passed between the two, or if there was even time for words before Uther succumbed to whatever sickness or poison riddled his body. Some say that Arthur arrived at court only after Uther had died, and that the only way he could prove his claim to the throne of high king was to draw the sword Excalibur from the stone – a feat which could only be achieved by the true heir. Some nobles, notably King Lot, who was married to Morgause, one of the daughters of Ygerna, spoke out strongly against a mere boy succeeding to the throne but, aided by his own prowess, and the subtle aid of Merlin, Arthur held his own against his detractors, and was crowned High King of Britain.

His mother, Ygerna, passed only a few words with her son before she retired to a convent, there to live out her days seeking forgiveness from God for the way she had betrayed Gorlois.

Soon after Arthur's coronation, possibly after his first victory in battle when his blood was hot, his half-sister Morgan came to Arthur, and seduced him into her bed. Arthur did not know her name, nor her blood-link to him, but only rejoiced in the seduction.

Morgan rose from that bed well pleased, for she knew she had conceived of a child from Arthur. That child was a boy, Mordred, and Mordred would grow to be Arthur's doom.

She would have good revenge for the deceit Arthur's father had played upon their mother so many years previous.

Morgan vanished from court, perhaps into the realm of the fairies, with whom she had good dealings, and eventually gave birth to her son. Too late did Arthur hear from Merlin's mouth the deceit that had been played upon him, and at Merlin's instigation, or perhaps even his own, had all boy babies born in the ninth month after that seduction put into a boat and set to sea. Mordred was among them. The boat smashed against rocks, killing all its occupants but one baby – Mordred. He was picked from the beach by a fisherman and eventually found his way through sundry devices into the household of Queen Morgause of Orkney, to be fostered among her own four sons, Gawain, Gaheris, Agravain and Gareth.

Arthur spent most of the first years of his reign subduing internal dissension and invasion, but eventually it was done, a peace made with the Saxons, and Arthur could rest and consider the realm he wanted to build. He decided on a capital, Camelot, built on a hill that overlooked the Island of Apples (or Glastonbury) where stood a Christian abbey. About his own person Arthur gathered a company of knights, or companions, gleaned not only from Britain itself, but from across western Europe. Among these knights was his foster-brother Sir Kay, son of Sir Ector, who Arthur made Seneschal of Britain. Also among them was his half-sister Morgause's eldest son, Gawain, who loved Arthur well, and was loved in return.

The most valiant and noble of these knights was Lancelot du Lake, so named for it was rumoured that the Lady of the Lake had fostered him as a child. Arthur loved Lancelot the best of all his company, and it was Lancelot whom Arthur chose to escort his chosen queen,

Guenevere, from her father Leodegan's realm. With Guenevere came her dowry: the Round Table.

Sending Lancelot to escort Guenevere was a fateful decision. Guenevere and Lancelot could not help loving each other, although many years were to pass before they consummated their love. Lancelot duly delivered the lady into Arthur's care and bed, and so as queen, Guenevere ruled beside Arthur.

But even though Guenevere regarded Arthur well, there was a sadness between them. As with Uther and Ygerna, there was no child, no son to come of their union. Pregnancies came and went, but so too did the miscarriages and stillbirths.

Arthur and Guenevere were to have no heir, save for the son of Arthur's incest.

Meanwhile, the wars resumed. The emperor of Rome taunted Arthur, and Arthur warred on him. There were more invasions, and other kings who thought to test Arthur's strength. Arthur spent many years away from Camelot, and for too many of those years he left Lancelot at home with Guenevere to keep the realm at peace. During these years, the love between Lancelot and Guenevere was finally consummated.

They tried to keep their guilty secret, but many at court wondered and watched, among them Morgause's sons. All five were now at court and the youngest, her foster-son Mordred, watched most closely of all.

It is said that Arthur also knew of the love between his wife and his leading knight – but what was he to do? He loved both Guenevere and Lancelot, and knew that to expose them to public ridicule and wrath would cause more damage than it would heal. So he said nothing.

Sometimes peace seemed an illusion during those years that Arthur stayed in Camelot. His elder half-sister, Morgan, now married to a northern king, Uriens, remained intent on his destruction. Merlin was of little help, as he spent years away from court on travels, and was eventually trapped in a crystal cave by Nimue, the Lady of the Lake. Once Morgan had sent to Arthur's court a magnificent cloak, but just as the king was about to sling it around his shoulders, Nimue (Merlin's successor in magic at Arthur's court) cautioned him against it. Instead, Nimue asked the girl who delivered the cloak to set it about her own shoulders. As soon as she did so the girl fell down dead from the poison that was twined among the weave. Another time, more disastrously, Morgan stole Excalibur and its magical sheath. This sword and sheath protected Arthur from grievous blood loss. Morgan gave the sword to her lover, Accolon, demanding of him that he challenge Arthur.

'With this sword,' she said, 'you will defeat Arthur and I will make you High King.'

Accolon listened to her, and challenged Arthur, but Arthur managed to defeat him even with the sorry sword Morgan had left in Excalibur's place. Arthur retrieved Excalibur from Accolon's dead grip, but he never found the magical sheath, for it is said that Morgan le Fay cast it into the waters of the Lake, where it was never seen again.

Meanwhile, a beautiful lady at the court, Elaine, had fallen in love with Lancelot. But Lancelot neither had eyes nor love for any woman save Guenevere. So Elaine determined to trick Lancelot, perhaps with the aid of Morgan, who was ever ready to cause disruption and tears. Elaine caused him to drink a drugged wine one night. She then had her serving maid tell Lancelot that Guenevere awaited him, but instead the maid led Lancelot to Elaine's chamber. They lay together, and that night Elaine conceived a child of Lancelot. Lancelot was sorely grieved when by morning's light he saw that he had been deceived by Elaine, and left her.

It is said that Lancelot wandered for many years away from court at that time, for Guenevere's anger was truly frightful when she heard he had betrayed her with one of the ladies of court. Elaine returned to her father's house, gave birth to a boy, Galahad, and later committed suicide when Lancelot continued to spurn her love.

Guenevere's place at court became ever more tenuous. Many had cause to be suspicious of her, and not only for reason of Lancelot. In the first years of her marriage Guenevere had been riding out one

May Day when the king of the Summer Country, Melwas, seized her and carried her into captivity in his castle. Some say that there he ravished her, others that she was a willing party to both abduction and rape, but Guenevere always swore her innocence and said her virtue had been unassailed.

It was left to Lancelot to rescue her from Melwas, although Arthur later defeated Melwas in a duel over the matter. In later years, another neighbouring king, Meliagaunt, also captured Guenevere for his own. Again, it was left to Lancelot to ride to the rescue. Guenevere surely lost her honour in Meliagaunt's castle, for although Meliagaunt lay not a finger on her, Lancelot made love with Guenevere in the chamber in which she was being held prisoner. When Meliagaunt discovered blood on Guenevere's sheets (from a wound Lancelot sustained in gaining entry to her chamber), he accused her of sleeping with one of her knights. Guenevere hotly denied the claim, and Lancelot challenged Meliagaunt to a duel over the slur to Guenevere's honour. Meliagaunt died in that duel, leaving Guenevere's honour intact, though she and Lancelot were in truth guilty of Meliagaunt's charge.

The queen also had misfortune in her role as hostess. At a banquet Guenevere held for the Knights of the Round Table, a knight named Patrise died when he ate of a poisoned apple. Patrise's cousin, Sir Mador, accused Guenevere of the murder (in reality a knight named Pinel had put the poisoned apple in the bowl of fruit hoping to poison Gawain). Arthur could not defend her, for he needed to be seen as a rightful and fair judge, and so determined that if the queen could find no knight to defend her in battle against her accuser, then she must needs be put to death by burning. So unpopular was Guenevere that all of the knights present at the banquet refused to represent her, and the only knight she could persuade to her cause was a reluctant Sir Bors, Lancelot being away from court at this time. However, Sir Bors managed to find Lancelot and tell him of the queen's dilemma, and Lancelot arrived in time to represent Guenevere in the armed combat, which he won, restoring her honour if not her popularity.

Suspicion of the woman continued. Many were jealous of her, others furious that she continued her affair with Lancelot under Arthur's nose. Mordred and Agravain decided to trap the lovers in such a compromising position that Arthur finally would be forced to do something about it. One evening the two knights led a company of knights into Guenevere's bed chamber when Lancelot was with her. A savage fight ensued, in which Lancelot fatally wounded Gareth, whom he loved dearly.

From this moment the slide into civil war was inevitable. Arthur's hand had been forced and he condemned Guenevere to the stake – he could do no less – but at the last moment Lancelot rescued Guenevere from the flames and rode off with her to his castle of Joyous Garde. Gawain, elder brother of Gareth, pushed for war against Lancelot (to avenge Gareth's death), to which Arthur reluctantly agreed. Gawain died in the battle which followed. Eventually Arthur and Lancelot made peace when the pope intervened, and Guenevere was restored to Arthur's side, although her position was now very uncertain.

At this point events become confused, but it appears that Arthur was once more required to travel abroad for war. Now he left his son Mordred in charge of the realm and of Guenevere. It was a fatal error, for this move allowed Mordred's ambition to flower into full-blown treachery. Mordred seized both Guenevere and the throne – some say Guenevere yielded to Mordred, others that she locked herself in the White Tower of London and refused to come out.

Arthur returned to Britain and met Mordred in a series of battles. At the last, father and son met in single combat. Arthur ran his lance through Mordred, but his dying son, filled with hate, wriggled down the lance until he could deliver a great blow to Arthur's helmet, fatally wounding his father.

As Arthur lay dying, he instructed Bedwyr to throw Excalibur into a nearby lake, which Bedwyr finally did. Then four queens came in a barge – among them Morgan le Fay – and carried Arthur away to Avalon, there to minister to his wounds so that Arthur might one day return to aid Britain.

Guenevere retreated to a convent, and Lancelot to a life of spiritual contemplation as a hermit. The throne passed to Cador, or perhaps to his son Constantine, but no man could unite the Britons in the same manner Arthur had, and the Saxons recommenced their inevitable crawl over the land of Britain until Arthur's realm and vision lay in ruins.

Part I

The BIRTH of a LEGEND

1

THE HISTORIC BACKGROUND

On the departure of the Romans, the Picts and Scots, learning they did not mean to return, were quick to return themselves, and becoming bolder than ever, occupied all the northern and outer part of the island up to the wall, as if it belonged to them. Here a dispirited British garrison . . . pined in terror night and day, while from beyond the wall the enemy constantly harassed them with hooked weapons, dragging the cowardly defenders down from their wall and dashing them to the ground. At length the Britons abandoned their cities and wall and fled in disorder, pursued by their foes.

BEDE, A History of the English Church and People, P. 53

*I*n the early twelfth century an English cleric called Geoffrey of Monmouth, who sometimes signed himself Geoffrey Arthuris, wrote his epic *History of the Kings of Britain*. From the stories of his childhood, and from his ambitious imagination, emerged the tale of Arthur of Britain, a man who united the Dark Age Britons against the Saxon invaders to become the greatest king that Europe had ever seen, only to succumb to the treachery of those he loved most dearly. In order to understand why Arthur failed, we need to understand the medieval world view. The Arthurian legend is not only a product of Geoffrey of Monmouth, but of the medieval mind which shaped its development from the twelfth to fifteenth centuries. Although the original stories of Arthur date back into the Dark Ages, the crucible for the development of the legend as we know it was the medieval age: a gallant and chivalric age, to be sure, but also an age balanced on the knife-edge of disaster in a world filled with the physical manifestations of evil. The literature and legends that emerged from that age are often far more than tales of adventure and romance. Many of them are moral parables and the Arthurian legend is no exception. The medieval authors of the Arthurian tragedy took a Dark Age tale and rewove it, intending to demonstrate how a flawed king, and a flawed man, will always fail. Arthur flawed? Indeed, and very badly, if often innocently. Arthur failed because of corruption and betrayal: within himself, within his realm, and among those closest to him – his parents (who planted the seeds of destruction), his sister, his wife, his best friend and his son, in whom betrayal grew to full flower.

THE DARK AGES

But first to the cauldron from whence strode the legend of Arthur: the Dark Ages. The Dark Ages date from the fall of the western Roman Empire in the late fifth century to the cessation of the Viking invasions of western Europe in the mid-eleventh century (the last great invasion to occur in western Europe was the Norman invasion of England in 1066). Waves of invasions and tribal movements of peoples characterise the entire Dark Ages: in the fifth and sixth centuries Germanic tribes moved from eastern, central and northern Eurasia into western and southern Europe, driven by land hunger and the Asiatic Hun nomads at their backs. In the seventh and eighth centuries Muslims invaded from the Arabian peninsula across Africa, through Spain and into central France. Finally, to complete the misery, in the ninth and tenth centuries Vikings swarmed out of their Scandinavian homelands over the British Isles and up the river systems of western and northern Europe. For six centuries three successive waves of invasions tore western Europe apart. No sooner was one tribe beaten back (or assimilated), then another attacked from a different direction.

To make life even more miserable, the invaders were not confined to marauding warriors. During the sixth to ninth centuries, tens of thousands died each year from the combined effects of epidemics and starvation. Europeans endured new diseases which decimated populations with no resistance – bubonic plague, measles and smallpox – as well as ergotism (a fungal disease of grain crops which killed as surely as did the plague). England suffered no less than forty-nine outbreaks of epidemics (of whatever nature) between 526 and 1087. Compounding the effects of disease were continuous years of crop failure, caused by a mini Ice Age. Starvation and disease were so rife that Church chroniclers reported masses of men and women who, preferring the grey embrace of the icy northern waters to starvation, leaped hand-in-hand from cliffs, and fathers who loved their sons more for the taste of their flesh than for the link of their blood. Corpses lay only hours in their graves before the hungry dug up their flesh and gnawed it raw. Those who lived survived only to hear the war cries of invaders, and the sweep of the axe through the air.

This grey and miasmic age was a time for heroes and for annihilation, and most regions endured both. From the pens of priests who lived long enough to hide their chronicles from the marauders, and from the oral traditions of those who clung to what uncertain life they could to murmur hope to their thin children, emerge the great heroes of fact and legend. Men who, for a year, ten years or a lifetime, managed to hold back the wrath of invading tribes and gods alike. This was an age that begot heroes, and the greatest of them all emerged from Britain's clouded hills and misty fens to drive back the Saxons and capture the heart and soul of a millennium.

THE GERMANIC INVASIONS

Both the legend of Arthur, as well what facts we know of the Dark Ages, are characterised by the successive attacks of invading Germanic or Scandinavian peoples. For at least two thousand years before the eleventh century, the tribes of central Asia and central and northern Europe migrated inexorably towards the warmer lands in the west and south. No-one completely understands what caused these migrations, although devastating climate change, land hunger, and the demands of a war-like culture are the most probable reasons.

In part, the Roman Empire had grown so massive as a reaction to these invasions. The empire existed for one purpose – to protect and feed Rome itself – but from its earliest days barbarian peoples[1] on the empire's northern and eastern frontiers threatened its security. The presence of the barbarians forced Rome continually to add buffer states between itself and the gathering barbarian hordes. Thus grew the empire, and thus it fell: eventually the empire grew so large that it could not man every one of the thousands of miles of frontier, nor effectively administer and govern its subject peoples. In one catastrophic century, from the early 400s to 478, the western Roman Empire[2] collapsed under its own weight and the pressure of hundreds of thousands of Germanic barbarians swarming over its frontiers.

The barbarians consisted of a number of different Germanic tribal groupings and peoples, warring and competing as much between themselves as they did with the Roman Empire. For generations before the fifth century, the Visigoths, Vandals, Franks, Lombards, Burgandinians and Sueves, among others, huddled on the northern frontiers of the empire, seeking land and shelter from the Huns at

---

1 The word 'barbarian' originally meant foreigner or outsider. In time it came to be associated with the concept of the uncouth or uncivilised.

2 During the third century the Roman Empire split into east and west, each with its own emperor, for administrative and military purposes. After the fall of the western empire, the eastern Roman Empire continued for another 1,000 years as the Byzantine Empire, based around Constantinople.

their backs. They managed occasionally to break through into Roman territory, and the Romans had allowed some few to settle on vacant land to try and ease the pressure, but before the early fifth century the majority of the barbarians still lived beyond the empire's frontiers. Then, in the winter of 406–407, several tribes – the Burgandinians, the Franks and the Sueves – crossed the Rhine into Gaul (France) and drove south along the well-maintained Roman road system. In response, the leader of the Roman forces in Britain, a common soldier who named himself Constantine, led the majority of their troops out of Britain to try and counter the flood of barbarians. He never returned. According to Bede, by 410 the Romans had left the Britons 'stripped of all troops and military supplies and robbed of the flower of its active youth'.

Britain now entered into 'a catastrophe, transacted over several generations'.[3] For centuries the Picts (tribes from what is now Scotland), and the Scots (tribes from Ireland)[4] had been harrying Roman Britain. To keep them at bay, the Romans had needed an army of some 50,000 men. Now the army was gone, and the raiders broke through what poorly-manned defences there were. But the ancient threat of the Picts and Scots was not all the Britons had to combat. From the coastlines of the North Sea came the Saxons, a generic name for three Germanic tribal groupings: Saxons, Angles and Jutes. All these raiders, Picts, Scots and Saxons, came by boat – and Britain's coastline is so riddled with creeks and rivers that an adequate defence of these waterways has been often more hopeless than feasible. Saxon war-bands harried and then settled the eastern and south-eastern coastlines of the island, moving ever inland. An initial trickle of invaders turned into a flood. The Britons could either stand and fight, or flee. Many Britons chose flight, seeking refuge across the narrow seas (the Channel) in Brittany, or Lesser Britain, which took its name from the refugees. Others moved to

3 Richard Hodges, *The Anglo-Saxon Achievement* (London, 1989), p. 20.
4 The Scots originally came from Ireland, invading east and then moving north through Britain to displace the Picts from what is now Scotland.

Spain. Yet more retreated into the easily defensible mountains of Wales, there to set up independent kingdoms where they hoped to ride out the horror. Others chose to put their backs to the sea and to stand and fight, sending sundry appeals to Rome for military aid.

'The sea drives us into the hands of the barbarians, and the barbarians drive us into the sea. Between the two of them, we have two deaths to choose from: we can either be drowned or have our throats cut.'

Monmouth quoting Gildas,
in *The History of the Kings of Britain*, p. 148

Whether or not Rome managed to send military aid is unclear. There may well have been attempts to send at least one legion back to reclaim the island. But whatever effort, if any, Rome made, was unsuccessful: by the mid-fifth century the Britons were on their own. By the end of the fifth century the people of the Byzantine Empire, the remnants of the once-mighty Roman empire, spoke of Britain only as the 'Isle of the Dead' or the 'land of legend'. They did not, and could not, know of the horrific fight for survival that continued within the island until the Saxons finally subdued the Britons in the sixth century.

Abandoned by Rome, the Britons were left to fight a savage war for their very existence. There is little in the way of 'fact' that survives from this time. The writers and recorders of society either fled, or died – pens were of little use against the battle-axes and swords of the invaders. The pagan flood decimated the Christian Church, and it survived only in isolated religious houses. Townsfolk abandoned their homes, for the beautifully crafted Roman roads led straight to their doors, and loose-waving grass conquered London. Men, women and children died in the battles to repel the invaders, or starved when they were driven off their land.

The fighting continued through the fifth century. Slowly the Britons strengthened their defences against the invaders. At some point at the turn of the fifth century into the sixth, the Britons won a major battle over the Saxons at a site known as Mount Badon.

Because this age has left us so little in the way of hard fact, the actual site and the dating of the battle of Badon is a matter of contention between historians. The battle may have taken place at some point between 491 and 516, possibly in one of the southern counties, perhaps either Dorset or Somerset.[5] Excavations of a hill fort in Somerset known as South Cadbury have revealed fortifications that date from c. 500.[6] The site is large, covering some eighteen acres, and overlooks the monastery of Glastonbury in the distance.

Whatever the reason, whoever the hero of Mount Badon, and over and above all the 'possibles' and 'perhapses', the sixth-century historian Gildas tells us that south-western Britain basked in relative calm between 500 and 550. Then . . . disaster. Renewed invasion, not by the Saxons, but by disease.

From the mid-sixth century the bubonic plague raged over western Europe, decimating British defences. Close following the black pustules of the plague came another wave of the flaxen-haired Saxons and, for whatever reasons – whether the effects of the plague, or the internal war and moral corruption that Gildas cites – the Britons were lost. Some scholars believe the decimation of the British was so extensive that the Britons were altogether driven out of the larger portion of their lands into the extreme southern and western parts of the island: Wales, Devon and Cornwall. Most of the island became a Germanic land tilled by Germanic peoples. By the end of the sixth century Britain had become 'Angleland' (England), and the almost 150 years of British struggle to expel the invaders was fading memory . . . and growing legend.

<hr>

5   'Possibly' and 'perhaps' are two words that characterise all studies of Dark Age Britain. No-one can write a credible history of this age and this land and not use these words.

6   The history of the hill fort dates back to pre-Roman days. The invading Romans destroyed the fort, but it was reoccupied and rebuilt by the Britons during the fifth-century invasions.

2

THE LEGEND IS BORN:
Geoffrey of Monmouth

Whenever I have chanced to think about the history of the kings of Britain . . . it has seemed a remarkable thing to me that, apart from such mention of them as Gildas and Bede had each made in a brilliant book on the subject, I have not yet been able to discover anything at all on the kings who lived here before the Incarnation of Christ, or indeed about Arthur and all the others who followed on after the Incarnation. Yet the deeds of these men were such that they deserve to be praised for all time. What is more, these deeds were handed down joyfully in oral tradition . . . by many peoples who had only their memory to rely on.

MONMOUTH, The History of the Kings of Britain, P. 51

By the mid-eleventh century England had survived a thousand years of invasion and disaster. Its landscape was littered with the fragmentary remains of hundreds of kingdoms that had risen, flourished and then collapsed, while the island peoples had witnessed the arrival of boatload after boatload of invaders before falling butchered into their peat-lined graves. Ploughshares had been beaten into swords, and then buried with the hands that wielded them.

This was a land of memory. This was a land of legend remembered. It was also a land that men lusted after.

England had one last invasion to endure after the struggles and cataclysms of the Dark Ages. In October of 1066 Duke William of Normandy landed on the south-east coastline of Saxon England armed with a burning ambition to have the isle for his own and a dubious claim to the English throne. Legend has it that when William stepped onto the sandy beach of Pevensey, he stumbled and fell over. The Duke quickly turned a disastrous omen into a victorious symbol. Grasping fistfuls of sand, William rose to his feet, turned to his chain-mailed knights, and thrust his hands skyward: 'England is mine!' he cried.

And so it came to pass. The armies of England's Saxon king, Earl Harold, had only recently turned back a Danish invasion at Stamford Bridge to the north. They were exhausted, not only from the draining battle against the Danes, but also from the forced march south to meet the Normans. And William had knights: mailed, horsed and courageous. The Saxons fought primarily on foot and without the protection of chain mail. The armies met just outside Hastings on the south coast and fought through the bloody day of 14th October. William won, although only just. England became a Norman state.

The Norman invasion had profound political and cultural implications. Over the next few years the Norman aristocracy completely replaced the Saxon elite. William, always fearful the Saxons would somehow manage to raise an army and stage a counter-offensive, built a series of forbidding castles around England not only to impose Norman authority on the Saxons, but also to secure a line of retreat back to the south-eastern ports should the Normans need it. Many of these castles still stand, as dark and imposing now as they were 1,000 years past: the most famous is the Tower of London.

The invasion also had dire implications for English–French relations. The dukes of Normandy were now kings of England, but they were *also* the vassals of the French king. The Norman kings resented these feudal ties to the French monarchy (how could one king be the vassal of another?), while the French kings loathed the amount of land the English kings held in France by virtue of their

Norman ties. The tension led to war after war between the two nations, resulting in the devastating Hundred Years War of the mid-fourteenth to the mid-fifteenth centuries in which the English finally, stunningly, lost the vast majority of their French land holdings (save the port of Calais, which they retained until the early modern era).

Politically, the English kings and aristocracy warred with the French, but culturally they felt at one with them. The Norman elite of England looked for cultural inspiration across the Channel. France was, after all, home and from the time of the Norman invasion until the mid-fifteenth century, England's nobility held as much, if not more, land there as they did in England. The language of the ruling class was a rough mixture of Norman French and English (the language of England's administration and law courts remained largely a curious dialect of Norman French, Latin and English until the sixteenth century). Despite this cultural closeness, the Normans – and the English generally – yearned to feel some kind of cultural superiority over France. Where was the heroic English heritage that the English, and their masters, the Normans, could flaunt before the French? It was a difficult ask, because the Normans could hardly praise Saxon political and cultural achievements (which were considerable) when they had trodden the Saxons and, to some extent, Saxon culture, into the mud of the field outside Hastings. To praise Saxon achievement would have been to illegitimise their own invasion. They needed a British hero to rival the French legend of Charlemagne, the Dark Age emperor of Gaul. The way was open for an ambitious and imaginative cultural revisionist: Geoffrey of Monmouth.

Little is known of Monmouth – nearly 1,000 years and the murkiness of Norman records have wrapped his life in almost complete obscurity. What we do know largely speaks through his writing. Monmouth was born about 1100, some thirty years after the Normans invaded, possibly, although not certainly, in or close to the town of Monmouth in eastern Wales on the modern border of the counties of Gwent and Gloucestershire. Monmouth's childhood years would have been spent during the time of ongoing cultural and political adjustment following the Norman invasion. He would also have been influenced by the rich oral culture of southern England, Wales and Brittany (his ancestral origins may have been Welsh or Breton). Much of Monmouth's life was associated with the Church and with Oxford, where he spent most of the years between 1129–1151, possibly in some teaching capacity, although a university as such did not exist at Oxford then. In 1152 Monmouth became the bishop of the backwater see of Saint Asaph in Wales, although there is no record of his ever visiting his diocese. He died in 1155.

Most of Monmouth's adult life appears to have been spent angling for promotion within the Church; his final reward for so many years' labour – Saint Asaph – must have been a disappointment. Clerical promotion in twelfth-century Norman England meant pleasing two masters, the Church and the Norman nobility. Ironically, the means by which Monmouth sought to please both sets of masters – his writings – have provided him with the fame and degree of influence he never achieved in his lifetime.

Monmouth's *History of the Kings of Britain* (finished about 1136) was a medieval best-seller. There are remaining some 200 medieval manuscripts of the book, testifying to its popularity. Many of these manuscripts are dedicated to different people: as Monmouth revised or had his original work recopied, he no doubt saw the opportunity to enlist the support and patronage of yet another nobleman. Originally Monmouth dedicated the *History* to the illegitimate son of Henry I, Robert, Earl of Gloucester and the majority of manuscripts have this dedication. Monmouth also tried his luck with dedicating the book to Waleran de Beaumont, Count of Meulan and Earl of Worcester. One manuscript has a dedication to King Stephen. Monmouth also mentions his debt to Walter, Archdeacon of Oxford. However, despite his efforts, none of these men apparently helped Monmouth attain the level of clerical eminence he sought. Disappointed with the results, but not the method, Monmouth dedicated a manuscript of *The Prophecies of Merlin* (later incorporated into his *History*) to Alexander, Bishop of Lincoln, again without success. Apparently undaunted, he then dedicated *The Life of Merlin* to Alexander's successor, Robert de Chesney. At last his efforts paid off and he was rewarded with the bishopric of Saint Asaph.

Monmouth's work lived far beyond the death of its creator. *The History of the Kings of Britain* was enormously influential, shaping English historiography for centuries . . . and it created the Arthurian legend as we know it. Originally written in Latin, the work was translated into French and English within a generation. The book had its contemporary critics and detractors, but most readers believed it to be a literal history: many later English medieval chronicles were based on Monmouth's *History*, and most were heavily influenced by it. It remained a standard history text for almost 400 years until scholarly suspicion destroyed its credibility in the sixteenth century.

Monmouth's *History*, and particularly his story of Arthur, is largely a work of vivid imagination. Other medieval scholars before Monmouth alluded to Arthur, but they did so only in passing. William of Malmesbury, for instance, briefly mentioned Arthur in his own history (which just predated Monmouth's) but commented that much of his life was mere fable. Whatever was known of Arthur in the early twelfth century, whether in dry chronicle or in oral tradition, Monmouth expanded a hundred-fold. He claimed to have worked from some mysterious and, to us, unknowable texts. Chief among these is the 'certain very ancient book written in the British language' kindly lent to him by Walter, Archdeacon of Oxford. From this book, 'attractively composed to form a consecutive and orderly narrative', Monmouth gleaned the deeds of all British kings from the time of Brutus to Cadwallader (who died, according to Monmouth, in AD 689). No-one since has been able to find, or even identify, this book, and its existence (or lack of it) has spawned many a scholarly feud in the past 200 years. Was this 'certain very ancient book' a fabrication? (All ambitious historians dream of finding a source that no-one else has ever used and which, most unfortunately, is lost in a house fire immediately after the historian has finished consulting it.) Or was this ancient text in fact the ninth-century *History of the Britons* (attributed to Nennius), or, even more enticingly, the original source from which Nennius worked? Was it something else? Something still unknown? However interesting, the debate is nevertheless sterile. No-one truly knows if Monmouth worked from a now lost text, or if he dreamed up the entire ancient book in order to give the workings of his own imagination the gloss of historic accuracy. All that we have left are the words that Monmouth scattered across his parchment.

From these words we know that Monmouth *did* use the stories and legends that he grew up with. Many of the characters in his Arthurian story – Arthur, Bedwyr, Kay, Guenevere, Mordred, Morgan le Fay – have precedents in Welsh folklore. Dark Age histories mention Arthur, or Arthur-like figures. But this historic and traditional framework is sketchy, and the majority of Monmouth's history of Arthur came from only one place: his ambitious imagination. Monmouth made Arthur a medieval chivalric king, probably because it suited his purposes to do so, although it is also likely that the author had no idea that life and warfare was very different in sixth-century Britain (for instance, knights did not exist in sixth-century Europe). Monmouth did not create a new hero, he took one that the English already had a rich folklore about and gave it new vigour and vibrancy.

Monmouth's lengthy Arthurian story is summarised at the end of the book (see Appendix A, page 293), but one or two points should be made about it here. Lancelot and the quest for the Holy Grail make no appearance in Monmouth's work: they are French imports of a later date. Nor do the majority of the company of knights ride through Monmouth's work. These, too, are later additions. The principal difference between Monmouth and the core legend as I have summarised it is that Monmouth's Mordred is Arthur's nephew rather than son, and Guenevere commits adultery with Mordred rather than with Lancelot. Apart from these sub-plots which were appended to other versions of the Arthurian story at a later date, Monmouth's work forms the foundation of the core legend.

Monmouth's interpretation of Arthur and of the king's life and times was heavily influenced by the world in which he lived – and by his own ambitions. Monmouth primarily wanted to give England a hero that everyone would be comfortable with: Norman nobles, Church clerics and the English people themselves. One of the things any ambitious twelfth-century English writer would *not* do was antagonise his Norman masters: Monmouth's Arthur is clearly constructed to pander to the Normans. In giving the Normans an acceptable hero, Monmouth had to be careful not to select a Saxon champion. The ideal historic choice for his hero would have been Alfred the Great. This real-life character had accomplished far more than a historic Arthur could possibly have done. Alfred was a ninth-century king of Wessex who, with the aid of his son Edward, managed to steady the Saxon resistance against the fury of the Vikings driving down into south-east England. If it were not for Alfred, England might well be Danish to this day. Alfred succeeded against the Vikings where Arthur eventually failed against the Saxons.

But as a Saxon hero Alfred was not a sound choice for Monmouth. Politically, it could have caused a resurgence of Saxon resistance against the Normans. Personally, it would have made Monmouth bishop of nothing but his own prison cell. So Monmouth took the only option open to him. He selected a Dark Age Roman–British hero who had fought *against* the Saxon invasions of the fifth and sixth centuries. The Saxons were the villains of Monmouth's tale; they had been the external reason for Arthur's fall, and the fall of post-Roman Britain. Looked at this way, the Normans had done the ancient British a favour by riding in and exterminating Saxon rule and culture and restoring to the British their ancient pride.

Monmouth was, however, somewhat careful not to paint too glorious a picture of Dark Age Britain. True, the deadly Saxon invaders had wrought death and destruction, but the British had also been at fault. Arthur had done his best – indeed, he had kept England safe for decades – but had finally succumbed to the internal betrayal of civil war rather than Saxon hostilities (the Saxons took advantage of the British disarray and completed the invasion that had been threatening for a hundred years). Thus even the British were not quite the ultimate heroes. They, too, had been at fault. All this reflected well upon the Normans. They had invaded in 1066, destroyed the rule of the hated Saxons, and had imposed stability and peace on a realm which had not seen either since the years of Roman rule.

Indeed, the Normans were to be commended for their actions.

Monmouth walked this political tightrope with consummate ease – not only had he 'discovered' a British–Roman figure who managed to justify the Norman invasion, his hero was a king so splendid his legend could rival that of Charlemagne.

Charlemagne is a historic certainty to Arthur's historic ambiguity. In the mid-eighth century the Martel family, headed by Charlemagne's grandfather, Charles Martel, set the Frankish tribes of Gaul on their path to greatness. Until then the region known as Gaul (slightly larger than France is now) had been dominated by sundry warring Frankish tribes and an ineffective dynasty, the Merovingian kings (unhappily known to posterity as the 'do-nothing' kings). Charles Martel displaced the Merovingians. He was a brilliant war-leader, winning the respect of the Frankish tribes and halting the Arab advance through the south of France at the battle of Poitiers in 732. His son, Pippin, and grandson, Charles the Great – known as Charlemagne – went on to establish the largest and most successful European empire of the Dark Ages (in fact, the most successful for almost a thousand years). Charlemagne, like his grandfather, was a man of war: in successive yearly campaigns in the eighth and ninth centuries (he reigned for some forty-three years) he defeated external tribes and subdued internal lords. He expanded his empire over most of western and parts of central and northern Europe. But Charlemagne was not only a man of war, he was a champion of the Church (he rescued a pope from kidnap in 800) and a cultural hero as well. Charlemagne was determined to make Gaul the cultural centre of the known world. He decided to effect a revival of classical learning. Schools, monasteries and centres of learning sprang up across the empire. Scholars came from far and wide to work for Charlemagne. His efforts remain today: even the handwriting we use is based on Carolingian minuscule, a style of writing developed in Charlemagne's monastic centres of learning. Charlemagne was an extraordinary man, a heroic war-captain, a splendid king and a cultural icon.

What did Norman England have? A few rough-edged British war-lords who had held a hill or two against the Dark Age invaders and a

Saxon king who was too politically sensitive to elevate to heroic status. So Monmouth took a name and a myth, and made of it a historic king to rival Charlemagne. Like Charlemagne, Arthur was a brilliant war-leader who won himself a huge empire which included Gaul, an addition sure to amuse and please the Normans. Also, like his Gallic rival, Arthur was as much a patron of culture as of the Church, and presided over a glittering court which all noblemen and kings of Europe attended. In almost every respect Arthur provided the perfect British counter-foil to the Gallic Charlemagne. The English, as their Norman overlords, could feel proud of their island's past.

The contemporary political situation in England could also have influenced Monmouth's depiction of Arthur's downfall, particularly Mordred's role. For some years the Norman monarchy had been troubled by rival claimants. Somewhat like Arthur, in 1135 Henry I of England had done the politically unacceptable thing and died without a male heir. His daughter, Matilda, took the throne, but in a patriarchal society, female monarchs were ever likely to face a challenge. The Anglo-Norman nobility was divided on whether it should accept Matilda, or the dead king's nephew, Stephen. In the end, the Norman nobles decided to accept Stephen, and he was crowned in Westminster Abbey in 1135. The compromise did not last long. Matilda and her husband, Geoffrey Plantagenet, Count of Anjou, rallied many dissatisfied Norman nobles to their cause, among them her bastard brother, Robert, Earl of Gloucester (one of the people to whom Monmouth dedicated his *History*). After a lengthy period of war, it was decided that Stephen should retain the throne, but that Matilda and Geoffrey's son, Henry, should inherit after Stephen's death (thus inaugurating the Plantagenet dynasty of England). Monmouth, in dedicating his work to the Earl of Gloucester, implicitly supported Matilda's claim to the throne. Thus, claim some historians, the entire story of Mordred's treachery is a commentary on Stephen's grab for the throne.

In fact, Monmouth's book was finished by the time the entire affair blew into war, and it is unlikely he made what would have been a massive revision on the spur of the moment. As well, the similarities between Mordred's treachery to Arthur, and Stephen's 'treachery' (or rightful claim, according to many nobles) to Matilda are few and far between. Finally, there was already a Welsh tradition that Mordred was in some way responsible for the destruction of Arthur's kingdom. Any similarities between Mordred and King Stephen were, perhaps, more a fortunate coincidence than anything else.

If the current political instability was unlikely to have influenced Monmouth, the current religious controversies surely did. Monmouth did not only have to please and flatter his Norman overlords, he also had to flatter his Church masters. He did this in two ways; first by creating for England a glorious Christian past where previously there was only pagan murkiness, and secondly by backing the Church's position in its conflict with the monarchs of Europe.

First to England's suddenly glorious Christian history. In reality, the Christian Church had a chequered past in England, just as it had across Europe. The Romans had first introduced Christianity into Europe, although most Romans were not Christian themselves (politically, it had suited the Romans to adopt Christianity as their state religion). Whatever thin veneer of Christianity the Romans gave to their empire, it was torn apart when the western empire collapsed in the fifth century. Isolated pockets of Christianity remained in the British Isles, but the majority of people through the fifth and sixth centuries reverted to paganism. Slowly Europe settled down during the fifth and sixth centuries. Determined to win back the 'island of the dead', as Britain had become known, in 597 Pope Gregory sent a very reluctant Saint Augustine to England to commence the reconversion of the island. It was a long and slow process (as was the reconversion process around all of Europe). In an intensely agricultural society, people found it hard to relinquish the earth and nature-orientated pagan faiths in favour of an intellectually abstract and esoteric Christian faith. The Church was forced to adopt questionable practices in order to gain converts: the cult of saints was expanded to include sundry pagan deities, the major pagan festivals of Eostre and Yuletide were incorporated into the Christian calendar, and priests found themselves muttering strange spells over bloodied clods of earth in ancient fertility rituals. Although the pagan faiths eventually died, pagan practices and ideas could not be stamped out. The Church was sensitive to the fact that they had not done as thorough a job as perhaps they should have done.

Monmouth presented them with a neatly repackaged history of the Dark Ages. He replaced a pagan past with a Christian one. The England of his *History* demonstrated a shining example of Christianity in which people called on the Virgin Mary, churches abounded and bishops were mentioned every second paragraph. It must have been very reassuring to his clerical masters.

Far more importantly, Monmouth included a moral in his tale of Arthur's rise and fall intended to be a grim warning to the contemporary monarchs of Europe. Since the reign of Pope Gregory VII in the late eleventh century, the papacy and many European monarchs had been involved in a power struggle that is now known as the Investiture Crisis. It was one of the great religious and political issues of the medieval period. The Catholic Church was a massive, wealthy and entirely independent international organisation. It paid no state taxes – and yet it tithed all state subjects. It was not subject to state law – yet it erected Church courts beside and even above state law courts. It owned huge swathes of territory in every country, and controlled vast amounts of income.

All self-respecting monarchs resented this situation. One of the only ways they had of controlling the activities of the Church in their own realm was to place their own men into the powerful bishoprics and archbishoprics. The ceremony in which a new archbishop or bishop received his office was called an investiture. Popes loathed lay investiture. It meant that many of the powerful Churchmen in Europe owed their allegiance to the monarch who had invested them rather than to the Holy Father. Popes claimed kings did not have the right to invest men into Church office; kings argued that, as they were anointed by God (via the Church), they had every right to 'oversee' the activities of the Church within their own realm. It all came down to the issue of ultimate power in a kingdom. Who held it – pope or king? The crisis erupted in the 1070s into war between the papacy and the Holy Roman Emperor (the Holy Roman Empire covered much of central Europe) and continued throughout the 1100s (in fact, the issue continued to simmer right through to the Protestant Reformation of the sixteenth century).

Monmouth was clearly on the side of the Church on this issue. As we will see in Chapter 10, Monmouth's Arthur violates the Church's dictum that no king should invest clerics into their offices. Not only that, but Arthur declares war on Rome itself (Monmouth disguised the Roman Church as the Roman Empire in his *History*, but no contemporary reader would have missed his meaning). For his misdemeanours, Arthur paid the ultimate price: loss of kingdom and life.

Monmouth's Arthurian tale is meant to enthral, to give the Normans and the English a hero to be proud of, but it is also a moral. Monmouth meant his history to teach, and there is a lesson to be learned from his Arthur. Here is a man who had it all: court, empire and glory. And yet here is a man who lost it all. Arthur was betrayed from within his own household, but he also betrayed himself. He was a king who went too far, who descended into the shadows of cruelty, unjust violence and what Monmouth clearly intended to be seen as an astounding attack upon the Church. No wonder he lost it all. Monmouth meant contemporary kings to take note: every king has a duty to his people, his country and his God. Descend into personal ambition, and God withdraws his grace. Monmouth also intended a moral lesson for the entire English race: civil dissent and war leads to destruction. Be loyal, be true, and trust in your leaders.

3

THE DEVELOPMENT
OF THE LEGEND

*T*he Arthurian legend has never been static. In almost every generation it has altered to meet the needs of new listeners and readers. Here one theme or one character is paramount, fifty years later another name or plot line assumes primary importance. Not only does the legend change to suit the needs of new societies, to confuse the issue there are actually two traditions that were combined in the fifteenth century to create the core legend we are familiar with today. The first of these traditions, as begun by Geoffrey of Monmouth, is the medieval English chronicle tradition which concentrates on Arthur and his military conquests. The second tradition is that of the medieval French romances, which concentrate on Lancelot and the quest for the Holy Grail. (The differences between the two traditions are summarised in a diagram on the next page.) The English chronicle tradition presents Arthur as historical figure, stoic and tragic, the French romances present a more glamorised mythical figure surrounded by the accoutrements of chivalric heroism. One of the main differences between the two traditions is with whom Guenevere betrays Arthur: in the chronicle tradition she has an affair (and often two children) with Mordred, Arthur's nephew, while in the French romance tradition she spurns the advances of Mordred (whom the French reworked as Arthur's son) in favour of Lancelot. In both, she is the adulteress who precipitates the destruction of Arthur and all his knights.

Major Differences Between The English Chronicle And French Romance Traditions

ENGLISH CHRONICLE	FRENCH ROMANCE
Concentrates on Arthur's conquests abroad.	Concentrates on the adventures of the Knights of the Round Table.
Lancelot does not appear.	Lancelot is a major character.
Mordred is Arthur's legitimate nephew.	Mordred is Arthur's incestuous son.
Guenevere takes Mordred as her lover.	Guenevere takes Lancelot as her lover.
Guenevere intentionally betrays Arthur.	Guenevere remains politically loyal to Arthur.
Guenevere gives Mordred two sons (in some versions).	Guenevere remains childless.
There is no quest for the Grail.	The quest for the Grail forms a major part of the legend.
Arthur's downfall is precipitated by Mordred and Guenevere's treachery.	Arthur's downfall is precipitated by Lancelot and Guenevere's affair.

Effectively, the English chronicle and French romance traditions were combined by another writer, Sir Thomas Malory, in the fifteenth century. Today we still use Malory's version of the legend, which only becomes a problem if one needs to believe in both the historicity of Arthur *and* the love affair between Lancelot and Guenevere (all of the French romance imports – Lancelot, Excalibur, Camelot, the quest for the Holy Grail – must be discarded in the hunt for the historic Arthur).

The tale of how these two traditions developed and eventually combined is vital in understanding the evolution of the various characters, as well as the central tragic betrayal of Arthur.

1. ARTHUR BEFORE MONMOUTH

But there was one who was a Red Ravager greater than all three: Arthur was his name. For a year neither grass nor plants used to spring up where one of the three would walk; but where Arthur went, not for seven years.

Welsh triad, cited in Korrel, *An Arthurian Triangle*, p. 52

Arthur enjoyed a full existence – in legend, if not, perhaps, in fact – well before Monmouth's *History of the Kings of Britain.* Arthur (or Arthur-figures) appeared in histories, lives of saints and chronicles and was a widespread and popular subject of the rich oral culture of the pre-twelfth-century world. He was not (as seen in the above quote) always depicted positively, being variously lustful, over-confident, stupid and a waster and destroyer of some renown. Welsh traditions used Arthur extensively, although as many of these were written down for the first time after Monmouth, it is difficult to be certain which ones are true to their pre-Monmouth origins, and which were corrupted by the post-Monmouth perception of Arthur.

The Celtic origins of the Arthurian legend have been the subject of much scholarly investigation, debate and publication. The principal dilemma with discovering the origins of the Arthurian legend in Celtic tradition is that Celtic culture and folklore were an oral tradition. Celtic folklore only began to appear in written form after Monmouth and the French romances popularised, and vastly altered, the Arthurian legend. To what extent are the Celtic tales that have come down to us of genuine Celtic origin, and how much was inserted by medieval scribes to fit the legend as they understood it in the twelfth, thirteenth and fourteenth centuries? When scribes transcribed a book, or wrote down oral tales, they often did not transcribe exactly, but altered, added and deleted to suit their own understanding of the book or tale: thus the old saying among scholars of medieval Europe that there are no copies among the medieval books that have come down to us, only originals. Of all the medieval manuscripts dealing with the Arthurian legend, no two are exactly the same. Therefore every Celtic oral tradition and tale that was transcribed by Christian monks and priests should be treated with caution.

Having sounded that note of warning, it is nevertheless apparent that there was a rich Arthurian tradition in oral Welsh culture before either Geoffrey of Monmouth or the French romances further popularised the legend. By decoding the variations of style and linguistics, a careful study of the Welsh poems can generally sort out the post-Monmouth insertions from the Welsh originals. So – who is the Celtic Arthur? He is not so much the king of a nation as the leader of a war-band performing valorous deeds. Sometimes the references to him are only fleeting, and assume a knowledge of Arthur by the listener (rather than reader in this preliterate world). One poem, the 'Verses on the Graves of the Heroes' in the *Black Book of Carmarthen*, indicates some mystery (an 'eternal wonder') surrounding Arthur's death and the site of his grave, possibly alluding to an equally mysterious return at some indeterminate point in the future. Some poems give Arthur a son (some as many as three); Llacheu is most frequently mentioned. The Arthur, and the Arthurian world, of these early poems bear little resemblance to the Arthurian legend that sprang from Monmouth's fertile imagination.

Arthur does assume a richer existence in the later Welsh tales *Culhwch and Olwen* and *Rhonabwy's Dream* (possibly dating from the late eleventh century and the early thirteenth century respectively). Although the earliest known manuscripts of these poems occur after Monmouth's time, the tales themselves show few signs of European or Anglo–Norman influence and *possibly* originated in Welsh oral tradition. In the first of these poems the hero, Culhwch, is Arthur's cousin. When Culhwch journeys to Arthur's court on a quest to find a bride (Olwen), we learn that Arthur is the prince of Britain, as well as of far-flung lands, and has a wife named Gwenhwyfar. Arthur has an impressive armoury: Caledfwlch his sword; Rhongomyniad his spear; Wynebgwrthucher his shield; and Carnwennan his dagger. (Interestingly, when Arthur lists his wondrous possessions, Gwenhwyfar comes last.) Cei (Kay) and Bedwyr head the list of Arthur's warriors. In *Rhonabwy's Dream* the title character meets with Arthur in a dream. Several characters from the Monmouth-inspired legend appear or are mentioned, Medrawd (Mordred) and Cei among them, and although the tale mentions the battles of Camlann and Badon, the action of the tale itself bears little resemblance to the core Arthurian legend as we know it now.

The Welsh triads[1] also make many a mention of Arthur and his court. The earliest manuscripts of the triads date from the thirteenth century – again, well after Monmouth – but their content and linguistic style date from a much earlier period. The triads also mention many of the characters and incidents that are now so well known to us: Cei (Kay) and Bedwyr again head Arthur's band of warriors, Medrawt (Mordred) appears, as does Guenevere. As long as one can accept the fact that the earliest known manuscripts of the Welsh tales date from *after* Monmouth, but that the tales themselves existed *before* Monmouth, then it is apparent that Arthur, Guenevere, Mordred, Kay and Bedwyr enjoyed considerable popularity within the Welsh oral tradition of the late Dark Ages.

A few of the Welsh tales of the lives of saints also refer to Arthur. These date from the twelfth century, some of them possibly post-dating Monmouth, but the material they contain is definitely pre-Monmouth. In the *Life of Saint Cadog* Arthur appears as the somewhat lustful captain of a war-band which includes Kay and Bedwyr. Inflamed with lecherous thoughts when he espies the abduction of a beautiful maiden, Arthur only barely overcomes his desires in order to effect a rescue of the girl and return her to her husband (the girl and her husband become the parents of the saintly Cadog). Further into the *Life*, Arthur has an altercation with

---

1 A triad is a tale which concerns three people or events.

Cadog himself, in which Arthur is greatly humbled. In other *Lives* (those of Saints Carannnog, Efflam, Padarn, Gildas and Illtud), Arthur is not portrayed as overly lecherous, but is nevertheless occasionally selfish, and, although brave, is a trifle hasty in his dealings with saintly persons. This occasions him some grief and the odd salutary lesson which causes him to lead a more virtuous life. Here, Arthur is patently a well-known figure, although not always a virtuous one – indeed, he sometimes slides perilously close to wickedness and selfishness.

Arthur also rates a brief mention in one or two Dark Age British histories, although these present problems for anyone trying to prove Arthur's historical existence (as we will see in Chapter 13). Gildas, who wrote within a generation of the life of any genuine historical Arthur, does not once mention his existence, although this in itself could be explained by the fact that Gildas omitted many genuinely historical figures, and his character of Ambrosius Aurelianus (brother of Uther, Arthur's father) who defeated the Saxons at the battle of Mount Badon, may well have been the genuine historical Arthur-figure. Bede, a notable historian of the early eighth century, also totally neglects to mention Arthur, although he follows Gildas in crediting Ambrosius with victory over the Saxons at Mount Badon.

The first mention of Arthur by name must wait until the ninth-century *History of the Britons* (sometimes attributed to Nennius, although current understanding of the chronicle is that it is the work of many authors over a number of years). This account relates that Arthur, a *dux bellorum* (leader of battles) fought alongside the kings of the Britons to drive back the Saxons in twelve major battles culminating in the victory at Badon in the year AD 516. In this version, Arthur is notably not a king, but a mighty war-leader and he has a hound, called Cabal. He is a devout Christian, who bears the image of the Virgin Mary into battle.

The *Annales Cambriae*, probably written in the tenth century, also mentions Arthur in two brief references. The first, the record for the year 516, mentions Arthur as the victorious Christian leader at the Battle of Badon, but the second is far more interesting. The record for the year 537 mentions the Battle of Camlann in which Arthur and Medraut (an early name for Mordred) fell. The record for 537 in particular is tantalisingly brief. What was Medraut's role in Arthur's death? Was he responsible for Arthur's death, or did he die fighting alongside Arthur? No-one knows, nor can they even hazard a guess from the paucity of the record. As to the source used by the *Annales Cambriae*, scholars still debate whether it was *The History of the Britons* (as the entry for 516 might indicate) or whether the *Annales Cambriae* and *The History of the Britons* both used a now-lost third source for their entries (a particularly enticing thought given that Geoffrey of Monmouth also claimed to have used a 'very ancient book written in the British language' which has never been found or even identified).

Thus, for 500 years from the time of the possible existence of Arthur (about the year AD 500) to the time of Geoffrey of Monmouth's seminal work on King Arthur in 1136, there are only tantalising glimpses of the man in Celtic tradition and in Christian historical record. Yet we know that tales of Arthur abounded well before Monmouth wrote. Celtic references to him, whether in legend or in the lives of saints, assume a knowledge of Arthur. The explosion of continental Arthurian romances from the twelfth century onwards cannot be explained merely by reference to Monmouth – the romances patently did not rely on Monmouth but on widespread popular tales (Celtic culture was not confined to the British Isles, and many of the figures in French romances are of Celtic origin). Finally, there is the reference to Arthur made by William of Malmesbury some ten to twelve years before Monmouth wrote. Malmesbury's *Chronicle of the Kings of England* follows Gildas and Bede in crediting Ambrosius with the defeat of the 'presumptuous barbarians', but adds that Ambrosius did so with the aid of 'warlike Arthur' at the Battle of Badon. 'It is of this Arthur,' Malmesbury wrote, 'that the Britons tell so many fables, even to the present day.' An indication, surely, that popular culture venerated Arthur, even if chronicle histories had yet to reflect that tradition. In the years before Monmouth, one other historian made mention of Arthur. Henry of

Huntingdon, writing his chronicle some time before 1133, repeats the history of Arthur as given in *The History of the Britons*: a warrior-general, rather than a king, he defeated the invaders in twelve battles culminating in Badon, always with the image of the Virgin Mary on his shoulders and with the aid of Jesus Christ.

After Monmouth, the legend of Arthur can be neatly divided into the chronicle tradition which accepted Arthur as a genuine historical figure (largely an English tradition), and the romance tradition (European or European inspired) which concentrated on romantic tales which used Arthur and his court as the base from which to launch a myriad chivalric adventures. In the English development of the legend, the two traditions remained relatively separate for several centuries after Monmouth, although manuscripts of both seemed equally popular, until Malory married the two strands in the fifteenth century to give us the legend we are now so familiar with. One of the prime reasons Malory's revisionist account of Arthur has assumed such significance (to the detriment of the scores of variations about England at the time) was because it appeared at the same time as the emerging printing press. William Caxton, the first English printer, took the manuscript, edited it, and published it in 1485. Malory's version of the tale became (and remains) the standard Arthurian legend in the English-speaking world.

2. THE CHRONICLE TRADITION

A priest named Layamon, son of Leovenath, lived among the people in Ernley at a splendid church on Severn's shore . . . . There came into his able mind a desire to chronicle the glorious history of England, to tell what these men were called and from whence they came who first possessed this land.

Prologue to Layamon's *Brut*, Bzdyl transl., p. 33

A Summary of the English Chronicle Tradition:

Arthur is a real historical figure. Conceived in sin by Uther and Ygerna and with the assistance of Merlin, Arthur assumes the throne at fifteen to become a world conqueror of renown. He establishes a fine court, and has a band of knights and kings at his back, led by Kay and Bedwyr. Arthur marries a woman called Guenevere who eventually betrays him with his nephew, Mordred. On Arthur's final campaign to conquer Rome, he learns that Mordred, whom he left as regent, has seized both the realm and Guenevere (obviously with her collusion). In many versions of the chronicle tradition, Guenevere compounds her betrayal of her husband by giving Mordred two sons. Arthur returns home, where his armies defeat those of Mordred, and where he eventually meets his nephew in single combat. Mordred dies, but in dying strikes Arthur a mortal wound. Arthur is spirited off into a mysterious undead existence, Guenevere retires to a convent, and the realm of Britain falls apart under Arthur's successors.

Medieval English chroniclers eagerly seized Monmouth's work, promoting King Arthur the historical figure for the next 400 years. Their Arthur was Monmouth's Arthur: the chivalric hero, conqueror of half the known world, destroyed and betrayed by the ambitions of his nephew, Mordred, coupled (in both senses of that word) with the treachery of Guenevere. The incest theme is rarely mentioned in the chronicle tradition,[2] or given as the reason for Arthur's betrayal. The medieval chronicles likewise ignore Lancelot and the quest for the Holy Grail although early modern chronicles very occasionally betray European romance influence.

Several French translations of Monmouth's work (which was written in Latin) had appeared by the mid-twelfth century to be eagerly read by the elite of England (since the Norman invasion of 1066 French was the language of the nobles). The most important of these was by a Norman poet called Wace, who produced a lively

2 Although, according to medieval cannon law, the adultery of a nephew with his uncle's wife was indeed incest.

version in 1155. In the tradition of all medieval scribes, translators or transcribers, Wace made his own additions to the tale (adding, for instance, three references to the Round Table).

The first English translation of Monmouth's chronicle appeared around 1205. Called the *Brut*, it was the work of an English priest by the name (or appellation) of Layamon (or 'lawman'). The *Brut* is not a direct translation of Monmouth, but a 'liberal' translation of Wace, with the additional use of Bede and presented as a poem rather than a historical prose account. Nevertheless, Layamon's rendering of Arthur's life follows Monmouth's account reasonably faithfully and it directly continues the chronicle tradition. The *Brut* introduces several new elements into Arthur's life. For example, soon after Arthur's birth, elves imbue his life with magic, enabling Arthur to become the best of knights, a powerful king, and to enjoy a long life. Layamon also infused Arthur's armour with magic: the supernatural elfin smith, Widia, forges Arthur's armour of woven steel (called Wygar), while Avalon's magic makes Arthur's sword, Caliburn. Layamon included a description of the Round Table, at which 1,600 men might sit at any one time. He also mentioned the many fables concerning the Round Table present among the English at the time he wrote. In another addition, Arthur is forewarned of Mordred's treason via a dream in which both Mordred and Guenevere (called Wenhaver in Layamon's version) destroy Arthur's great hall. Indeed, Layamon placed equal blame on Mordred and Guenevere for the betrayal of Arthur. Mordred was 'always about the queen' prior to Arthur's departure for Europe, and once Arthur had left, both his wife and his nephew conspire to snatch the throne for Mordred: 'Evil it was that they were born, for they ruined this land with their greedy plunder.'

Following Layamon came numerous medieval chronicles, all in the Monmouth tradition, although all adapted and added to the legend: Robert Mannyng of Brunne's *Chronicle*, written in verse between 1327–1338, is but one example. Without exception, however, all the chronicles treated Arthur as a genuine historical figure, a conqueror unparalleled in European history, but a king eventually betrayed by his ambitious nephew Mordred in alliance with the treacherous Guenevere.

The chronicle tradition reached its peak in the sixteenth century as histories of England poured off the by now widely available printing presses. The sixteenth-century chronicles, or histories, however, tended to be far more terse than their medieval predecessors. As we will see in Chapter 14, the sixteenth century was a watershed in demolishing the belief in Arthur as a historical figure, as well as in the development of the legend itself. As a result, sixteenth-century English men and women must have found it increasingly difficult to believe in the glorious hero of medieval tradition (and more uncomfortable to read accounts of the lechery at Arthur's court in the romantic tradition). By the early seventeenth century, histories either glossed over Arthur with a few brief words, or preferred to omit him completely, citing as reason the lack of genuine historical records from before the tenth or eleventh centuries.

3. THE FRENCH ROMANCE TRADITION

As to Arthur, it is hard to recognize the proudly self-willed, fearless and impetuous champion of the Britons presented in the Vulgate Cycle . . . . *Though depicted as the flower of chivalry throughout . . . Arthur is continually besmirched, belittled, degraded and vilified.*

Korrel, *An Arthurian Triangle*, pp. 179 & 181

A *Summary of the* French Romance Tradition:

Generally the romances begin well into Arthur's reign, assuming a background knowledge of Arthur's conception and birth by the reader or listener. In this tradition Arthur is a great British king, although not a world conqueror (and certainly not a conqueror of France). Arthur has had an incestuous affair with his sister, Morgan le Fay (or sometimes another sister) which has produced a son, Mordred. Morgan continues as Arthur's foe throughout his reign, her efforts to destroy him thwarted only by Merlin's successor, Nimue, the Lady of the Lake (Merlin generally has little success against Morgan).

Arthur's court serves as the base for the Knights of the Round Table, Lancelot du Lake chief among them, and the knights engage in many adventures, among them the quest for the Holy Grail. Lancelot and Guenevere fall in love and for many years conduct an affair which all in the court know about (Arthur generally pretends an ignorance). Eventually the issue is forced into the open by Mordred and some of his foster-brothers. Civil war ensues between Arthur and Lancelot, during which Mordred makes his move, seizing the throne and attempting to seize Guenevere (she does not co-operate). Arthur returns home from his war on Lancelot, defeats Mordred's forces in battle, but is himself mortally wounded when he kills his son. Arthur is carried off to Avalon by Morgan le Fay and several other queens. Guenevere retires to a convent, Lancelot to a monastery.

The continental writers, particularly the medieval French poets, have bequeathed us an entirely different view of Arthur. The first of the major Arthurian romances appeared in the Champagne area of France in the mid to late twelfth century, some three or four decades after Monmouth. Its author, Chretien de Troyes, lived at the court of the Countess Marie de Champagne, and under her patronage he wrote four romances dealing with the adventures of Arthur's knights Gawain, Yvain, Erec and Lancelot: *Erec et Enide; Cliges; Lancelot, or The Knight of the Cart*; and *Yvain, or The Knight with the Lion.* Later in life at the court of the Count of Flanders, de Troyes added *Perceval le Gallois* to the original four romances. Although these romances, as all of the continental Arthurian romances, appeared after Monmouth, it is unlikely that Monmouth had any major influence on their composition. Chretien very possibly knew of Monmouth, or had heard versions of his Arthurian tale – there were strong cultural links between Norman England and France, and Champagne was at the heart of the northern French trade routes – many a troubadour must have passed through the Countess' court. Yet there is little to recognise of Monmouth in Chretien's work, or any of the later romances. It is far more likely that Chretien tapped into the same spring of Celtic legend – as widespread in Brittany and parts of France as in the British Isles – as did Monmouth; many of Chretien's characters have Celtic origins (for example, Tristram and Isolte, Gawain, and Kay).

Virtually all the continental romances (the best known is the *Vulgate Cycle*, a thirteenth-century collection of separate Arthurian romances) are epic tales of chivalry, and clearly distinct from the Monmouth-chronicle tradition in England. They use Arthur's court as the base for their epics, but the romances are largely tales of the adventures of Arthur's knights, rather than of Arthur himself. From Arthur's court sally forth the best and most glorious of chivalry's knights. Back to Arthur's court ride these glorious knights to relate the tales of their semi-magical adventures, and to grab a quick bite to eat and get their armour laundered before they sally forth once more.

Arthur, as suggested by Korrel, above, does not come out of the continental romances well. Chretien, and other poets of the romance tradition, praise him as a great chivalric king – he is mighty, noble and famed about the world for his magnificent court – yet in most of these romances Arthur's actions belie the authors' gaudy words. Arthur comes across as indecisive, weak and petulant, malicious, selfish and cruel. When Guenevere is captured by a renegade king, it is Lancelot or Gawain who must ride out to rescue her while Arthur sits at home and wrings his hands. Arthur appears far too ready to believe ill of Guenevere, and is constantly sentencing her to death by burning from which someone else (generally Lancelot) must save her (true, Arthur does have his hands somewhat tied as he must appear to remain above the law, but he still comes out of these episodes badly). Finally, Arthur's lack of common sense in allowing Gawain's lust for revenge to persuade him to make war on Lancelot presents Mordred with the perfect opportunity for treason, and as well prevents Lancelot from once more riding to Arthur's side and saving the day.

Of course – what else might you expect from French writers? In an age when the French were pitted against the English it was hardly to be expected that they would not take every opportunity to taint England's heroic king. Peter Korrel, in *An Arthurian Triangle*, shows how the French romances were a combination of British heroes (Arthur, Gawain, Kay and Perceval) and French (Lancelot, Galahad, Lional, Bohort and Hector). By the time of the *Vulgate Cycle*, the French heroes are generally treated sympathetically, while the British are not only often villainous, they generally 'serve as mere foils to the French heroes to demonstrate the superiority of the Frenchmen'.[3] Guenevere is customarily treated sympathetically (in contrast to the English chronicle traditions which generally treated her badly), perhaps because the French wanted Lancelot to come out of the romances well, and thus Guenevere was whitewashed so that Lancelot's love of his life is not presented as a 'treacherous harlot'.[4]

Despite their somewhat unkind treatment of British heroes, the French romances exerted a huge influence on English treatment of the Arthurian legend. By the fourteenth century English versions of the French romances were circulating within society – culminating in Sir Thomas Malory's fusion of both romance and chronicle traditions in *Morte Darthur*. The French romances added several major elements: the Grail story; Lancelot, and his adulterous affair with Guenevere; the story of Mordred's incestuous conception; and, as well, the adventures of sundry knights and lovers. During the fourteenth and fifteenth centuries the two differing traditions, chronicle and romance, circulated within England and Scotland. Both appeared equally popular, both were revised, altered and refurbished as the mood took either author or audience. Scores of differing poems, ballads and oral tales circulated. Most of these have now been lost, and all we are left with is the haunting knowledge that

3 Korrel, p. 202.
4 Korrel, p. 201.

they once *did* exist. (Although there are available in modern translation a number of variant medieval Arthurian legends, and still more that remain untranslated, the vast majority of oral culture regarding Arthur is gone.)

4. MALORY TO BRADLEY

White was thirty when he rented the gamekeeper's cottage. He had done with his past, he was on good terms with himself, he was free. His solitude was peopled by a succession of hawks, a rescued tawny owl, a setter bitch on whom he unloosed his frustrated capacity to love. Now in the Morte d'Arthur, *he had a subject into which he could loose his frustrated capacity for hero worship, his accumulated miscellany of scholarship, his love of living, his admiration of Malory.*

Sylvia Townsend Warner's
afterword to White's *The Once and Future King*, p. 816

In the mid-fifteenth century an Englishman, Sir Thomas Malory, whiled away the time in his prison cell combining the English chronicle tradition with the French romance tradition. His effort, *Morte Darthur*, was the last major revision of the Arthurian epic for almost five hundred years. The Arthurian legend we know so well today is a result of Malory's blending of traditions, although *Morte Darthur* is more French chivalric romance than sober English chronicle. William Caxton, who set up one of the first presses in England, found Malory's work, revised it and published it in 1485. *Morte Darthur* became an instant success, and remains so today, although it languished almost unknown for some hundred years from the late seventeenth century. While the printing press has undoubtedly enriched western society – it made books cheaply available to the masses for the first time in history – it also destroyed oral culture. Where there had once been a rich and varied oral culture surrounding any one legend, the printing press promoted only one version of the legend.[5] Nowhere is this more apparent than with the Arthurian legend. Where once scores of Arthurian tales circulated, now we have but one: Malory's. Once one version of a varied tradition is published, it tends eventually to become the *only* version. People read from the single version available in the book, rather than re-telling the stories their parents told them, or listening to the tales and songs of troubadours from distant lands. Today, the process of the destruction of the richness and depth of traditional culture is continuing apace with film.

Caxton also printed chronicles with brief summations of the legend as well, but it was Malory's version that dominated. By the 1560s, the scholar Roger Ascham grumbled that *Morte Darthur* was more widely read at Queen Elizabeth's court than the Bible:

> *In our forefather's time . . . few books were read in our tongue, saving certain books of chivalry . . . As one example,* Morte Arthur; *the whole pleasure of which book standeth in two special points, in open manslaughter and bold bawdry.*

> Ascham, *The Scholemaster*, p. 159

By the early 1600s, however, Arthur's star was on the wane. As suggested by Ascham's comment, the increasingly puritanical English were finding the Arthurian story a trifle bawdy at best, outright lascivious and sinful at worst. These knights apparently committed murder on a whim, and adultery at the mere whiff of a passing lady's scent. At the same time, people were beginning to realise that the Arthur of tradition – glorious knight, chivalric hero, conqueror of half the known world – was a historical improbability. Not only could people no longer believe in Arthur's existence, as a cultural icon he had become an embarrassment.

By the mid-seventeenth century the Arthurian legend had faded from view; a demise corresponding with the decline in popularity,

---

5 This is a well documented process; see, for instance, Elizabeth Eisenstein, *The Printing Press as an Agent of Change* (Cambridge University Press, 1979).

and eventual murder, of the English monarchy itself. Glorious and all-conquering monarchs were an anathema to a Parliamentary-led and puritanically-souled nation obsessed with fighting against any idea of royal absolutism and court depravity. Doubtless the commoners still told stories of Arthur about their cottage fires at night – the fact that the majority of geographical features named after Arthur (Arthur's Seats dot the English countryside) date from this time in history indicates that Arthur was still a well-known name among the rural labourers, but elite society had chosen to forget him.

By 1700, Arthur as the king of romance, legend and myth was effectively dead. He made the occasional embarrassing appearance as a dandified fop in Restoration drama, but the mythical hero largely lay as forgotten as his grave in Avalon. Within sixty years, however, a curious collection of poems and ballads signalled Arthur's resurrection. Bishop Thomas Percy, an eighteenth-century antiquarian, spent his most happy hours rescuing old manuscripts from oblivion. Among his ancient and fire-damaged manuscripts Percy found six poems relating to Arthur, and in 1765 he published what remained of them in *Reliques of Ancient English Poetry, Consisting of Old Heroic Ballads, Songs and Other Pieces of Our Earlier Poets, Together with Some Few of Later Date.* Over the next fifty years more Arthurian poetry appeared in print, although much of it was merely poor rendering of continental romances. Then, in 1816–1817, three new editions of Malory's *Morte Darthur* appeared. England, entering the glorious century of empire and world domination, rediscovered its ancient hero.

The king had been reborn.

The eighteenth-century enthusiasm for Arthur was nothing compared to the nineteenth century which was awash with Arthur-mania and chivalric glory generally. Tournaments and re-enactments of battles and processions cluttered the English countryside, and poets, novelists and artists sat down at desks and before easels and churned out poetry, prose and painting after painting depicting the Arthur of legend. Malory's influence was paramount, although Arthur and his court were heavily sanitised; the nineteenth-century

Arthur was a glorious, faultless king betrayed by his wife and his son by incest. The Victorians adored the invitation to pretentious moralising about the sins of loose-moraled wives and perverse sisters while at the same time venerating the chivalric ideal. Guenevere, poor girl, spent most of the nineteenth century grovelling at Arthur's feet begging forgiveness for her womanly sins.

And thus to the twentieth century. Despite the continued popularity of re-enactment societies and university fraternities devoted to dressing in peaked velvet caps and chain mail, the Arthurian legend has lost most of its chivalric gloss. Instead, the tale has undergone a period of intense revisionism not witnessed since the twelfth century. While the basic structure of the story as popularised by Malory has not changed to any marked extent, the characters and their motivations have been markedly reinterpreted, while a (sometimes histrionic) belief in the historicity of Arthur – again, not evident to any great extent since the fifteenth century – has re-emerged. As films, novels and sundry Arthurian handbooks have inundated the market, historians and archaeologists have engaged in their own quiet Arthurian quests. Did he truly exist? Can there ever be smoke without fire? Surely . . . surely there must have been *something* to have kicked the entire legend off? Hills have been dug up, 1,000-year-old refuse pits pondered over, and historical records studied anew – all without conclusive evidence to prove or disprove the existence of Arthur.

4

THE BETRAYAL THEME

The principle of women, so they say, is the principle of all evil; through women, so they say, Evil entered this world; there is some fantastic Jewish tale about an apple and a snake.

BRADLEY, The Mists of Avalon, P. 13

That is why we have to take note of the parentage of Arthur's son Mordred, and to remember, when the time comes, that the king had slept with his own sister. He did not know that he was doing so . . . but it seems, in tragedy, that innocence is not enough.

WHITE, The Once and Future King, P. 335

*S*ince Monmouth put quill to parchment, the betrayal of Arthur has taken place through two main means: in the chronicle tradition, internal treachery results in civil war which results in disaster both for Arthur and for Britain; and in the romance tradition (and in most modern versions), it is original sin which brings Arthur to his knees, albeit via the vehicle of civil dissension and war.

It takes no great time or understanding of the Arthurian legend to realise that sex, and particularly illicit sex, plays a major part in Arthur's story. But few people realise the full import of that 'illicit sex', nor understand the medieval fear of sexuality, of incest and, by the later medieval era, the distinct antipathy towards women that underlay the fear of sexuality. To the medieval mind, the Arthurian tale was largely a lesson in what can happen, even to the brightest and best, when lust rears its frightful head. Arthur was a product of sinful lust, he indulged in sinful lust, as did his wife, as did his best friend, as did his son (who was himself the product of sin), and as did most of the knights and their ladies at one time or the other. One of the major reasons the Arthurian legend lost much of its appeal in the later sixteenth century was because of a growing distaste for the amount of illicit sexual activity taking place at every turn of the page.

Nowhere is the medieval legacy more apparent in the Arthurian legend than in the original sin motif. To understand the depth of the sexual betrayal around Arthur, one must understand the legacy of the medieval Church and its teachings regarding sexual activity, women generally, and Eve particularly. The shadow of Eve falls over the entire legend: the dark and often tragically uncontrollable sexual desires of women too often result in unparalleled destruction and grief. Medieval authors revelled in the theme, and even modern novelists find it hard to escape this profoundly mysogynist legacy.

The medieval Church in western Europe (then the Catholic Church) exerted a control over society that today we, living in a largely secular society, may find difficult to comprehend. The medieval world was pre-scientific and non-technological. People understood life, the world, the universe, and everything that went bump in the night in wholly religious and superstitious terms. This helps to explain the influence of the Christian Church. This life, explained the Church, was not important, it was the next one which was paramount. This world was the horrible, evil wasteland into which Adam and Eve had been expelled in punishment for their (or rather, Eve's) sin, and only by extensive spiritual effort in this life could people overcome their innate sin and make it into an eternity spent with God and his saints in heaven. Repair the damage of original sin in this life, pay the price in penance and contrition and a lifetime of good works, and you could reap the reward in the next life.

But to achieve the bliss of eternity in heaven, one had to appease the gate keeper – the Church controlled the pathways into the next life. Only a few would make it; at one point a cleric preached that only one in 1,000 souls would be saved. In a world of back-breaking labour, constant fear of crop failure and starvation, of buboes and unexplainable plagues and chronic pain, people clung to the only hope open to them: the next life would be better. If you were good. The medieval European's typical superannuation scheme did not involve saving spare cash towards a comfortable old age, it involved constant penances, good works, desperate attempts to overcome his or her natural aptitude for sin . . . a lifetime of appeasement for Adam and Eve's original sin. Medieval Christianity was a faith of fear – the fear of sin, the fear of the horrors of purgatory and hell and the fear of transgressing Church law. Medieval people would have listened to the Arthurian epic and known from the start what they were hearing: the story of a man's fall from grace through sin. It didn't matter that often the sin was unwitting and unknowing. It was still sin, and it damned Arthur to everlasting failure and heartbreak.

The betrayal theme in the Arthurian epic begins – as it begins for all Christians – in the story of Adam and Eve. This biblical story was a favourite of the medieval Church, and clerics lost no chance to drive the lesson of mankind's fall home: many churches had representations of Adam, Eve and the serpent carved about their doorways so that every time the devout stepped through the doorway into church (or, more appropriately, from the church into the outside world) they would be forcibly reminded of mankind's fall from grace and expulsion from the Garden of Eden.

Adam and Eve's fall from grace had nothing to do with sex, although sex soon became associated with it, if only because of the story's pervading theme of temptation. In the Garden of Eden, Adam and his 'help meet', Eve, lived in harmony with all creatures and all things. They were not tempted with carnal thoughts, because in this paradise lust played no part in the generative process. Because of God's commandment to be fruitful and multiply, Adam and Eve would certainly have had to have intercourse at some point (although theological scholars generally feel that the Fall intervened before they did), but in Paradise our original father and mother could control their genital organs in the same manner as we control a finger. Lust (and certainly not enjoyment!) played no part in the reproductive technicalities of Paradise. Sex was simply a task to be accomplished with no more than a shrug of the shoulders and as much economy as possible.

In the Garden of Eden Adam and Eve wandered naked and unashamed among the flora and fauna. There was only one thing they could not do: eat of the Tree of Knowledge in the centre of the Garden. But Eve was weak, and when the serpent spoke to her and told her that if she ate of the fruit of the Tree of Knowledge her eyes would be opened, and she would be as a god, knowing all things, Eve was sorely tempted. Full of womanly weakness as she was, Eve succumbed, and ate of the fruit, and persuaded Adam to eat of the fruit as well. Knowledge infused them, and suddenly they became aware of their nakedness. Ashamed, Adam and Eve covered themselves with the leaves of the fig tree and hid from God.

God was righteously wrathful when he learned Adam and Eve had eaten of the forbidden fruit. He expelled them from the Garden of Eden, cursing Eve with pain and sorrow in childbirth, and making her the handmaiden of her husband: *I will greatly multiply thy sorrow and thy conception; in sorrow thou shalt bring forth children; and thy desire shall be to thy husband, and he shall rule over thee.*[1] Having given Eve her due, God then cursed Adam with everlasting toil in the fields: *Cursed is the ground for thy sake; in sorrow thou shalt eat of it all the days of thy life; thorns also and thistles shall it bring forth to thee; and thou shalt eat the herb of the field: in the sweat of thy face shalt thou eat bread, till thou return to the ground.*[2]

1 Genesis 3:16.
2 Genesis 3:17–19.

Thus was humankind cursed. Sons of Adam toiled unceasingly in the wasteland, daughters of Eve wailed incessantly in the agony of childbirth. Pests multiplied, and creatures forgot their duty to serve mankind. Thistles and stones sprang from the earth to break apart ploughs. Floods and storms and droughts ravaged the face of this wasteland as men and women alike battled to redeem themselves from their original sin.

And it was all Eve's fault. The medieval Church never, never let their flock forget it. Women were seen as weak and prey to the temptations of evil: and as the serpent had also been expelled from Eden to writhe his vile way through the world, evil was constantly present to ensnare the weak and the unwary. Women had to be controlled, because, out of control, they would give in to the temptation of evil and subsequently wreck the hopes of all mankind. And when not succumbing to temptation, women *were* temptation, inviting men to partake of the sinful pleasures of the flesh. Thus, women were to be wives, help meets, to be ruled over by their husbands and controlled within the bounds of marriage. Marriage provided the walls which would protect women from themselves, and mankind generally from women. Never let it be forgotten that it was Eve who led Adam into temptation, and not the other way around.

Concomitant with an almost morbid fear of the potential evil of all women (a fear which led to the witch hunts of the fifteenth to seventeenth centuries), the Church was also obsessed with the vast potential for evil and sin within all forms of sexual activity. In part this was based on the movement within the early Church towards monasticism and hermitism: renouncement of all the pleasures and temptations of fleshly desires. Only when one led a chaste life, forswearing the evils of gluttony, luxury and sexuality, could one attain a higher spiritual plane. The sexual ideal within the early and medieval Church was one of sexual abstinence: chastity and, preferably, virginity. Thus the Catholic Church's eventual decree of celibacy for its priests, a decree which remains problematical because nowhere in the Bible does it forbid priestly marriage (and in fact, biblical texts seem to encourage it).

No doubt the Church would have liked to enforce celibacy on the entire Christian population, but that was not only impossible to enforce but, *had* it been enforced, would have resulted in the ultimate destruction of the Church itself. So the medieval Church did the next best thing, it decreed that sexual activity was to only take place between a husband and wife within the sanctity of marriage. Sexual intercourse should never be undertaken purely for enjoyment (it was a sin to enjoy oneself), but should be only for purposes of procreation, although intercourse could also take place (again, only within marriage) to alleviate the temptations of lust. A husband could not have sex with his wife if she was menstruating (the corrupted menstrual blood might 'infect' a resulting foetus – any child born with red hair was regarded suspiciously), nor if she was pregnant (no point, a child had already been conceived). Once a wife had given birth, she was then considered unclean for a period of some forty to sixty days and could not be touched until shriven by the Church.

To aid the millions of struggling souls battling the temptations of lust, the Church also banned sexual activity during various times of the year: Lent, Advent and Rogationtide (a moveable feast about mid-year) being the major seasons of enforced abstinence. Lent and Advent were periods leading up to the holiest times of the year, Easter and Christmas, for which Christians had to prepare themselves by cleansing their souls in the weeks leading up to them. Sexual activities were also banned on Sundays and the numerous saints days observed throughout the year, on Mondays, Wednesdays and Fridays (for reasons lost in the mists of clerical absurdity), and on wedding nights (to avoid corrupting the sanctity of the nuptial mass: this decree eventually lapsed under the unavoidable temptations of newly-wedded lust).

Because all men were sons of Adam and all women daughters of Eve and thus would always succumb to temptation, the Church came up with a corpus of spiritual punishment for all transgressions, but particularly for sexual transgressions: the penitentials, books detailing a penance for every sin. The medieval penitentials make extraordinary reading: did they reflect the sexual habits of our forefathers and mothers, or the twisted minds of the clerics? For example, lengthy penances were set for wives who removed their husbands' testicles, dried them, ground them up, and fed them back to their husbands in soup (the patient husband received no penance). Mixing a husband's semen in food to act as an aphrodisiac was likewise forbidden. It was recommended that men who fornicated with donkeys receive twenty-five years' penance, and the offending donkey be flayed alive. Sometimes animals 'polluted by coitus' were to be butchered and their flesh thrown to dogs (although the animals were to be spared if doubt remained of their guilt). More ordinary penances might consist of saying a certain prayer a set number of times each day, it might involve living on bread and water a set number of days per week for a number of years, it might involve going on pilgrimage, not changing clothes except on Sundays, and so forth. If all this wasn't enough to drive any medieval European into a morass of sexual frustration, there were always the Church laws regarding sexual relationships between blood kin: incest. The penances for incest with mother, sister or father's widow were generally severe and might involve anything up to fifteen years of hard work to absolve oneself of the sin.

Medieval marriage was a relatively informal affair, its only formal requirements that both parties speak their consent before witnesses, and that both partners should be free to consent to the marriage. In part, this meant that neither had a prior contract of marriage and that they were of an age to give free consent, but it also meant that the pair should not be related. Today, most societies are careful to avoid marriage, or sexual activity, between close blood relatives (siblings, parents and children, grandparents and grandchildren, uncles and aunts; some societies also frown at sexual relations between first cousins), but medieval taboos were vastly more problematical. The Church prohibited sexual activity and marriage between blood relatives out to the *sixth* cousin and most village communities were blood-related from about the second cousin outwards. To make matters worse, sexual relations with anyone tenuously connected to people who married *into* your family were also prohibited: thus, a brother-in-law's relatives also represented the road to hell. The Church did not leave it there: the relatives of any person a man or woman had slept with also automatically became taboo.

Naturally, these taboos (and the resulting difficulties attaining salvation if they were broken) caused numerous frowns, frets and tracings back through family trees and records – if records were kept at all.[3] Any claims of innocence ('But I didn't *know* she was the fifth cousin of a girl I slept with eighteen years ago at a drunken harvest feast!') were futile. A cleric only had to mouth the verse from Leviticus to damn the sinner for all time: *And if a soul sin, and commit any of these things which are forbidden to be done by the commandments of the Lord; even though he wist it not, yet is he guilty, and shall bear his iniquity.*[4] The implications of this single verse for the Arthurian legend are immense, as they were for medieval Europe generally.

The best example of the horrors these laws could visit on a person's life is the sad and sometimes sordid tale of Henry VIII and his desire to wed Anne Boleyn while still encumbered with the inconvenience of a first wife. Henry was the second son of Henry VII. His elder brother, appropriately enough for this book, was named Arthur – a deliberate attempt by Henry VII to tie his new dynasty's shaky legal claim to the English throne back to the glorious past. He managed to secure his son's engagement to Princess Katherine of Aragon – a spectacular diplomatic coup for Henry VII. Unfortunately, Prince Arthur failed to live up to his father's expectations. He was a sickly lad and died shortly

3 The fourteenth-century Cathar heretics of southern France shrugged off many of the Catholic Church's sexual taboos, recommending, 'With a second cousin, give her the works'. Emmanuel le Roy Ladurie, *Montaillou* (Penguin, Harmondsworth, 1978, reprint 1984), p. 185. These happy-go-lucky peasants were eventually nabbed by the Holy Inquisition and compelled to see the error of their ways.

4 Leviticus 5:17.

after his marriage. The Spanish were horribly offended, and to prevent all-out war, Henry VII promptly engaged the widowed Katherine to his second son, and now heir to the throne, Henry. To do so, Henry VII had to obtain a papal dispensation because of yet another verse from Leviticus: *And if a man shall take his brother's wife, it is an unclean thing: he hath uncovered his brother's nakedness; they shall be childless.*[5] By taking Arthur's wife, young Prince Henry was technically committing incest: however, the papal dispensation allowed him forgiveness in advance.

After some twenty years of marriage Henry and Katherine remained son-less and Henry began to brood on the verse from Leviticus. After all, he knew *he* was not at fault, for he had bastard sons a-plenty scattered among the de-flowered womanly nobility of England. Besides, Henry had fallen in love with his wife's lady-in-waiting, Anne Boleyn. Obviously, his marriage had to be dissolved: but Henry also needed a papal dispensation to marry the Lady Anne, because he had once slept with *her* sister, and so marriage to Anne was also, technically, incest. Henry's request and, later, increasingly enraged appeals to the pope, met with stubbornly firm refusals from Rome. The dilemma eventually proved the catalyst for the English Protestant Reformation when Henry seized the power of the pope in England and married Anne just before she managed to give birth to a daughter – a grievous error that doomed the hapless bride.

The moral of the tale – of *any* tale, whether that of Henry VIII or the humblest serf – was that sexual sin, particularly incest, even if committed in innocence, would condemn you. The Arthurian legend is no exception. The legend is rife with sexual sin resulting in utter havoc and disaster: any medieval person listening to or reading this tale would have read this meaning into it. Uther deceives Ygerna and sleeps with her while she is still married to Gorlois: Arthur is conceived in sexual sin. Arthur innocently sleeps with his sister and

5 Leviticus 20:21.

58

begets Mordred, deepening his own inherited sexual sin,[6] and the child of this sin results in the downfall of Camelot and the destruction of Britain. In many versions of the legend, Mordred then sleeps with Guenevere, contravening yet *another* verse from Leviticus: *And the man that lieth with his father's wife hath uncovered his father's nakedness: both of them shall surely be put to death; their blood shall be upon them.*[7] Uther and Ygerna deceive Gorlois, Guenevere and Lancelot dupe Arthur, Elaine tricks Lancelot, Morgan le Fay – the ultimate medieval icon of sexual depravity – not only knowingly seduces Arthur, but she also cuckolds her husband Uriens with Accolon and other knights, Nimue traps Merlin through sexual temptation . . . and not to mention the galaxy of knights who dull their shining armour of virtue at many an opportunity.

Original (and sexual) sin stains this family like no other in our mythical past. Nowhere is this more apparent than in the treatment of the women of the Arthurian legend. In pre-Monmouth Welsh poems, Guenevere and Morgan appear in positive lights; Monmouth and Layamon also treat Morgan well, although they depict Guenevere as the treacherous seductress. But they are the medieval exception rather than the rule. Almost without fail, all the women of the Arthurian legend are representations of Eve, and of the destructiveness of female sexuality.

Guenevere is Eve barely under control. She tries to be the dutiful, loving and loyal wife, but ultimately fails. Guenevere is 'womanly weak', and she succumbs to the blandishments of Lancelot or, as in the chronicle tradition, Mordred. She also represents the temptation of women: how often does Guenevere's beauty tempt rival kings to kidnap and ravish her? While many medieval authors forgave Guenevere her lapse with Lancelot (depicting Arthur's treatment of

---

6 And again Leviticus: *And if a man shall take his sister, his father's daughter, or his mother's daughter, and see her nakedness, and she see his nakedness; it is a wicked thing; and they shall be cut off in the sight of their people: he hath uncovered his sister's nakedness; he shall bear his iniquity* (Leviticus 20:17).

7 Leviticus 20:11.

her as cool at best), nineteenth and twentieth-century authors often chose to condemn her out of hand, or at least make her the weak link that, when snapped, propels the entire land into tragedy. If Guenevere is barely under control, Morgan le Fay is Eve run riot: the dark witch, the evil seductress, the wanton. Guenevere's and Morgan's betrayal of Arthur is invariably accomplished through sexual means. Ygerna, Nimue and Elaine also betray their men sexually (though Ygerna does so innocently, the act still damns her, and damns her offspring).

Except in the very earliest chronicles, this theme of sexual betrayal, depravity and sin leads invariably to the civil war which is the means by which Arthur and his realm are torn down. Guenevere's adultery with Lancelot (or with Mordred in the earlier chronicle tradition) provides the catalyst for war, while Morgan's incest with her brother provides the weapon – Mordred – by which the fateful blow is struck.

No author since the twelfth century has been able to ignore this theme of sexual betrayal and the eventual calamities provoked by original sin.[8] Even Monmouth and Layamon touch on it, if only subtly: Monmouth was, after all, the one who conceived of the Uther and Ygerna deception. Even modern authors are profoundly affected by it and must certainly address it, even if they wish to deny its potency and rehabilitate the female culprits (Bradley, for example). To exorcise the element of original sin would be to cut the heart out of the Arthurian legend. Arthur lost his kingdom the instant Eve reached for the apple.

8 Although the Arthurian legend is moralistic in the extreme, it is possible to view the medieval epics as a means by which people could indulge in otherwise illegal sexual activity without the guilt or the threat of an eternity spent in hell. Through Arthur, his household and his table of knights, people could explore sexual activities otherwise denied them – through their imaginations, if not their flesh. Arthurian legend as medieval pornography, if you like.

Part II

ARTHUR'S HOUSEHOLD

5

THE BED OF BETRAYAL:
Ygerna, Uther and Gorlois

Ygerne went into the room and had a bed made, a kingly bed covered with splendid cloth. Having observed it well, the king reclined upon it. Ygerne lay beside him, believing truly that he was Gorlois, never suspecting that he was King Uther. The king approached her as a man should a woman, engendering on Ygerne, dearest of women, the most valiant of kings . . . . Ygerne knew not in whose arms she lay, thinking always that it was Earl Gorlois.

LAYAMON, Brut, BZDYL, TRANSL., P. 185

Pendragon broil'd with flames of filthy fires,
By Merlin's mists enjoy'd Igerna's bed . . .
Who sows in sin, in sin shall reap his pain:
The doom is sworn: death guerdons¹ death again.

HUGHES, The Misfortunes of Arthur, ACT I, sc. iv

1 Rewards.

Whoever determined the manner of Arthur's conception, whether Merlin, some dark, unknowable god, or the caprices of Fate, they did so in such a manner as to ensure his inevitable doom. As civil war couched Arthur's conception, so also would the ring of British steel against British steel herald his passing. Arthur was not conceived by husband and wife in the safety and legitimacy of the marriage bed; instead, he was conceived amid the betrayal and deception of his mother's rape.

Monmouth firmly established the tradition of Arthur's conception. In his version, Uther Pendragon, King of Britain, summoned his nobles to a council at London. Gorlois, Duke of Cornwall and staunch supporter of Uther, came with his beautiful wife, Ygerna. Smitten with lust, Uther could not keep his eyes off her, nor keep his attentions even vaguely decorous. Fearful he should lose his wife, Gorlois left court. Uther ordered his return, Gorlois refused, Uther mobilised for war. Leaving his wife in his cliff-hugging stronghold of Tintagel, Gorlois took refuge in a fortified camp elsewhere, hoping thereby not to accomplish both their dooms by staying in the one place. Uther ravaged through the Duchy of Cornwall, burning towns and castles, then laid siege to Gorlois' camp, all the time sliding deeper into all-consuming desire for Ygerna. He had to have her, no matter what the risk. His friend and subordinate, Ulfin, suggested he should ask for Merlin's help. Uther concurred, and sent for the magician. Merlin agreed to aid Uther. He changed the king into the likeness of Gorlois, so that Uther could access Tintagel. The guards at the gate,

> *opened the gates and [Uther] was let in. Who, indeed, could possibly have suspected anything, once it was thought that Gorlois himself had come? The King spent that night with Ygerna and satisfied his desire by making love with her. He had deceived her by the disguise which he had taken. He had deceived her, too, by the lying things that he said to her, things which he planned with great skill.*
>
> Monmouth, *The History of the Kings of Britain*, p. 207

Meanwhile, as Uther lay with Ygerna, his army acted without his instructions and attacked Gorlois' camp. The duke fought valiantly, but was among the first to be killed. Messengers came to Tintagel to inform the duchess of her husband's death, but were astonished to find Gorlois apparently alive and well at Ygerna's side. Uther, maintaining his deception, said he would ride forth and parley with the king, and left. Later that day he returned to Ygerna in his true guise, informed her that her husband was dead, and took her for his own wife. They lived together in great love, having two children, Arthur and Anna.

It is the medieval chronicle tradition rather than the romance that deals with Uther and Ygerna: the romances largely deal with Arthur's latter life and death, and the manner of his conception is often passed over lightly.

Monmouth's version of Arthur's conception – which rapidly came to be the accepted version – is extraordinary. Most remarkable is the deliberate planning behind the story. Arthur's character had to bear some stain from the very beginning, and Monmouth accomplished this through the manner of his conception. Arthur is not conceived in innocence, safety and legitimacy, he is conceived amid the most contrived betrayal that one can imagine. His conception not only stains his character, but it also casts a shadow over his moral and legal right to the throne. The later authors and narrators who addressed the issue of Arthur's conception largely continued with this version: without it, it is difficult to justify much of the tragic betrayal (particularly by the women in his life) which later overwhelms Arthur.

Uther betrayed both Gorlois and Ygerna in his determination to sate his lust. Gorlois was not only one of the highest nobles in the realm – a difficult person to move against under any circumstances – he was also Uther's strongest and staunchest supporter, and of vital military importance in the king's battles against the Saxon invaders. Uther's single-minded destruction of this trust and support for the solitary purpose of seducing Gorlois' wife is close to unbelievable. Uther could have had any woman in the realm, and others, as beautiful as Ygerna and of similar nobility, must have been available. But, no, Uther had to pick the one woman sure to cause civil war. Moreover, this civil war is made further contemptible in that Uther, not the aggrieved duke, pushed it into life. Gorlois did not provoke Uther beyond retiring from court without permission in order to save his beloved wife's honour. But Uther acted without thinking, save in his deliberate haste so that tempers (and desires) had no time to cool. Once armies were mobilised, Gorlois again did nothing to antagonise the king (other than refusing Uther permission to seduce Ygerna) and simply attempted to wait out the king's fury. The war, and the destruction it caused, were entirely of Uther's making. He almost destroyed his kingdom, and he certainly destroyed a good man, in order to have a woman. His pursuit of Ygerna can in no way be seen as romantic; it was single-mindedly cruel, reprehensible and utterly stupid.

Yet this was the man legend chose to father Arthur.

The other person Uther betrayed was Ygerna. In Monmouth's version, as in most medieval versions of the tale, Ygerna is the faithful wife of Gorlois. She does not encourage Uther, nor does she have any idea she is betraying her husband when she takes the disguised Uther into her bed. Ygerna never consents to sexual intercourse with Uther, only with her husband. Thus, both legally and morally, Arthur is the child of a rape and this rape inevitably sends frightful reverberations through his entire life. It is the first, critical step in the long years of sexual betrayal ahead which would cripple Arthur's reign.

Who sows in sin, in sin shall reap his pain:
The doom is sworn: death guerdons death again.

What sort of man was Uther, father of Arthur? In most accounts Uther is the brother of Aurealis Ambrosius, and takes the throne after Ambrosius' death. This is not always the case. In Rosemary Sutcliff's *Sword at Sunset*, Uther barely rates a mention: Arthur (or Artos, as he is in this tale) was begat by Uther on some serving wench under a hedge one night with, one assumes, the minimum of betrayal, fuss or magical disguises. In fact, Uther does not appear in the novel at all as he dies in Arthur's youth, and so Sutcliff allows a middle-aged Arthur to succeed on Ambrosius' death.

But Sutcliff's scenario is rare: there is almost always a hiatus between the two great kings, Ambrosius and Arthur, that is filled by Uther. Uther is a capable king, but not a great one. He is a competent – sometimes brilliant – soldier and war-leader. Uther can not only wield the sword of war with ease, he is also generally depicted as having a soldier's ease of lechery; this is a man with easy desires. However good a warrior and serving-maid seducer, Uther often fails in the diplomatic side of kingship: witness the catastrophically mishandled events surrounding Arthur's conception. He is not, according to Layamon, either wise or quick-witted. While sometimes arrogant, there is some sense of conscientiousness about him: Stewart has Uther feel as 'guilty as Judas' about Gorlois' death, which makes him seek desperately to place the blame for the betrayal on someone else's shoulders (in this case, Ulfin and Merlin).[2] Whatever the regrets and guilts Stewart's Uther has, the easy coupling of his name with that of the supreme betrayer, Judas, does his character no credit at all.

Uther's 'glory days', such as they were, tend to end from the moment he plants Arthur in Ygerna's womb. Uther's task is done; now the legend merely bides its time as Arthur grows to a suitable age to assume the throne; Uther lives only fifteen years from the time of Arthur's birth. During these fifteen years, as before, Uther is depicted as capable but not brilliant. There is no seed of greatness in his makeup, and he barely manages to hold the realm together for his son. As Arthur and Ambrosius do, although much less successfully, Uther must hold back the invaders, and most of his reign is spent in the field of war. Modern authors have treated him with a little more sensitivity than their medieval predecessors. Stewart makes Uther an impatient and impulsive man, but nevertheless one with a sharp edge of 'almost' greatness about him.

2 Stewart, *The Hollow Hills*, p. 324.

In *The Mists of Avalon*, Marion Zimmer Bradley creates an impressively sensitive man, someone capable of generating great love (certainly in Ygerna), but also bumbling, as characterised by his physical clumsiness: 'She drew her skirts aside, feeling awkward as he stumbled – *how clumsy he was! Like a big, friendly puppy!*'[3] From unthinking rapist to big, friendly puppy: Bradley allows Uther to escape the charge of rape by making Ygerna a party to her husband's deception. Ygerna knows it is Uther tapping at her door and, when he hesitates – awkwardly – she is the one to take his hand and lead him to her bed.

Whatever the treatment of the man himself, all manipulators of the Arthurian legend have Uther gently fade – both physically and metaphorically – from the time of Arthur's conception. His task is now only to keep the throne warm – and to avoid begetting another heir. Depending on the version, Ygerna only has daughters within matrimonial legitimacy, or Uther begins to suffer from some disease which makes him impotent and incapable of siring another heir. Meanwhile, the wars continue, and the Saxon invaders become ever more threatening, oftentimes ravaging through the entire island. Half-dead from his illness, Uther raises himself from his sick bed and leads his army into battle against the Saxons. He defeats them soundly, and those Saxons who are left conspire to do away with Uther once and for all, managing to poison him. Dead, Uther is buried with his brother in the Giants' Ring that we call Stonehenge.

On the face of it, Ygerna is treated relatively gently by the legend and its authors, though she also has her faults – she cannot excuse her betrayal of Gorlois. As faithful to Gorlois as she might be, and as unwitting of the deception visited upon her as she generally is, like her son, Ygerna cannot escape that doom-laden verse of Leviticus: *And if a soul sin, and commit any of these things which are forbidden to be done by the commandments of the Lord; even though he wist it not, yet is he guilty, and shall bear his iniquity*[4]. In the medieval mind Ygerna would

3 Bradley, p. 39.
4 Leviticus 5:17.

also have borne the guilt of her beauty. She could never be entirely 'innocent' of the wars and destruction Uther visited on Cornwall, nor of her rape, because it was her beauty in the first instance that inflamed Uther's lust.

Yet as a woman, albeit a sinning one, Ygerna is almost, but not quite, the Madonna-like mother of the hero. In medieval and nineteenth-century literature Ygerna is faithful and loyal to her first husband, Gorlois, and accepts Uther into her bed only when tricked. The chronicles that deal with Ygerna depict her as Monmouth did, as a beautiful woman who drove Uther to such a distraction of lust that he pushed Britain into war and deceived Ygerna in order to lie with her.

Tennyson stands alone in managing to place Arthur's conception within the boundaries of marriage. In the first of his revised twelve *Idylls of the King*, 'The Coming of Arthur', Tennyson very carefully makes Ygerna as sinless as he does Arthur. In order to have a blameless hero, Tennyson must also have a blameless mother (although one wonders how much angst that would have caused the poet; Ygerna would have made a perfect 'false' woman to add to his other 'false women'). The winsome Ygerna is a 'stainless wife' to Gorlois, and abhors Uther's lustful attentions. Uther and Gorlois fight, Gorlois is killed, and Uther storms Tintagel where:

> . . . *compass'd by the power of the King,*
> *Enforced she was to wed him in her tears,*
> *And with a shameful swiftness: afterward,*
> *Not many moons, Uther died himself.*

Tennyson, 'The Coming of Arthur' (1898), p. 312

The choices, as Tennyson listed them, were three: Arthur could have been conceived in shame (i.e. conceived on Ygerna by Uther adulterously); he could have been the posthumous child of Gorlois; or he could be the legitimate son of Uther (even if got amid a great many tears from the stainless Ygerna). In the circumstances, Tennyson had no choice – alone among Arthurian authors he went with the third option.

The latter twentieth-century – perhaps in an attempt to liberate Ygerna from being the mere toy of other people's ambitions – has managed to paint her in a different and far more guilty light. Bradley not only has Ygerna hate Gorlois (she prays that Uther will kill him), but she also plays a witting part in his betrayal (even using sorcery to thwart Gorlois' night attack on Uther's camp). It is true that Bradley's Ygerna is manipulated by the Lady of Avalon and the Merlin of Britain, but the larger part of her betrayal of Gorlois is all of her own design. In *The Crystal Cave* Mary Stewart also has Ygerna play a complicit role in her 'seduction'. In this version, she is no true and honest wife, but hungers for Uther (a hunger fed by the fires of political ambition) as much as the king hungers for her. Ygerna needs Merlin's aid to bring Uther to her just as Uther also needs the magician's help to fulfil his desire under the cover of deception. 'I am no trashy Helen for men to fight over, die over, burn down kingdoms for,' Ygerna says proudly, consumed with self-justification, 'I cannot go to him secretly and dishonour myself in my own eyes'.[5] And yet, isn't her dishonour exactly what she *does* accomplish? As well as the war, the deaths of many men and the scorching of a kingdom? Stewart manages to absolve Ygerna to some degree by having Merlin promise her that no bloodshed nor dishonour shall arise from their deception of Gorlois, and that her husband will not suffer – thus we feel that even if Ygerna's actions do actually harm, then she *meant* no harm. Although comforted by this, Ygerna is no fool: 'If you have brought bloodshed to Cornwall through me,' she tells him, 'or death to my husband, then I shall spend the rest of my life praying to any gods there are that you, too, Merlin, shall die betrayed by a woman.'[6]

Prophesy indeed, for Merlin in his turn is betrayed by Nimue, Lady of the Lake. Betrayal continued through to another life, and always accomplished by the daughters of Eve. Perhaps Stewart's Ygerna should have held her tongue and accepted dishonour with bowed head, for her curse eventually affected her son as much as it ever did

5 Stewart, *The Crystal Cave*, p. 265.
6 Stewart, *The Crystal Cave*, p. 268.

Merlin. Both Stewart and Bradley have a remorseful Ygerna retire to a convent after Uther's death: the perfect retreat for any deceitful wife needing to rehabilitate her soul.

Thus, only Tennyson, in order to create his 'blameless' and 'stainless' king, depicts Ygerna as totally innocent, Arthur being conceived in the innocent (if tearful) safety of the marriage bed. In the latter twentieth century (T.H. White and Rosemary Sutcliff ignored the issue), Ygerna has been made as deceitful as Uther – both contrive Gorlois' betrayal – so that the modern reader, though not attuned to medieval nuances of medieval sin and perceptions of Eve, can fully understand her part in the disaster of the future.

If we put to one side Ygerna's guilt, implied or explicit, the question of *exactly* when Arthur was conceived is one often specifically addressed by Arthurian authors. Two points must be made, both of which later impact upon Arthur's perceived 'fitness' for kingship. First, was Arthur conceived within marriage? With the exception of Tennyson, no-one has the boy conceived within the sanctity of marriage: born, certainly, but not conceived. As far as a legal claim to the throne goes, conception outside of marriage would not have been a problem as Uther weds Ygraine within hours (days at the most) of Gorlois' death. The second consideration, however, has a far greater moral impact on Arthur's fate: *was he conceived before Gorlois' death, or after?* If conceived before, then Arthur is the child of a shameful adultery (not to mention a rape); if conceived after, then, although the entire conception remains shadowy and fraught with nuances of shame and deceit, at least technically it wasn't a conception via adultery which would carry a greater burden of sin.

Monmouth begins the tradition of having Arthur conceived while Gorlois is still alive. However, Monmouth's wording is a little unclear: more sensationally, it might be that just as the deadly sword enters Gorlois' body, so does Uther enter Ygerna. In this second scenario, Arthur will never be able to escape the implications: his life is stained from the outset by Gorlois' simultaneous death and the adultery forced on his mother. Closely following Monmouth, Layamon has

Arthur conceived before Gorlois' death. Many hours before, in fact, as the duke is slaughtered while Uther lies by Ygerna's side, languid with 'amorous delight'.

In the fifteenth century Malory alters the tale, just slightly, but enough to give Arthur a more honourable conception. Firstly, Gorlois is at war against Uther for a long time before Uther decides to seduce Ygerna, thus Uther was not the one to provoke war against the duke (he merely exacerbates it). Arthur is conceived more than three hours after Gorlois' death, declares Malory's Merlin, and thus has no stain of bastardy over his claim to the throne. Malory's line was taken up by many an Arthurian apologist in later centuries: in 1602 Richard Carew, in describing Tintagel in his *Survey of Cornwall*, proffered the aside that this was where 'our victorious Arthur' was conceived, and 'that without taynt of bastardy, saith Merlyn, because her husband dyed some houres before'.[7]

Some half a century earlier, Arthur's greatest apologist, John Leland, working from Monmouth, reluctantly agreed that Arthur was conceived in adultery. However, this should not rebound to Arthur's prejudice,

> *that the father being an adulterer did leave after him a sonne borne to valiant courage, prosperitie, & triumphant victories: seeing he was not in fault, that he the lesse proceeded from lawful matrimony, seeing that he afterwardes proved both a valiant and honest person.*

> Leland, *The Assertion of King Arthure*, p. 19

Writing as he did amid the turmoil of Henry VIII's remarriages and adulteries and the constant questioning of which of his children were bastards and which (if any) were not, Leland no doubt felt it prudent to argue that the virtues of any child wiped out any stain of their conception. Interestingly, Leland's Arthur is not only conceived outside marriage, he is also born outside marriage.[8] (Which begs the question, which of Henry's children was he trying to curry favour with?)

7 *Survey of Cornwall*, folio Ii verso.
8 Leyland, p. 20.

The majority of versions of the legend that mention it, make it clear that Arthur was conceived before Gorlois died, and amid the most horrible deceit and adultery. In earlier versions Ygerna had no knowledge of the deception, but in the medieval mind her innocence could not negate the shadow of Eve, while in later-twentieth-century novels, Ygerna plays as horrid a role in the deceit as Uther does.

After Ygerna is brought to bed of a son, Arthur is sent away immediately. Legend generally has him raised by Sir Ector, a faithful knight who lives in the north of Britain, or sometimes in Brittany. Again, this device is meaningful. Uther will not acknowledge Arthur as his heir, perhaps wondering himself if the boy was truly Gorlois' child. Ygerna, in those versions which have her deceived by trickery, must also have wondered. Monmouth at least very carefully states that Uther continued the deception even after word of Gorlois' death was brought to them. The timing of Arthur's birth would have called into obvious question his legitimacy, for he could have been Gorlois' son, in which case Uther would not only not have wanted to claim him as his own, but also would have wanted to send the boy as far away as possible in case he tried to revenge Gorlois' death.

It was not unusual for any noble lad, generally about seven or eight, to be sent away to be raised to knighthood in another noble's castle. Feudal nobles sent their sons away for several reasons: it removed the boy from the dangers of parental love (they might be too soft on him); it strengthened feudal bonds and loyalties between nobles if they shared their sons about; and it also gave any noble a houseful of potential hostages should feudal loyalties fail. So the fact that Arthur is raised at another court is not unusual, but the fact that he was sent away at birth is. The primary reason given is that Uther was not sure of the boy's paternity, and so he would have several reasons to remove him from his court.

But there is a more subtle reason the chroniclers and authors of the Arthurian legend removed the baby almost instantly from his mother's arms, and that was in order not to give Ygerna time to suckle the child. Medieval people believed that a child suckled a woman's character as well as her milk, thus great care was taken in choosing a wet nurse. Michelangelo, for instance, always claimed that he had imbibed his sculpting skills from the breast of his wet nurse, the wife of a stone-mason. Ygerna, of suspect character, was not a good wet nurse for her son who was going to have to work from birth to overcome (if he could) the stain of his conception. Tennyson, unsurprisingly, gives Ygerna a far more noble reason for so readily disposing of her son after birth: she gives the child to Merlin to raise in order that the barons warring over Uther's throne would not tear him apart. A stainless, blameless motivation in abandoning her son.

Thus Arthur's conception is critical. It sets the scene for the later tragedies in his life, and it sets the parameters of those tragedies. Arthur will be betrayed from within his own household, and by those who should have loved him best. Ygerna's deception (witting or not) rebounds on her son as first Ygerna's daughter (whether Arthur's twin, Anne, or Ygerna's daughter by Gorlois, Morgan le Fay) deceives Arthur into her bed to conceive the son who will kill him, and as then Guenevere takes Lancelot (or sometimes Mordred) into her bed to eventually incite the civil war that gives Mordred the opportunity to strike home the mortal sword thrust. Nowhere are the consequences of this reverberating tragedy more clearly defined than in Thomas Hughes' sixteenth-century play, *The Misfortunes of Arthur*. Gorlois' vengeful ghost opens the play, swearing that Arthur shall be made to suffer as he, Gorlois, has suffered. He curses Arthur and his twin sister, Anne (on whom he begets Mordred), with a frightful fate.

> *Let traitorous Mordred keep his sire from shore;*
> *Let Britain rest a prey for foreign powers;*
> *Let sword and fire, still fed with mutual strife,*
> *Turn all the kings to ghost: let civil wars*
> *And discord swell, till all the realm be torn!*
> *Even in that soil whereof myself was Duke,*
> *Where first my spouse Igerna brake her vow,*

Where this ungracious offspring was begot:
In Cornwall – there let Mordred's death declare,
Let Arthur's fatal wound bewray, the wrong,
The murder vile, the rape of wife and weal,
Wherewith their sire incens'd both Gods and man.
Thus, thus Pendragon's seed, so sown and reap'd,
Thus cursed imps, ill-born and worse consum'd,
Shall render just revenge for parents' crimes.

Hughes, *The Misfortunes of Arthur*, Act I, sc. i

6

GUENEVERE:
'The Empty Vessel, the Shore Without a Sea'[1]

I *cannot touch thy lips, they are not mine,*
But Lancelot's: *nay, they never were the King's.*
I *cannot take thy hand; that too is flesh,*
And in the flesh thou hast sinned.

ARTHUR, IN TENNYSON, *Guinevere* (1898), P. 464

And I *look at Gwynhwyfar and think, 'My God, I could have ended up like*
that myself, an absolute idiot'.

BRADLEY, IN FRY, 'THE GODDESS ASCENDING', P. 78

Next to Arthur, Guenevere is the most complex figure in the Arthurian legend. She is also the saddest. Arthur is glorified, Guenevere is almost universally reviled. She is the faithless wife, the treacherous queen, the womanly failure. Only Mordred can elicit more blame, and yet the majority of the revulsion is reserved for Guenevere. Mordred has no choice but to

---

1 White, p. 511.

betray for he was conceived within evil and thus can do nothing but evil. In most versions of the legend, Guenevere *does* have a choice, and she chooses to deceive: so how can anyone regard her sympathetically?

The medieval English chronicles certainly did not. In the chronicle tradition Guenevere plots, and commits adultery with Mordred, Arthur's nephew. She may be noble and beautiful, but the chroniclers reviled Guenevere for deceiving her king with the usurper Mordred. Modern authors rarely allow themselves much sympathy for Guenevere either: Stewart, perhaps; White almost; Sutcliff retains a cool distance; while Bradley treats the queen with revulsion – her Guenevere is hardly allowed a moment of integrity. The nineteenth-century Tennyson reviled Guenevere as well; she is the false woman, the weak and corruptible harlot, who betrayed her blameless king. Alone among this general repugnance, the medieval French romancers regarded Guenevere with compassion: she is the true lover of the best knight in the world, Lancelot, and she remains true to Lancelot, if not to her husband (whom the romancers portray with considerable contempt). If Guenevere deceives, then she is driven to do it.

Like her husband, Guenevere fills many roles. She is a beautiful and compellingly desirable woman. She is a wife and a queen; her responsibilities soar above those of all other women in Arthur's realm. She is a lover. She is not a mother. She is a Christian. She is a betrayer. She is the figure who assumes the blame and carries the guilt of Arthur's eternal failure. Guenevere is, above all, a daughter of Eve, forever sliding over the precipice of temptation and effecting the ruination of all about her. She is never quiet or still, never quiescent. She is the bright, dangerous flame that propels Camelot and the Fellowship of the Round Table into the ultimate, disastrous conflagration.

THE WOMAN

Like Arthur and numerous of his companions, Guenevere comes from a Welsh background, but her appearances in pre-Monmouth

Welsh tradition are somewhat fragmentary. Her reputation is not bad as such – she is not faithless – but neither does her presence guarantee a serene household. Several of the Welsh triads mention that the Battle of Camlann (where, according to the *Annales Cambriae*, Arthur and Mordred fell) started because of a spat between Guenevere and her sister Gwenhwyfach. Another triad relates that Medrawd (Mordred) strode into Arthur's court, dragged Guenevere from her throne, and struck her (possibly then instigating the battle which killed Mordred and Arthur, although none of the triads are specific on this point). Thus Guenevere is again the cause, however innocent, of the battle that killed Arthur and Mordred. The other incident that occurs numerous times in Welsh tradition is the abduction and rape of Guenevere by Melwas: this became very prominent in the French romances. In the Welsh tradition, as in the French romances, Guenevere must be rescued by one of Arthur's knights (generally Lancelot in the romances). There is never any suggestion in the Welsh tradition that Guenevere is anything but unlucky. She may have been the catalyst for Camlann, but Gwenhwyfach struck the first blow in their argument, and Guenevere had nothing to do with Mordred's behaviour in dragging her to the floor and striking her. Neither did Guenevere invite the abduction and rape by Melwas. There is never any suspicion that she is faithless to her husband, or that there was any discord between them. Guenevere is, however, as barren to her husband in the Welsh tales as she remains through the English chronicles and French romances (save for the odd child she bears to Mordred), while Arthur manages to have several other children (possibly by other wives). To all intents and purposes the ancient Welsh Guenevere is noble, beautiful, desirable and fateful, although not deliberately so.

These traits continue through Geoffrey of Monmouth and into the present day. In the earlier English chronicle tradition Guenevere is bred of Roman stock, has been trained in the household of Duke Cador of Cornwall and is the loveliest woman in the realm. She has beautiful manners, speech and deportment. As the French romance tradition developed the legend, Guenevere became the daughter of

King Leodegan, a respectable king who furnishes his daughter, and Arthur's Camelot, with the Round Table as dowry (interestingly, it could be argued that when Guenevere destroys the Fellowship of the Round Table she may have every right to do so as the Table itself is hers). As the woman who is to become wife and queen of King Arthur, she appears perfect.

But as the tale progresses, we discover that Guenevere is not perfect at all; indeed, she is seriously flawed. The English chronicles do not develop Guenevere's character, merely making her the treacherous wife who plots with Mordred. It has been left to French romances and modern interpretations to provide Guenevere with the psychological frailties that can explain her otherwise inexplicable behaviour. Guenevere is a woman who desperately needs to be loved; Arthur can never give this to her. She is a warm and compassionate woman who feels keenly the isolation of sitting on a throne, and loathes the absences and unavoidable coolnesses of her husband. If Guenevere cannot have the love and support of a husband, then she needs a child – her inability to bear children deepens her desperation to be loved and cherished. Having been let down by husband and her own infertility, Guenevere must seek her love elsewhere.

Lancelot gives Guenevere the love she cannot find within her marriage. Guenevere knows their love is wrong, but she cannot help herself, even though the risks are so enormous. Here she is portrayed as the typical daughter of Eve. Guenevere is weak, she is tempted, and she tastes. The two medieval traditions treat Guenevere slightly differently in this weakness: in the English chronicle tradition (where her lover is Mordred, not Lancelot), Guenevere's weakness is more likely naked political ambition than anything else; in the French romances, Guenevere still manages to cling to her nobility and dignity through her womanly weaknesses. But nobility and dignity are denied Guenevere in post-medieval portrayals of her character. The early-modern ballads generally regarded Guenevere very poorly. One seventeenth-century ballad described her in vile language:

Shee is a bitch and a witch,
And a whore bold.

The Boy and the Mantle[2]

Guenevere has fared little better in modern literature where she is generally depicted as a fragile character. Her weakness is exacerbated by her central tragedy of being unable to bear a (living) child – and is there anything more dangerous than a weak character consumed with failure? In the twentieth century Guenevere's character failings are sometimes reflected in her appearance. T.H. White has her over-dressed and too heavily made-up at the age of forty-two; she is reported among the people of Camelot to be growing old ungracefully, she has no sense of style, and cries and makes disgraceful 'fishwife' scenes. She is 'poor Jenny'.

Guenevere cannot trust or rely on herself, and so she needs to be able to lean on someone or something; if not Arthur, then Lancelot, if not Lancelot, then perhaps the Church. Bradley has Guenevere clinging desperately to religion for support, a woman blind to the beauty of the pagan ways, terrified of her femininity and sexuality, and who sets out to destroy Avalon (a magical island associated with pagan religion) and all it stands for because she is afraid of it (and perhaps afraid of the power of the women who inhabit it). Even our first glimpses of Guenevere as a child are hardly flattering. Although secure within her father's house, the girl-Guenevere only barely feels safe – the open spaces of the world beyond the kitchen garden walls terrify her, and she needs somewhere enclosed to be able to control the strangling panic she feels whenever she catches sight of the outside world. 'You're afraid of everything,' Guenevere's father says to her, and sends her off to marry Arthur (unfortunately, with Lancelot as escort, with the result that Guenevere immediately designates him her 'enclosed safe space') so that she can make a 'good marriage with a trusty man to look after my pretty little featherhead.'[3] Bradley's

---

2 http://www.lib.rochester.edu/camelot/percyboy.htm.

3 Bradley, p. 295.

Guenevere is beautiful, learned and gracious, but she is also shy, retiring, tremulous and fragile: she will never be able to cope with the demands of being a queen to Arthur and leading the court of Camelot.

Sutcliff and Stewart allow Guenevere more strength, but even so she is a woman weak and sometimes lost. In Sutcliff's *Sword at Sunset* Guenevere (as in Bradley) is afraid of the 'Dark People' (the pagans) and the old ways, and blames Arthur's sympathy for the Dark People for the death of their only child, Hylin. Guenevere cannot reconcile the fact that Arthur spends more time with his men than he does with her; the final break comes when Arthur is unable to attend his child's death. Guenevere perceives (perhaps rightly, perhaps not) that the struggle for the land will always come first in Arthur's preferences, his family second, and thus she turns from him to the emotional support offered by Sutcliff's Lancelot figure, Bedwyr; even Arthur's dying daughter cries out for Bedwyr and his harp before she falls into her fatal slumber. Stewart's Guenevere is more mature than most other depictions of her, and with more strength, but even so she is sometimes a lost and lonely figure, and it is this loneliness and uncertainty that eventually makes her turn to Mordred (after having lost Lancelot).

THE WIFE AND QUEEN

Guenevere's marriage to Arthur is a political union rather than one of romance and passion. As king, Arthur needs an heir, and he needs a central figure to provide his court with a focus during his frequent absences of conquest.

Guenevere's roles as wife and queen are inseparable and as both she has one primary obligation: to bear Arthur and the realm an heir. Her central tragedy is that she cannot do this. In Welsh tradition, and in medieval and nineteenth-century literature, Guenevere remains stubbornly barren, *except* in the occasional English chronicle where she bears Mordred children (the ultimate betrayal – she will not bear an heir for Arthur, but she will give his rival two sons). Medieval literature does not comment much on this; Guenevere's barrenness is well known, and the medieval audience did not have to have spelt out for them the tragic consequences of this. Some late twentieth-century novels, mirroring contemporary expectations, allow Guenevere to experience the pain of pregnancy, as well as the loss of her children – the superwoman syndrome? Somehow Guenevere must hold down a successful career as a queen *and*, potentially, a mother (though she doesn't actually produce a living heir). Sutcliff gives Arthur and Guenevere a daughter who dies from an unnamed disease when she is a toddler. In this sole instance it is Arthur who is stubbornly impotent (his sister Ygerna, having first got herself with child by Arthur, then curses him). Bradley's Guenevere falls pregnant, but loses her children before their birthing time. In *The Last Enchantment*, Arthur's first wife, Guenever (there has long been a tradition that Arthur had two, even three, wives with similar or identical names), dies in childbirth; the child is lost as well. Modern readers are left with tantalising glimpses of the child-that-might-have-been; Guenevere is left with double the tragedy.

Without fail in these texts, everyone close to Guenevere shows her nothing but sympathy for her failure to bear a child. Even Arthur never berates or blames her. This naturally makes it worse for Guenevere. She is consumed by a sense of crippling failure (*every* woman can bear a child, why can't I?) and is gnawed by guilt. Other women have borne Arthur children (even his *sister!*) but she cannot. 'Whatever else a queen might do for her lord, her first duty was to give him a son, and she had not done that.'[4] Even Lancelot has a son, Galahad, by Elaine's trickery. As a woman, wife and queen, Guenevere is a failure, and she knows it. No-one makes more of this than T.H. White. He might portray Guenevere as a shrewish fishwife, over-dressed and over-rouged, but nevertheless she is a woman who lives with a tragedy that, in the end, she can share with no-one.

4 Bradley, p. 357.

Guenever's central tragedy was that she was childless. Arthur had two illegitimate children, and Lancelot had Galahad. But Guenever – and she was the one of the three who most ought to have had children, and who would have been best with children, and whom God had seemingly made for breeding lovely children – she was the one who was left an empty vessel, a shore without a sea.

White, The Once and Future King, p. 511

And so Guenevere breaks, she turns into a 'raving woman', emotionally unstable because of her childlessness. White believes her lack of motherhood so dominates her life that it controls her perceptions of everything else: thus she loves Arthur as a father, and Lancelot only as the son she can never have.

Besides producing an heir, Guenevere has other duties to fulfil as both wife and queen. The medieval wife had to be humble and obedient: 'it is the command of God that wives be subject to their husbands as their lords.'[5] God, after all, had made woman as Adam's help meet. As queen, Guenevere was also married to the kingdom; she was required to remain as faithful to it as she was to her husband.

Bradley portrays their marriage not as a love-match, but a political arrangement, a 'painful duty' on Arthur's – and certainly Guenevere's – part.[6] Generally in the literature Guenevere is rarely passionately in love with Arthur – passion she reserves for Lancelot – although she does like, respect and love him, but more as a father-figure than as a lover. Her perception is not surprising – Arthur is usually much older than his wife. He has warred and won a kingdom by the time he settles

---

5 The Goodman of Paris' advice to his young wife in 1393. (*The Goodman of Paris*, Folio Society, London, 1992, p. 75). Elsewhere The Goodman advises his wife to be as a dog, who always has his heart and eyes upon his master, even though his master might whip him and throw stones at him (p. 73). The Goodman was a loving husband, and his views, extreme as they seem now, merely reflected medieval perceptions of the duties of wife to husband.

6 Bradley, p. 320.

down and marries; he comes to the throne at fifteen, then spends some ten to fifteen years before he believes the realm is stable enough for him to set aside the hunt for the invader in favour of the hunt for a wife. Arthur is generally ten or fifteen years older than Guenevere, but often the age difference is much greater. In the early-thirteenth century French romance *La Mort le Roi Artu* (*The Death of King Arthur*) Guenevere is 'at least' fifty and Arthur is ninety-two (the French romancers always liked to give their characters some maturity). Lancelot is always closer to Guenevere's age: a fifty-five to her fifty in *La Mort le Roi Artu*. The age difference naturally tells on their relationship. Guenevere is not the wife of Arthur's youth, but of his heroic middle-age. She often feels over-awed, and sometimes frightened, of her husband. She must live up to his awesome reputation – as well as provide a suitable figurehead for his court – and this often proves difficult for her. Guenevere longs to please him, yet often fails . . . especially in her task of providing an heir. Arthur is also often away, and this does not help the relationship. The medieval romances, as most modern novels, leave Guenevere's deepest protestations of love for Lancelot, not her husband.

The English chronicle tradition gives Guenevere a bit more strength in her dealings with, and feelings for, her husband, but only in the sense that premeditated treachery and betrayal tend to strengthen one's resolve not to get caught. Guenevere often mouths loving words to Arthur, but these are generally lies to further her treacherous adultery with Mordred. In the fifteenth-century alliterative *Morte Arthure* Guenevere is crestfallen and sobbing as she bids Arthur farewell on his departure for war on the continent. Arthur is her 'life's delight', and she would rather die than have him leave her like this. Fine words, but utterly false. In this version Guenevere has already given herself to Mordred and is plotting her husband's death: she is a fine actress, not a woman in love. In Hughes' sixteenth-century *The Misfortunes of Arthur*, Guenevere turns to Mordred for love during her husband's nine-year-absence. Arthur is a 'stranger and a foe' to her, and so she gives her love and loyalty to Mordred (whom she quickly abandons in order to enter a convent and escape her husband's 'sore revenge'). The chronicle tradition makes it clear that Guenevere's marriage to Arthur is purely political, as is also her treachery with Mordred.

Even in modern literature, where you might expect it, rarely does Guenevere love her husband with a passion. In White she adores him, but with affection rather than love. She 'felt respect for him, with gratitude, kindness, love and a sense of protection ... she felt everything except the passion of a romance.'[7] Bradley's Guenevere spends much of her time feeling frightened and over-awed both of court and of husband. Guenevere loves Arthur, but more from a sense of gratitude than anything else: she is grateful that Arthur does not turn on her for not producing an heir; for not putting her aside after the Melwas affair; and she is supremely grateful to him for sanctioning her affair with Lancelot. Guenevere 'loves' her husband with awe, respect and gratefulness.

She is also terrified of him. Whenever we see her fail at something, we can also see her wince at Arthur's reaction (or imagined reaction). Medieval literature (often influenced by the French romances which portray Arthur in a poor light) gives Guenevere good reason to fear her husband: on several occasions he sentences her to death at the stake, and on one of these occasions there is no good evidence that she has done anything wrong. His fervour in sentencing his wife to death is explained to some degree by the fact that Guenevere is also a queen – thus any disloyalty to her husband is also treason to the realm and carries an automatic death sentence. Guenevere is truly terrified of Arthur's return to England after Mordred has made his attempt on the throne: even if she has not succumbed to Mordred's sexual advancements, Guenevere fears that Arthur will *think* she has. Before the final battle against Mordred, Guenevere flees to a convent, not only to assuage her sense of guilt and escape Mordred's spite, but to evade her husband's wrath:

7 White, p. 392.

if my lord has the honour of the battle, nothing will prevent him from thinking that Mordred has slept with me, because of the great force [Mordred] has used to capture me. I am sure the king will kill me as soon as he can get his hands on me.

La Mort le Roi Artu, p. 197

Having survived Arthur's attempts to put her to the stake on several previous occasions, Guenevere no longer trusts his sense of justice and mercy. It is not that she feels Arthur is personally jealous or spiteful – after all, he tolerates her adultery with Lancelot for a very long time – but whenever her frailties become public, then she knows that Arthur will be forced to act, and it is the king Guenevere is terrified of, rather than the man.

As queen, Guenevere also has a highly significant symbolic role to play. She is married to the realm as much as she is married to Arthur, and her behaviour affects the realm as much as does Arthur's. Their marriage, their union and their unity reflects the unity and health of the nation; if they should fail, then so will the nation. Marion Bradley writes that as queen, Guenevere 'created a symbol of the central strength behind all the armies and the wars – the home and center for which the men rallied their strength.'[8] Thus Guenevere's role as queen is of vital importance; she cannot simply shut herself away in her boudoir and while away the hours in embroidery . . . as much as she may have liked to. She is the twin figure-head of the nation, and she must be as strong as Arthur. Because Arthur is often absent, it falls on Guenevere's shoulders to run the court. Guenevere does this as well as she is able, but often she finds this task distasteful, and more often she finds it overwhelming. One of her problems is that apart from Lancelot (who she cannot publicly lean on) Guenevere has no real friends at court; she necessarily is a remote and royal figure. Thus Queen Guenevere attracts resentments and jealousies (especially from her husband's knights), is never freely given

8 Bradley, p. 318.

friendship and, in combination with her frailties of character, it means she has many problems in fulfilling her duties.

Guenevere appears perfect for the job; the chronicles stress her regal appearance. She appears in stately settings, wearing her crown and wondrous robes, and with a train of minor queens and noble women waiting attendance upon her. At the great state feasts Guenevere sits alongside Arthur to receive the banqueters, then walks with Sir Gawain to supervise the serving of spices and wine to all diners. Her conduct and deportment on these occasions is faultless. In the effort to create a suitably wondrous lover for their hero, Lancelot, the French romancers imbue Guenevere with even greater attributes. She organises tournaments so that the Knights of the Round Table may have a chance to gain glory in jousting, clothes herself in the most splendid of raiments, and is gracious and welcoming.

However, even in her role as royal hostess she sometimes fumbles. The best example of this is the 'poisoned apple' episode. Guenevere decides to give a banquet at court. To this banquet she invites most of the Knights of the Round Table. Unfortunately, one knight who resents Gawain determines to poison him, and, as Gawain has a well-known preference for fruit, especially apples, the would-be-murderer places a poisoned apple on a fruit platter. Unwittingly, Guenevere offers this fruit platter about, and a minor knight happens to take the poisoned apple; he dies at table. Though it is certainly unfortunate for the hapless knight, it is a major disaster for the queen. Guenevere is the host, and she must take responsibility for everything that happens at table. The knights accuse Guenevere of murder (by this stage, well into her affair with Lancelot, most of the knights have grown to despise her), Arthur agrees with them and sentences his wife to death by burning unless she can find a champion to fight for her in trial by battle against the revengeful brother of the knight who died.

But Guenevere cannot find a knight to champion her cause (Lancelot is away from court at this stage). Knight after knight turns down an increasingly hysterical Guenevere's pleas. Sir Lionel, whom she had ever thought her friend, replied to her thus:

> *'Madam, how can you demand of me,'*
>> *He answered, 'when you know*
> *That you with ill-will forced Lancelot*
>> *Away from us to go . . .*
> *By Christ who created me a man,*
>> *We are glad you suffer thus!'*

Stanzaic Le Morte Arthur, Ll. 1380–1383, 1386–1387

Sir Bors, previously one of Guenevere's champions, is even more outspoken:

> *'By the body of God on the Holy Cross,*
>> *You well deserve to be burned!*
> *The noblest body of flesh and blood*
>> *That ever breathed here below*
> *Was forced by your vile capricious mind*
>> *Away from us to go.'*

Stanzaic Le Morte Arthur, Ll. 1350–1355

Arthur's role in this episode is both weak and reprehensible (as is much of his treatment of his wife), but Guenevere's is pitiful. Unwittingly she oversaw a murder, a murder that brought into the open the accumulated resentment of the Knights of the Round Table. It is highly significant that Guenevere offers an apple (in some legends, she picks up the poisoned apple and hands it personally to the knight) – here is Eve resurrected in the flawed queen, handing over the apple that will destroy.

Guenevere's credibility at court is undermined very seriously by this incident. To add to her troubles, the most powerful medieval queens have always been those who attain power through their fecundity. Barren, Guenevere is haunted by the rounded bellies of her pregnant ladies-in-waiting. Guenevere might be as gracious and queenly as she can, her deportment and speech might be regal, but she constantly must search for some way to redefine her role; give herself something else to do, if you like, other than provide an heir.

Unfortunately, in any medieval society, this was virtually impossible to do. The medieval queen was essentially a glorified housewife. Guenevere's search for 'something to do,' eventually leads her into the arms of Lancelot and the Church (or, in the English tradition, into the political ambitions of Mordred), and, depending on the version of the legend, both of these 'affairs' can be equally as disastrous.

Guenevere's main sexual failing as wife and queen is her adultery with Lancelot (and/or Mordred). She is Eve who succumbs to temptation and destroys Arthur's 'perfect' realm because of it. Yet there is one other way Eve's failing manifests itself in Guenevere. All wives, and most certainly all queens, should keep themselves chaste. But Guenevere is abducted and raped by a neighbouring king, Melwas, and abducted and almost raped by another, Meliagaunt (or Meliagaunce). Naturally she cannot be blamed entirely for this, but there are very uncomfortable overtones about this entire episode: firstly, Guenevere is seen to be 'at fault' for having allowed her beauty to inflame Melwas and Meliagaunt in the first instance; and secondly it is always hinted that Guenevere herself had a hand in the Melwas abduction, that it was not an abduction at all, but a seduction by mutual consent.

During the early years of her marriage, and before she consummated her love for Lancelot, Guenevere went out riding. Arthur was away, although not too far distant, and an escort of some eight or nine armed men rode with Guenevere. At one point Guenevere spurred her horse away from her escort, and they lost her in a dark forest. The guard later found her horse wandering, but no queen. It was discovered that Melwas had seized her and taken her to a fortified island. It was left to Lancelot to rescue Guenevere. Late that night he braved the fortifications, rescued Guenevere, and carried her home. Guenevere swore that nothing had happened between her and Melwas (in different stories her accounts vary – sometimes they play chess all night, sometimes they just talk) but whatever the truth, Guenevere's reputation was ruined. Arthur later dealt with Melwas personally (although he did not kill him).

There is always a degree of great discomfort about this episode in Guenevere's life. She and Arthur had been married long enough at this stage to realise there probably would be no child. For that and other reasons Guenevere was restless and unhappy. Melwas was a man of high repute, breeding and good-looking in the bargain. Had Guenevere and Melwas planned the 'abduction' together? How had Melwas known where to find Guenevere that day – to all intents and purposes her desire to go out riding was a spur of the minute decision. Again, as with the Mordred episode, Guenevere was terrified at Arthur's reaction. This time, at least, Arthur proved himself more magnanimous than affronted.

The second abduction by Meliagaunt (in some accounts a knight, in others a neighbouring king) occurs some unspecified time later. Like Melwas, Meliagaunt seizes Guenevere while she is out riding in the woods. He has long desired her, and thinks to enjoy her at his leisure within the safety of his castle. Again Lancelot rescues Guenevere, although this time he decides to take the opportunity of achieving some illicit love himself. Finding the chamber in which Guenevere has been locked (together with her guard of wounded knights and some ladies-in-waiting), Lancelet removes the bars from the window, cutting the heel of one hand badly. For a knight with lust on his mind, this proves no deterrent. He spends the night with Guenevere (somehow managing to wake none of the knights or ladies who were also in the chamber), then departs before dawn, carefully rearranging the bars on the window.

But Lancelot has left blood all over Guenevere and her bed linen. When Meliagaunt (generally now repentant after spending a night regretting her capture) arrives to wake the queen, he sees the blood, and accuses Guenevere of sleeping with one of her wounded knights. She pleads a nose bleed, Meliagaunt does not believe her, and denounces her to Arthur. Ironically, it is a true accusation, save in the naming of the adulterer. Lancelot must defeat Meliagaunt in combat to (again) save Guenevere's reputation. Lancelot himself does not come out of this well. He kills Meliagaunt, even though Guenevere was substantially guilty of the charge.

The Meliagaunt episode is very similar to the Melwas episode, in that Guenevere unwittingly keeps putting herself, her maids, and her guard in great danger (especially by riding thoughtlessly out into the untamed landscape of forest). With each abduction Guenevere damages her reputation further. Even though she is not to 'blame' for the abductions, she is still 'at fault'.

Thus Guenevere is hardly a chaste woman, wife or queen, as is her duty; in fact, she is an abysmal failure at chastity. She commits adultery with Lancelot (and Mordred, in the chronicle tradition), but she is also abducted by two other men, and is raped by one of them. She is the fateful woman, the Eve who cannot help driving men mad with desire. Men commit foolishness in order to taste her beauty, men die in order to save her.

For love of her, a kingdom is destroyed.

She is the medieval Helen of Troy.

THE LOVER AND THE UNLOVED

If Guenevere fails in her genuine many-yeared attempt to be a faithful, chaste wife, how does she fare as a lover? Does she embrace her heritage as a daughter of Eve, or does she try to deny it? In both traditions Guenevere is not blessed with an overly happy marriage to her husband. Arthur, as any medieval man, peasant or emperor, has always been concerned far more with external matters than with the peace, harmony and general well-being of his household. He can hardly bear all the blame for this: Arthur *does* have to spend an extraordinary amount of his life on the campaign trail (although, as we shall see, not always justifiably). The chronicles, which catalogue his earlier campaigns, have him spending at least ten to fifteen years away from home; these are years he leaves Guenevere alone to cope with domestic issues and courtly crises. Unfortunately, this is the undoing of the marriage, especially as Arthur often leaves Lancelot (or Mordred) as regent while he is away.

Guenevere first meets Lancelot before her marriage. Arthur, having concluded negotiations with King Leodegan, sends Lancelot to escort Guenevere to Camelot. On the way, Guenevere and Lancelot fall in love (Bradley has them meet much earlier than this; Lancelot rescues Guenevere as a young child from the marshes surrounding Avalon). Thus the tragedy is set. The would-be lovers *could* have eloped at this point. It would have caused a major diplomatic incident, as well as embarrassment to both Arthur and her father, but at least at this stage Guenevere had not been formally married to Arthur.[9] Their elopement would not have been the treason their adultery eventually made it, and it would not have caused the ruination of the Fellowship of the Round Table. In Bradley's novel, *The Mists of Avalon*, a still unwedded Guenevere pleads with her father to give her to Lancelot rather than Arthur, but she meekly accepts his decision to bond her with the king (perhaps an understandable choice for an ambitious father to make).

Bright eyes and thudding hearts notwithstanding, Lancelot does the outwardly honourable thing and hands an untouched Guenevere over to Arthur. They are married, and for a number of years Guenevere remains faithful to her husband. She tries her best to love Arthur, although that love is composed more of respect, awe, gratitude and overwhelming duty than passion. Gradually the relationship sours. Inevitably, Guenevere turns to Lancelot. He can give her what her husband cannot: spiritual companionship, friendship and passionate love. He is literally her champion: it is *never* Arthur who rescues Guenevere from the continual scrapes that ensnare her. Guenevere also feels a sense of pride in her achievement in snaring Lancelot. He is the most handsome man at court;[10] he is

---

9 This is a legal nicety, however. In medieval Europe, all that was ever needed for a marriage to be legally contracted was a formal consent. By accepting Arthur's proposal (in whatever diplomatic manner or form it was couched), Guenevere would have been legally married to him, even though she had never met him. Formal consent made a marriage, a ceremony did not. Whether or not a marriage was *truly* legal before it had been consummated was a legalistic grey area.

10 This is not always the case, sometimes Lancelot has a homely, if not ugly, face, but he is always highly sexually attractive.

certainly the most accomplished. Lancelot is known as the best and loveliest knight in the world: no-one can outdo him in the lists or on the battlefield – even Arthur runs a poor second to Lancelot's chivalric accomplishments (the number of times a be-armoured Arthur thumps into the dirt in tournaments is a regal embarrassment). Moreover, Lancelot remains true to his love for Guenevere even after her marriage. He strays on one occasion only, and even this was through trickery.

It is generally unclear at what point Guenevere and Lancelot consummate their love. To some degree the physical consummation is unimportant, as Guenevere has already been unfaithful to her husband in her mind and her affections if not her body. For years she has shown Lancelot the face of love – noted by many, not the least Arthur himself – and the first time they actually bed comes with the accompaniment of a gentle sigh of inevitability, rather than with a warning clarion of alarm bells. Sometimes their first bedding takes place after Lancelot's rescue of Guenevere from Melwas' clutches, sometimes after Guenevere has endured many years of neglect from her husband.

Once they have become physical lovers, Guenevere and Lancelot cannot stop themselves. Whether in medieval romance or modern novel, they enjoy a fabulous sex life (always intimating that Guenevere did not enjoy a good sexual relationship with Arthur). Initially they are discreet and for the first years of their adultery people either do not realise the affair, or actively protect the lovers (Guenevere's ladies-in-waiting often know). Those who are aware generally are content to let the affair run its course so long as the lovers remain discreet.

In many aspects, Guenevere is more Lancelot's wife than she is Arthur's. She loves him far more, has a far deeper emotional and spiritual bonding with him – and Lancelot is *hers*. He remains unmarried and gives his heart entirely to Guenevere; on the other hand, Arthur is married more to his duties as king than he ever is to Guenevere. She feels safer with Lancelot than with any other man, she adores him heart, body and mind, and he is true to her as any loving husband should be (save for his occasional flirtation with God, but that Guenevere does not resent at all). He shares his body with no-one else save Guenevere . . . or so she believes.

Many ladies at Arthur's court had tried unsuccessfully to seduce Lancelot, but one, Elaine,[11] was determined not to fail. Elaine has long held a passion for Lancelot, but, enamoured as he is with Guenevere, she knows she has no hope of catching him through legitimate means. Thus, one day when Lancelot is a guest at her father, Pelles', castle, Elaine contrives to get Lancelot drunk (possibly she gives him a love potion she had obtained from Morgan), then sends her serving woman to Lancelot with a message that the queen awaits him in a pavilion in the castle grounds. Lancelot needs no urging. He goes to the darkened pavilion. As soon as he steps in he smells Guenevere's scent (with which Elaine had drenched herself). He throws himself on to the bed and the woman it contains.

In the morning when he wakes and discovers the identity of his lover Lancelot is horrified. But there is nothing he can do about it. Elaine lies there, and she lies there with his child already conceived in her belly.

How is he going to tell Guenevere?

In most accounts Lancelot does not tell Guenevere at all, she finds out when news of Elaine's son reaches court. She is appalled, and consumed with a gut-wrenching sense of betrayal – Lancelot has been unfaithful! Having heard the news, Guenevere takes refuge in flight.

The Queen said not a single word,
  But to her chamber fled,
And there, demented at the news,
  Fell down upon her bed.

Stanzaic *Le Morte Arthur*, Ll. 648–651

11 Sometimes there are two Elaines, one the daughter of King Pelles, who bears
   Lancelot a child, and the other Elaine, the Lady of Ascalot (the Lady of
   Shallot), who commits suicide when Lancelot refuses her love. More normally,
   these two Elaines are fused into the one character, as in T.H. White.

She sobs, almost losing her reason, and her maids become fearful, thinking that the rest of the court will guess the reason why she has been upset so badly at the news that, apparently, Lancelot has taken up with Elaine. Even worse is the news that Elaine has fallen pregnant to Lancelot and given birth to a son, Galahad. In other words, Elaine did for Lancelot what Guenevere can do for no man, *she gave him an heir.* To Guenevere the betrayal is double; not only did Lancelot sleep with another woman, but he did not immediately confess his betrayal to her. Indeed, his silence constitutes a lie. Sometimes the betrayal is compounded when Elaine and her chubby, beautiful son arrive at court. Again Elaine tricks Lancelot into her bed, again with the same lie that it was Guenevere who awaits him there (Lancelot is so utterly careless it is appalling), again Guenevere is confronted with Elaine's smug face and always, always, always the baby squirming in the woman's arms.

Her reaction, given her emotional 'marriage' to Lancelot, is understandable, and in T.H. White's account she gives vent to her betrayal and hurt when she summons both Lancelot and Elaine to her chamber. Balling a handkerchief in one fist, Guenevere accuses Lancelot and Elaine of betrayal, calling Lancelot a traitor and Elaine a strumpet. Lancelot quails under her increasingly hysterical attack, but Elaine calmly stands her ground, informing Guenevere that Lancelot had, indeed, spent the previous night in her bed. At this Guenevere loses all control, disintegrating into a sobbing, raving madwoman, her hair tumbling down as she repeatedly stabs her finger at the door, demanding that both the traitor and the strumpet leave. White makes Guenevere a helpless, tragic figure – shrewish, hysterical, ugly – all a measure of her sense of betrayal.

Eventually she accepts Lancelot's apology and reconciles with him in a flood of tears (Lancelot also weeps). Abandoned, Elaine commits suicide (she becomes the Lady of Shallot in Tennyson's nineteenth-century verse), an action that reflects badly not only on herself, but Guenevere and Lancelot as well. She leaves a suicide note, explaining she killed herself for love of Lancelot:

'I knelt and wept with woeful moans,
   But to every plea I made,
He replied he would never be my lover:
   He'd none of that, he said.
So for his sake my sad heart, lords,
   Was stricken with grieving sore,
And at the last death took me off,
   For I could live no more.'

Stanzaic Le Morte Arthur, Ll. 1084–1091

Lancelot has some quick explaining to do to Arthur in order to hide the fact that Elaine killed herself because she could not win Lancelot away from Guenevere. Fatefully, the episode earns Lancelot the hatred of one of the strongest knights at court, Gawain (and a personal favourite of Arthur), for Gawain had been in love with Elaine himself. In years to come it is Gawain who pushes Arthur into civil war with Lancelot.

Even though Guenevere and Lancelot remain undiscovered (or at least, unremarked upon ... it is difficult to equate Guenevere's behaviour in the scene above with 'undiscovered'), guilt drives a wedge into their relationship. Both Guenevere and Lancelot are deeply spiritual people, and they are too well aware that they sin in the sight of God (even if they are not too distressed about cuckolding Arthur). T.H. White explains this as an Eternal Quadrangle; there were four people involved in the sexual liaison between Lancelot and Guenevere: the two lovers, the cuckolded husband, Arthur and the cuckolded God. Lancelot always felt as if he betrayed two people whenever he bedded Guenevere – Arthur and God – and the guilt of betraying God was always the stronger guilt for the best knight in the world. To Guenevere's dismay, Lancelot breaks off the affair when he sets off on the quest for the Holy Grail. Determined to achieve as pure a spiritual plane as he can (necessary to be able to attain the Grail), he forswears carnal knowledge of Guenevere (it does not help him: it will be the genuinely chaste Galahad who attains the Grail). After years searching for the Grail, Lancelot returns home. As much as he loves Guenevere, he is determined not to resume their sexual relationship. T.H. White has Lancelot very carefully explain all this to Guenevere:

> *Lancelot . . . said, apologizing and begging her not to think him offensive, (1) that they could not very well go back to their old way, after the Grail; (2) that, had it not been for their guilty love, he might have been allowed to achieve the Grail; (3) that it was dangerous in any case, because the Orkney faction was beginning to watch them unpleasantly, particularly Agravaine and Mordred; and (4) that it would be a great shame to themselves and also to Arthur. He numbered the points carefully.*
>
> White, *The Once and Future King*, p. 513

Naturally, when any lover has to carefully justify his new-found morality in these terms, it is only going to be a matter of (not too much) time before he slips back to his old sin. White's Guenevere is not too concerned.

> *The Queen smiled outright. He was a darling. She had agreed with every word he said – was a regular convert already.*
>
> White, *The Once and Future King*, p. 513

She knows Lancelot's strengths, but she also knows his weaknesses, and she is right in thinking that it will not be many weeks before Lancelot slips beneath her bed coverlet again.

> *Then, as the book saith, Sir Launcelot began to resort unto Queen Guenever again, and forgat the promise and the perfection that he had made in the quest . . . . and so they loved together more hotter than they did toforehand.*
>
> Malory, *Morte Darthur*, Vol. 2, Book XVIII, Chap. 1

As their love deepens, the lovers become careless: in *La Mort le Roi Artu*, 'They acted . . . with such a lack of discretion that many people at the court discovered the truth about them'.[12] But Lancelot remains uncomfortable with the affair, and his betrayal of God, and he sometimes seeks consolation in solitude. Guenevere pines when Lancelot is away, and, on one occasion where none know where he has gone, she weeps and wails and begs a troop of guards to search out her lover.

> *But none of them knew where they should search,*
> *Or where he wished to go,*
> *And so that noble troop returned*
> *To court with sighs of woe.*
> *They found the Queen there, swooning still,*
> *All lank and loose her hair,*
> *And they were so sad they could not speak*
> *To ease her pain and despair.*

Stanzaic Le Morte Arthur, Ll. 800–807

Guenevere never acts this way when Arthur is away (generally at war) and she has no news of his well-being. Her emotional outbursts, centred on Lancelot and driving her into illness, are extraordinary in their indiscretion, even given that Lancelot is beloved of all at court, and it raises eyebrows.

Eventually the two younger Orkney boys, Agravain and Mordred, force Arthur to confront the issue. The two knights trap Lancelot in Guenevere's bedroom. A fight ensues in which Lancelot kills a number of knights, and flees. The affair is now public, and Arthur is forced to act. He condemns Guenevere to death yet again (it is treason for a queen to share her body with anyone save her husband the king), Lancelot intervenes, pulls Guenevere from the burning stake, and flees with her. Arthur wages war on Lancelot, Mordred seizes the throne while he is away, and Camelot falls.

Guenevere's affair with Lancelot is foolish in the extreme. Her marriage to Arthur may have left her emotionally unsatisfied, but it

---

12 *La Mort le Roi Artu*, p. 108.

cannot excuse, first, her unfaithfulness and, secondly, the sheer ineptitude with which she conducted her adultery. She, even more than Lancelot, increasingly courted disaster with her behaviour. She met with her lover in indiscreet places and moments, and her conduct in public was revealing, to say the least. As a woman and a wife, Guenevere behaved stupidly; as a queen she behaved appallingly. She allowed her own needs to rule her conduct as queen, to betray the realm as much as she betrayed her husband. Nevertheless, even though the entire court became aware of the affair (how could they not, given Guenevere's behaviour?), and even though Arthur himself probably knew about it, and tolerated it, it was left up to the Fellowship of the Round Table to expose her.

The Knights of the Round Table loathe Guenevere. Not so much for her betrayal of Arthur, although that was bad enough, but for the fact that her love distanced Lancelot from the Fellowship. The knights might have forgiven her anything – God knows they were ready enough to tumble other men's wives themselves – but not that Lancelot cleaved more to her than he did to them. Not only did Lancelot betray the fellowship of his fellow knights for a woman, but Guenevere's frequent attacks of jealousy drove Lancelot from court time and time again, driving him away from the Fellowship of the Round Table at the same time: the Fellowship are spurned lovers themselves. For that betrayal the knights are determined to see her dead. Preferably after she has suffered a bit.

The knights are instrumental in persuading Arthur to sentence Guenevere to death after the poisoned apple affair, and all refuse to act as her champion. Arthur eventually persuades a very reluctant Sir Bors in this matter. When Sir Bors agrees, he must answer to the still-angry Fellowship. 'I do it for the king,' he says, 'and for the king only.'

Many answered him again: 'As for our most noble King Arthur, we love him and honour him as well as ye do, but as for Queen Guenever we love her not, because she is a destroyer of good knights'.

Malory, Morte Darthur, Vol. 2, Book XVIII, Chap. 5

Once Agravain and Mordred have 'discovered' his and Guenevere's adultery, Lancelot must leave for good. In doing so he farewells the Round Table. The sadness of the Fellowship is extraordinary, for the knights understand that now not only is their company of knights broken, but so also is the realm.

Guenevere is best known as the lover of Lancelot, but that is the influence of the French romance tradition only. In the English chronicle tradition Guenevere betrays Arthur with another man, his nephew, Mordred. This affair is a clear-cut case of political treachery. Arthur decides to wage war on Rome, he leaves Guenevere and realm in the care of his nephew Mordred, and Mordred takes the chance to seize both.

The chronicles treat this subject with some terseness, as they do all relationships: for the chronicles, the more important things were Arthur's wars and his personal glory. When Mordred seizes power, Guenevere apparently consents to become his *de facto* wife, in some accounts giving him two sons. Sometimes, however, they are lovers beforehand. Layamon notes that Mordred was 'always about' the queen prior to Arthur leaving for Europe;[13] it is a slightly ambiguous statement, but does intimate they were lovers beforehand. Here the guilt, as such, descends on Mordred rather than the queen, although nothing could excuse her actions. The alliterative *Morte Arthure* also has Guenevere conspiring with Mordred beforehand – a clear case of political treachery on her part.

The chronicle tradition reviled Guenevere for this action, and the revulsion only grew stronger as the centuries passed. In the early sixteenth century John Leland considerably expanded Guenevere and Mordred's liaison in a book aimed at proving Arthur's existence and extolling his virtues in an increasingly disbelieving climate of public opinion. Leland would have nothing to do with the French tradition (Guenevere the betrayed wife, the lonely wife, the woman

13 Layamon, p. 232.

only seeking love) and took to Guenevere with a knife sharpened with moralistic outrage:

> as it is sufficiently apparent that she was beautifull, so it is a thing doubted, whether she was chaste yea or no. Truly so far as I can with honestie I would spare the impaired honor and fame of noble women: But yet the truth of the historie pluckes me by the eare, and willeth not onely, but commandeth me to declare what the Ancients have deemed of her . . . . she had not onely carnall knowledge of Mordred the Pict, but also that she was joined to him in mariage. O mischiefe, O lewd life, O filthy dayes!

Leland, The Assertion of King Arthure, p. 63

True, Leland wrote during the early Tudor dynasty, a time of particular preoccupation with the various guises political treachery might take, but his comments prefigure the later puritanical outrage at the sexual misconduct that witnessed the demise of the Arthurian legend in the seventeenth century.

The French romances deal with Mordred and Guenevere's (almost) adultery, but alter it slightly. Arthur goes to war (usually against Lancelot rather than Rome), and leaves Mordred in charge. Mordred seizes power and *attempts* to seize Guenevere as well. Here Guenevere shows a little more sense and a great deal more spunk than in the chronicles. She agrees to Mordred's proposal of marriage (with suitable shudders at the idea of marrying her father's son, as Mordred is in the romances), then begs leave to go to London to shop for her trousseau. Mordred agrees, and Guenevere travels to London, avoids the department stores entirely, and locks herself inside the White Tower (the Tower of London). Nevertheless, as we have seen, Guenevere still fears that Arthur will believe she has slept with Mordred, and it is just one more reason she eventually flees to a convent when Arthur lands once more on England's shores. In the twentieth century, Mordred's 'affair' with Guenevere has been differently handled. Some, like Sutcliff, ignore it completely. Others, like Mary Stewart, tend to excuse it. Stewart's

Guenevere thinks that Arthur has died on the continent, and she agrees with Mordred's plan to seize the throne as quickly as he might in order to limit the inevitable political instability at the sudden death of a powerful king. Likewise, she agrees to become his wife; Mordred's claim to the throne as bastard son of Arthur will be substantially increased with Guenevere as his wife. Stewart's scenario is a highly probable historical one. 'Pretenders' to the throne were always wont to seize power as quickly as they could, and then to wed either the wife or daughter of the previous monarch. However, Arthur was not dead, and Guenevere and Mordred's actions quickly disintegrate into utter disaster. Whatever she does, however well-meaning she is, Guenevere inevitably precipitates the ultimate betrayal of her lord and husband.

THE BETRAYER

There are two 'logical' betrayers in the Arthurian legend: Guenevere and Mordred. Of the two, Guenevere's is the deeper sin, simply because her betrayal is by far the deeper emotionally and physically. Arthur's coolness as a husband, Guenevere's barrenness and her isolation as queen may drive her into adultery, but the adultery plays a critical role in Arthur's downfall. In the medieval mind Guenevere's betrayal is that of Eve: the temptress leads men, and eventually a kingdom, into disarray and disaster.

While the romance tradition concentrates on Guenevere's adultery with Lancelot as a prime force in Arthur's downfall, the chronicle tradition has her clearly the political traitor. Guenevere's role as treasonous wife begins in Monmouth. Mordred seizes the throne while Arthur is away, and takes Guenevere as his wife at the same time. There appears to be no force or intimidation on Mordred's part, and Guenevere does not, as in the romances, flee to the Tower of London and lock herself in. She has broken the vows of her earlier marriage and is now living adulterously with Mordred.

This is such an appalling scenario that Monmouth literally has to take time out. One can almost see him lift quill from parchment, purse his lips and repress a shudder. He writes: 'About this particular matter, most noble Duke, Geoffrey of Monmouth prefers to say nothing.'[14] It is an interesting comment in itself: what was there to say nothing about? The fact that a queen could behave so treacherously, and to such a noble lord as Arthur . . . or is there something else that Monmouth thinks too unspeakable to comment on? It is possible that Mordred was already recognised as Arthur's son in popular belief, thus Guenevere moving into his bed was not only political treachery at its height, but a horrifying case of incest as well.

Whatever, we will never know what it was that Monmouth decided it prudent to remain silent about – but which his contemporary reader would already be aware of (Monmouth's comment is clearly designed to refer the reader to popular knowledge). The known fact is that Guenevere committed a heinous crime by supporting Mordred's treachery: her flight to a convent when Arthur comes home is proof enough of her own fear of retribution. Layamon compounds her guilt by having her involved in an affair with Mordred well before Arthur leaves to conquer Rome; Mordred is always 'evilly' about the queen, and they conducted their affair 'secretly in court and in hall'.[15] In the next breath Layamon calls Guenevere the worthiest woman in the realm, then reviles both her and Mordred as traitors who ruined the land with their greedy plunder; a typical medieval inconsistency.

The alliterative *Morte Arthure* takes Guenevere's sexual and political treachery even further. She and Mordred have obviously been lovers well before Arthur leaves his queen and realm in Mordred's care. Arthur has two swords, Clarent (his ceremonial sword) and Excalibur (his battle sword). Arthur farewells Mordred and Guenevere. He,

14 Monmouth addresses himself to one of his patrons, p. 257.
15 Layamon, p. 232.

Kissed them kindly and commended them to Christ.
She suddenly swooned when he asked for his sword,
And fell down fainting as if fated to die.

Alliterative *Morte Arthure*, Ll. 714–717

At this point Arthur takes little notice, as perhaps, does the reader. Guenevere is merely emotional at the leave-taking, it seems. Only later do the meaning of these lines fall into place. When Arthur returns to do battle with Mordred, the full extent of Guenevere's treachery becomes apparent. She has given Clarent – the symbol of Arthur's kingship – to Mordred, and Arthur is appalled:

Now I see Clarent unscabbarded, crown of all swords,
I am aware that my wardrobe at Wallingford is plundered;
No one knew where it was but Guinevere alone;
She herself had safekeeping of that sword of high renown.

Alliterative *Morte Arthure*, Ll. 4202–4205

Guenevere has not only given her body to Mordred, but she has also given him the state regalia of office. State regalia were highly important in a largely illiterate medieval Europe: visual symbols of power were everything. Pretenders to a throne invariably made a grab for the state regalia (whether sword, orb or crown) before they made a sword pass at the body of the reigning monarch. Here Guenevere has not only given the state regalia to Mordred, but, apparently, *before* Arthur even leaves the realm (else why faint in fright when Arthur asked for his sword?).

In the romance tradition, it is Lancelot with whom Guenevere commits adultery, although Lancelot never makes any attempt to seize the throne. Indeed, apart from their affair, Guenevere and Lancelot are consistently loyal to Arthur. Nevertheless, their adultery results in the fall of Arthur, the Fellowship of the Round Table and Camelot itself.

The medieval romances make no real attempt to lay the blame entirely on Guenevere. Arthur himself has massive failings as a king and a husband (the chronicle tradition also gives Arthur many royal and personal failings); against him Lancelot shines as an example of (almost) perfect man and knighthood. But neither do the romances absolve her. Both she and Lancelot recognise their guilt, and both enter religious houses after Arthur's death in order to try and atone for their guilt in destroying Camelot. Guenevere has a second motive in entering a religious house: she fears that should she leave her convent refuge she will succumb once more to Lancelot's sexual charms.

It is the nineteenth and twentieth centuries which have shifted almost full responsibility for the fall of Camelot on to Guenevere's frail shoulders. Nothing before or since can compare with Tennyson's patriarchal outrage. He alone has Arthur confront Guenevere at the convent. Tennyson thrusts Guenevere onto the floor, grovelling before Arthur who stands, legs set stiff and well apart, before her. Arthur blames Guenevere for everything that has ever gone wrong at Camelot, a blame that rests on her weakness as a daughter of Eve:

> *Then came thy shameful sin with Lancelot;*
> *Then came the sin of Tristram and Isolt,[16]*
> *Then others, following these my mightiest knights,*
> *And drawing foul ensample from fair names,*
> *Sinn'd also, till the loathsome opposite*
> *Of all my heart had destined did obtain,*
> *And all through thee!*

Tennyson, *Guinevere* (1898), p. 463

Guenevere has infected the entire court as Eve's sin has infected all humankind. Arthur meant to encourage high thought, amiable words, truth and courtliness at Camelot's court. Instead, Guenevere brought the entire lot tumbling down. What are high ideals in the face of a woman's inevitable sin?

16 Another adulterous triangle. Isolte was married to Mark, King of Cornwall, but had a disastrous affair with Tristram who, like Lancelot to Guenevere, was her true love.

He paused, and in the pause she crept an inch
Nearer, and laid her hands about his feet.

Tennyson, Guinevere (1898), p. 464

Via Arthur, Tennyson verbally batters Guenevere, the epitome of the unfaithful wife. His stainless king had been virgin but for her, her flesh is 'polluted', Arthur loves her no more, and yet, he forgives her. In 'The Figure of Guinevere', Elisabeth Brewer wrote sarcastically: 'Tennyson humiliated his Guinevere, as only a Victorian male writer could. Of course he had the good of the nation at heart.'[17] Whatever his motivation (upholding moral standards?), and whatever his skill (the imagery employed in this poem is extraordinary), Tennyson's treatment of a hapless woman trapped in an unhappy marriage remains sickening.

THE CHRISTIAN

So thus we find Guenevere, once-proud queen, once consummate woman, grovelling on a convent floor, unable to even look on the wrathful face of her righteously angered husband. Having failed Arthur doubly – she could not give him an heir and she committed adultery – Guenevere is a soul wracked with guilt. She cannot find either solace or forgiveness, either from her husband or her lover, so it cannot be surprising she seeks it from the Church. Guenevere is a life-long committed Christian, but as her world crumbles about her, her faith becomes ever more fervent, sometimes bordering on the fanatic. Guenevere also feels guilt that Lancelot did not succeed in the quest for the Holy Grail because of his sin with her. It is very rare that Guenevere is depicted as anything but a Christian. She leans towards (and very often leans heavily on) Christianity all her life, and once Arthur falls she retreats to the Church and into religion.

17 E. Brewer, 'The Figure of Guinevere', p. 315.

Guenevere may be Christian, but she is a daughter of Eve, and her sins and betrayals are those of Eve. She is the wanton temptress, even though she does not set out to be; she simply cannot help it. Many men desire her, all suffer because of her. Guenevere's honour, constantly being compromised, constantly results in death and war. She may not plot in the same manner that Morgan does, but the results are even worse – her actions cast Arthur, Camelot and all it stood for, into the wasteland of despair. Thus her only redemption can be through Christianity. She must battle the evil within in order to combat the evil she spreads through Camelot. Devoutness notwithstanding, to the medieval mind, there can be only two fates for Guenevere. She could die, but she does not (it is a remarkable thing that *none* of the 'sinful' women of the Arthurian legend die, they all survive the demise of their men). Guenevere lives through the horror of the collapse of Camelot and the death of her husband so that she can truly repent of her sins. As a daughter of Eve, Guenevere does the truly medieval thing, and the *only* thing a medieval woman in her state of sin can do: she enters a convent, takes the veil, and spends what is left of her life repenting.

Thus the medieval Guenevere is necessarily religious, although this only becomes apparent when she takes the veil in a too-late attempt to repent once Arthur has returned to England to deal with Mordred's treachery.

> *Guinevere, learning of the battle*
> *And the deadly ruin done,*
> *Took five ladies and went away*
> *To Amesbury as a nun,*
> *And there she remained in holy prayer,*
> *Weeping evermore.*
> *She never would be happy again:*
> *Yes, white and black she wore.*

Stanzaic *Le Morte Arthur*, Ll. 3566–3573

Malory has Guenevere 'steal' away to Amesbury when she hears of Arthur's death: she must creep through the night, so sinful is she. Once at Amesbury, Guenevere takes the veil and wears the white and black:

> and great penance she took, as ever did sinful lady in this land, and never creature could make her merry; but lived in fasting, prayers, and alms-deeds, that all manner of people marvelled at how virtuously she was changed.

Malory, Morte Darthur, Vol. 2, Book XXI, Chap. 7

Here the remorseful and repentant queen cannot even laugh, and Malory is very careful to point out how 'virtuously' she had changed from her former, 'temptress' self.

There is a very slight variation of the accepted story in the French *La Mort le Roi Artu*. Guenevere, as mentioned above, flees to the convent out of fear of both Mordred and Arthur: she thinks either one will kill her if they find her. But she does not immediately take the habit of the nun. Apparently this Guenevere decides to hide in the convent and wait out the inevitable battle, then reassess her options once one or the other man has won. Neither Arthur nor Mordred win, both fall, and on the face of it, Guenevere now has no-one to fear and can come out of hiding. But there are still men she must fear: Mordred's two grown sons, 'good hardened knights'. At the death of their father and grandfather, these two unnamed men at once set about seizing the country. Guenevere, now terrified that these two will kill her if they catch her, finally takes refuge in the habit of a nun: a slightly less devout reason to take vows than those previously seen.

In the medieval English chronicle tradition, where Guenevere is usually actively involved in Mordred's treachery, this ambiguity is even more pronounced. Layamon, whose Guenevere sleeps with Mordred well before Arthur sets off to conquer Rome, has her flee to the convent at Caerleon because 'she wished not for all the world to see Arthur again'.[18] The alliterative *Morte Arthure* of the early fifteenth

---

18 Layamon, p. 253.

century, where Guenevere not only connives with Mordred, but bears him two sons, has her flee to a convent to become a nun when she learns that her husband has landed back in England at the head of an army:

> *To Caerleon she came, and took the veil,*
> *Asking for the habit for the honour of Christ –*
> *All in falseness and fraud, in fear of her lord!*
>
> <div align="right">Alliterative <i>Morte Arthure</i>, Ll. 3916–3918</div>

The Guenevere of the English chronicle tradition, then, flees to the convent less out of a sense of repentance, but because she fears Arthur will kill her.

Once in the convent, Guenevere's fate becomes less clear. In the chronicle tradition she simply fades from view: Layamon wrote that 'Men knew not what became of her then, and years later they knew not whether she had died or drowned herself.'[19] The romance tradition gives Guenevere and Lancelot two alternative deaths. In the first, Lancelot invades England to deal death to Mordred's two sons. He wins his battle against them, then proceeds to the convent where he finds that Guenevere has just died (sometimes half an hour before, sometimes a few days previously). Lancelot then enters into a period of deep repentance himself, sometimes becoming a monk or a hermit, before he also dies. Having repented, Guenevere and Lancelot spend eternity with God, not each other.

The alternative scenario has Guenevere meet with Lancelot in one final, emotionally fraught meeting. Arthur is dead, and technically the lovers now are free to become husband and wife; indeed, this is what Lancelot has on his mind as he spurs his horse to the convent door. The meeting is traumatic: Guenevere faints when she sees him and must be carried to her bed. There Lancelot confronts her, but Guenevere will have none of him. Arthur has died, hundreds if not thousands of men have died, and all because of their lust. Now both

19 Layamon, p. 253.

must atone for their sins. She pleads with Lancelot to leave her be, and tries to persuade him to take a wife and settle down. But this Lancelot refuses to do. If he cannot have Guenevere then he will have no other woman. Like Guenevere, he will seek repentance in the habits of some religious order. 'Kiss me,' he says, 'and I will go.'

> 'No,' said Guinevere, 'that I will not;
>   Think about that no more.
> We must resolve to deny ourselves
>   What brought us bliss before.'

Stanzaic Le Morte Arthur, Ll. 3714–3717

Chastity has won out. After succumbing to the sins of Eve for so many years, now Guenevere must redeem Eve's sin. Lancelot agrees, albeit reluctantly. At this they part, never to see each other again, living their final years in states close to a dementia of repentance and grief.

Guenevere has tended to become more intensely devout in the modern age. This is generally because modern authors, setting their Arthurian plots within the historical Dark Ages, almost always depict the conflict between the ancient pagan ways and the new, aggressive Christianity that is slowly but inevitably filtering into Britain. Almost always Guenevere is made the representative of the new Christianity: historically, this is quite viable, as the Dark Age Christian missionaries invariably converted a king's wife first, hoping that she would then use her considerable influence to convert the king, who would then convert the kingdom.

This is largely the scenario in Bradley's *Mists of Avalon*. The main theme of the novel is the conflict between the aggressive and all-consuming Christian religion and the old ways of worship of nature and the mother goddess of the earth. Frail, witless Guenevere clings to Christianity as a light and a comfort in a world that frightens her. In full denial of her own femininity, Guenevere is terrified of the power of women – especially Morgan le Fay. Morgan represents the old pagan ways, encompassing the power of the female, Guenevere represents the new Christian way, in which the female symbolises sin, temptation and evil. She hides within Christianity, and she eventually converts a somewhat reluctant Arthur to the extent that he begins to discriminate against traditional pagan practices. Battle is enjoined between the old ways and the new and the battleground is Arthur. The battle is intense, the hatred extreme, and neither win nor lose, although Christianity finally firms its grip over the land and Avalon retreats into the mists (taking with it Arthur: if the battle cannot be won outright, then one can at least cut one's losses by kidnapping the battleground). Guenevere retreats to a convent, but, after a lifetime of fearing the outside world and seeking the comfort of retaining walls, she suddenly feels trapped: '*The walls, the walls, they would drive her mad, closing her in, she would never be free again . . .*'[20]

Poor Guenevere, she always meant well, and all she ever needed was love. Now here she sits, trapped for eternity within the silent and unforgiving walls of a convent, an empty vessel, a shore without a sea.

20 Bradley, p. 995.

7

LANCELOT DU LAKE:
The Best of Lovers,
the Most Secret of Foes

King Arthur answered, fierce and hard:
 'I never thought that you
Would cause me damage, Lancelot,
 As you have come to do,
Or that beneath our comradeship
 You were my secret foe.'

STANZAIC *Le Morte Arthur*, Ll. 2388–2393

*L*ancelot is a sweet, loving man and a glorious chivalric knight, but only on the surface. As a knight he is obsessed with his own glory and fame and finds it difficult to cope with the realisation that his sins mean he will never attain the Holy Grail. Lancelot is also the supreme lover, but he is a man so fixated by love he will lie, he will betray friendships, he will wreck innocent lives and he will murder to protect that love – and to protect himself. He understands the dangers into which he leads Guenevere, Arthur, and all that Arthur has fought to build, and he gives not a damn while still managing to be unutterably pious about his motives and his relationship with God. Lancelot has generally been treated well over the past 800 years: popular opinion can forgive Lancelot (the glorious boy, the supreme knight) his part in Arthur's betrayal, but it can still blame Guenevere, the misused wife and the lonely woman. Once Lancelot's actions are viewed with a dispassionate and unromantic eye, however, his motives and his personality become highly questionable. Lancelot may not be the conniving traitor that Mordred is so often portrayed to be, but he is most certainly weak – as chivalry allowed any glorious knight to be weak when it came to matters of love – and his weakness provides one of the most critical cracks in Arthur's household.

Lancelot comes late to the Arthurian legend, and he is very literally a foreigner in Arthur's court. Some scholars, Roger S. Loomis for example, like to trace Lancelot back through Welsh tradition to ancient pagan gods (tracing Lancelot du Lac – Lancelot of the Lake – to the Welsh Llwch Lleminawc or to the Irish god Lugh Lionnbheimionach).[1] Redacting medieval Arthurian characters back to their supposed Celtic origins is a thriving cottage industry for today's neo-pagans, but the effort so far as Lancelot is concerned is generally useless. All of the Arthurian characters take on vastly different roles after Geoffrey of Monmouth twisted them to his own purpose, and Lancelot was not only a much later addition, but an entirely medieval chivalric construction rather than a pagan throwback. Lancelot first appears in Chretien de Troye's late twelfth-century *Le Chevalier de la Charette* (*The Knight of the Cart*). He appeared in English literature only gradually, and was not fully incorporated until Malory's fifteenth-century *Morte Darthur*.

Thus Lancelot is a true addition of the French romances. The continental romances always concentrated on the sundry adventures and scrapes of the knights of the Round Table rather than on Arthur himself. Arthur does not fare well in the romances, being largely a bumbling foil for the true hero, Lancelot. Thus in the romance

---

1 August J. App, 'Lancelot in English Literature: His Role and Character,' PhD thesis, Catholic University of America, 1929, p. 3.

tradition Lancelot, rather than Arthur, is the epitome of chivalric glory, and Guenevere a much nobler and stronger character in order to provide the glorious Lancelot with a suitable lover: Lancelot could never be allowed to throw away both glory and the Grail for the love of the cold political traitor of the English chronicles.

Lancelot's role has not changed a great deal since his character first appeared in Chretien's *The Knight of the Cart* (the title comes from an incident where an unhorsed Lancelot must take to a cart for transport, a singularly ignoble thing for a knight to be forced to do). He is the son of King Ban of Benoic, a kingdom in western France: the name 'du Lac' (of the Lake) derives from the rumour that Lancelot was adopted, or, at the least, spent some years being educated by the Lady of the Lake. Once grown, Lancelot arrives at Arthur's court, and quickly becomes the darling of the Round Table set, joining Gawain and Kay as one of the king's favourites. Lancelot establishes himself as a favourite of the queen as well, and they become lovers. Lancelot spends many years away from court, at war, on his futile Grail quest, and sometimes because of madness. Always Lancelot comes home to his lover.

Lancelot is handsome (or sometimes attractively ugly), he is desirable, he is often called the best knight in the world, he appears a sensitive and sweet man: especially in his devotion and friendship for Guenevere. Because of his attributes, many trust and lean on him, but Lancelot lets most of these people down. His God he infuriates with his constant adultery, Arthur he cuckolds, the Fellowship of the Round Table he abandons for a woman, and the mother of his child he drives to suicide with his indifference. The only person he is constantly true to is Guenevere. She can drive him literally to madness, but he never, never abandons his love for her.

Lancelot is an anachronism within Arthur's court: a deeply sensitive and spiritual man who nonetheless revels in his own hero-status as the best knight in the world. Lancelot actively courts adoration and yet this inevitably brings him into conflict with the spiritual aspect of his nature: only the humblest can attain the heights of spirituality.

Lancelot's arrival at Arthur's court creates a storm of excitement: here at last is a knight worthy of Camelot, and a knight worthy to be called the best knight in the world! Lancelot can even unhorse Arthur himself, although, if we read Malory, this is in itself not a particularly unusual event as Malory has everyone but the milkmaid unhorse Arthur at some point or the other. But Lancelot can best any knight of the Fellowship of the Round Table, let alone the various renegade knights who try to kill him. Lancelot can also slay sundry giants, outwit the worst enchantments that various witches throw at him, and proves himself a deft hand at rescuing maidens from the various scrapes that chivalric romances insist they endure. Elaine, for instance, who eventually tricks Lancelot into her bed, is left boiling in a tub of water for some five years before Lancelot rescues her! No wonder Lancelot basks in the admiration of not only Camelot, but of every Arthurian enthusiast for some 800 years. In the English chronicle tradition Gawain, Arthur's nephew by his sister, was always the most important knight at Camelot. However, once Lancelot was incorporated into the core legend, Gawain was unceremoniously supplanted. Interestingly, Gawain is the one who eggs Arthur into the final and ultimately destructive war against Lancelot. Revenge? Perhaps, but not only for losing his prime place at Camelot to Lancelot. Gawain is also an erstwhile lover of Elaine, the woman who bears Lancelot's child and then kills herself: Gawain has many reasons to hate Lancelot.

But none of this matters during Lancelot's early, rosy years at Camelot. All love him, and all admire his prowess. In Malory's *Morte Darthur*, Arthur holds a series of tournaments and jousts after returning from his successful war on Rome. Some knights,

> . . . *increased so in arms and in worship that they passed all their fellows in prowess and noble deeds, and that was well proved on many; but in especial it was proved on Sir Launcelot du Lake, for in all tournaments and jousts and deeds of arms, both for life and death, he passed all other knights, and at no time he was never overcome but if it were by treason or enchantment, so Sir Launcelot increased so marvellously in worship, and in honour.*

> Malory, *Morte Darthur*, Vol. 1, Book VI, Chap. 1

Having proved himself on the tourneying field, Lancelot then decides to seek greater glory in 'adventuring', or questing. This is questing merely for the sake of it, or, more properly, for the sake of glory. When the quest for the Holy Grail is announced, Lancelot is ecstatic. Here, finally, is a quest worthy of the best knight in the world: to find the vessel used by Christ at the Last Supper. The quest for the Holy Grail was an addition by the French romancers to the Arthurian legend, primarily as a literary device to send the Fellowship of the Round Table on various adventures, although the Holy Grail story has antecedents in European pagan fertility rites. Only the best knight in the world could attain the Grail (find the hiding place of the Grail), and naturally Lancelot believes this will be himself. But he fails, and in the end the Grail is attained by Lancelot's son, the chaste and pure Galahad,[2] who dies in ecstasy as he experiences divine visions as reward for his success.

As evidenced by his failure to attain the Grail, Lancelot is judged a sinner. According to the chivalric code it was quite permissible for a knight to love a married lady, but the love had to remain platonic. Lancelot is a deeply spiritual man, and the sin of bedding Guenevere weighs deeply on his soul. However, rarely is Lancelot concerned that he is cuckolding Arthur by sleeping with Guenevere, only that he is cuckolding God. Lancelot spends many sleepless nights wondering how he can deceive God while he spends equally happy hours basking in Arthur's favour. In White's *Once and Future King* Lancelot's questing is a desperate attempt to escape Guenevere and save his honour rather than achieve fame and glory.

When the quest for the Holy Grail is announced (rather like the medieval crusades, it was a quest designed to give peace-moribund knights something to do), Lancelot is sure that he – the best knight in the world – will be the one to obtain the Grail. But he does not, and he

---

2 Interestingly, both Arthur's and Lancelot's sons are conceived amid trickery and sin. Unlike Mordred, however, Galahad remains pure of spirit and of body, and his holiness allows him to achieve the Holy Grail. Nevertheless, whether sinner or saint, both Mordred and Galahad die at the end of their respective 'quests'.

cannot. His sin of adultery stains his character so badly that God will not allow him to achieve the Grail. At one point during his quest for the Holy Grail, Lancelot comes to realise what is hindering his efforts. He confesses to a hermit that not only has he long loved the queen in an adulterous relationship, but that his many previous years of questing and adventuring have either been on her behalf (presumably to make her love him more) or in order to win himself more worship and 'to cause me to be the better beloved, and little or nought I thanked God of it'. The hermit berates him, for God had given Lancelot good looks, quick wits, and prowess and hardiness beyond any other man. And yet what had Lancelot done with all his gifts? Befouled himself with lechery.[3] Lancelot does penance, and promises never to commit lechery again, but even that is not enough, and Lancelot not only fails in his quest for the Holy Grail, but before long he also resumes his adulterous relationship with Guenevere. 'Sin is so foul in him,' remarks another holy old man, 'he may not achieve such holy deeds, for had not been his sin he had passed all the knights that ever were in his days.'[4] In White, Lancelot confesses his sins to Guenevere herself:

> *Jenny, all my life I have wanted to do miracles. I have wanted to be holy. I suppose it was ambition or pride or some other unworthy thing. It was not enough for me to conquer the world – I wanted to conquer heaven too. I was so grasping that it was not enough to be the strongest knight – I had to be the best as well.'*

> White, *The Once and Future King*, p. 414

Pride and vaunting ambition characterise Lancelot, and it is possible that in some part of his unconscious mind, his love for the most unobtainable woman in the world, Guenevere, Queen of Arthur, was part of that ambition and pride.

Lancelot's character is frail in other ways as well. Love for Guenevere weakens Lancelot to the point of madness. One day he is

3 Malory, Vol. 2, Book XIII, Chap. 20.
4 Malory, Vol. 2, Book XI, Chap. 7.

trapped (both by Elaine and by Guenevere) in the Lady Elaine's bed. Appalled at Guenevere's fury, Lancelot's mind snaps and he leaps from a window into a thorny bush. Struggling from the bush, his body scratched and torn by the thorns, Lancelot flees where he:

> . . . *ever ran wild wood from place to place, and lived by fruit and such as he might get, and drank water two year; and other clothing had he but little but his shirt and his breech.*

Malory, Morte Darthur, Vol. 2, Book XII, Chap. 1

When Lancelot finally returns to court after two years, Arthur asked what had caused his madness. Was it Elaine? the king wondered. Lancelot implies that it was – the stress of the seduction and then the child – but, as Malory wrote cynically, 'all Sir Launcelot's kin knew for whom he went out of his mind.' [5]

If there is one thing that Lancelot does well, does truly, and does consistently, it is love Guenevere. Whatever his subconscious motives, once Lancelot admits his love for Guenevere he does not ever remit it. He is Guenevere's true champion in a manner in which Arthur never is (or is never allowed to be). Lancelot is far more Guenevere's emotional and spiritual husband than is Arthur.

The actual timing of their first adultery is generally left uncertain. Once lovers, however, neither can help themselves. Guenevere is a jealous lover, and Lancelot gives her two reasons to exhibit that jealousy: his relationship with God, and his relationship with Elaine.

Lancelot never intends to betray Guenevere. His love for her is so strong and so committed that he never entertains any thought of sleeping with another woman. Trickery and enchantment are the only reasons Elaine manages where all other women, save Guenevere, have failed. She either manages to get Lancelot extremely drunk or slips an enchanted potion into his wine, and then has her serving maid inform Lancelot that Guenevere waits in bed for

---

5   Malory, Vol. 2, Book XII, Chap. 10.

him. With nary a second thought, and not a moment's hesitation, Lancelot takes advantage of the unexpected opportunity to bed his love, never knowing it is the virginal Elaine he makes love to rather than Guenevere. Drunk or not, enchanted or no, one might expect Lancelot to have suspected that matters were not quite as they seemed at some point, but he enjoys an entire night of love with the delighted Elaine without ever realising she isn't Guenevere. They finally slip into sleep, he sated from love, she dreaming of the son she will bear from the night's passion.

Lancelot is furious when the morning sun reveals the deception, and perhaps the more enraged because the best knight in the world has finally proved himself capable of being 'unhorsed', even if it is in the bedchamber rather than the tourneying field. Without fail he draws his sword and threatens Elaine's life – hardly a chivalric gesture, even if he has been deceived.

And anon as he had unshut the window the enchantment was gone; then he knew himself that he had done amiss . . .
So then he gat his sword in his hand and said: Thou traitoress, what art thou that I have lain by all this night? Thou shalt die right here of my hands.

Malory, *Morte Darthur*, Vol. 2, Book XI, Chap. 3

Elaine is reduced to cowering naked on the floor, begging for her life. Granted she is no innocent in this affair, but Lancelot is surely hardly the man to go about being sanctimonious about being cuckolded in matters of the bed. Rarely does Lancelot's anger last long. He is saddened by the deception, but he puts aside all thought of murdering Elaine. Instead, he leaves her and rides back to Guenevere (in White's Arthurian rendering, this is the point where Lancelot first makes love to Guenevere. Having sullied himself with Elaine, he decides he might as well do so with Guenevere as well). Guenevere eventually discovers Lancelot's infidelity, and her resulting fury sends Lancelot mad and he spends two years wandering the wilderness.

But this is not the end of Elaine. The girl constantly pines for him, but Lancelot either ignores her or treats her with indifference. Sometimes they spend some years together (generally after Elaine or her father rescues him from the wilderness). But Lancelot cannot forget Guenevere, and Elaine cannot hold him. He refuses her love, and she commits suicide, leaving behind a plaintive note:

> 'To tell truly of the man
>   For whom I suffered so,
> I say I died a fearful death
>   For the noblest knight I know.
> None was so regal or richly graced
>   Or dealt a braver blow,
> Yet baser in field and hall I never
>   Met as friend or foe.
>
> 'Yes, such discourtesy friend or foe
>   Has never shown, I say.
> His manners were of churlish mode,
>   All courtliness cast away.
> I knelt and wept with woeful moans,
>   But to every plea I made,
> He replied he would not be my lover:
>   He'd none of that, he said.'

Stanzaic *Le Morte Arthur*, Ll. 1072–1087

Elaine's death causes the final break between Lancelot and Gawain. Gawain had long loved the maid, and blamed Lancelot entirely for her death. Lancelot should not have shunned Elaine's love, Gawain declares, and thus her death is implacable proof of Lancelot's 'evil fame'. Later Gawain will do all he can to destroy Lancelot, pushing an unwilling Arthur into all-out war against his former friend. But Lancelot is not entirely unfeeling. In White's *Ill-Made Knight* he is consumed with guilt and responsibility by all the things he should have said to, and done for, Elaine, but never did. His peace of mind is not helped by

Guenevere herself who, having reviled him for sleeping with Elaine in the first instance, now berates him for not doing enough for her:

'Why were you not kinder to her?' cried the Queen. 'Why could you not have given her something to live for? You might have showed her some bounty and gentleness, which would have preserved her life.'

White, The Once and Future King, p. 535

Lancelot is not entirely responsible for the problem of Elaine, for the girl herself tricked him. Nevertheless, as Guenevere perhaps too righteously points out, he could have done more for her. But Elaine had become a further sin on Lancelot's conscience, and he could never forgive Elaine the guilt she made him feel.

Guenevere's other rival for Lancelot's affections, and a far more potent and dangerous one, was God. Lancelot may have slept with Elaine, even married her in some tales, but Guenevere always knew that he truly lusted for her. But Lancelot often loathed himself for that lust. As a direct result of his lechery he failed to obtain the Holy Grail, something the proud Lancelot felt should have been his. At certain times he swears to forgo Guenevere, not through any guilt that he is cheating on Arthur (this never appears to cross Lancelot's mind), but because he is cheating on God. God expects him to be pure, and so he must be. Lancelot makes a determined effort during the quest for the Holy Grail, but he can never stay away from Guenevere for very long. Once the quest is over (and has been achieved by his son, Galahad), Lancelot slides back into his old sin.

Then . . . Sir Launcelot began to resort unto Queen Guenever again, and forgat the promise and the perfection that he made in the quest. For . . . had not Sir Launcelot been in his privy thoughts and in his mind so set inwardly to the queen as he was in seeming outward to God, there had no knight passed him in the quest of the Sangreal; but ever his thoughts were privily on the queen, and so they loved together more hotter than they did to-forehand.

Malory, Morte Darthur, Vol. 2, Book XVIII, Chap. 1

Back in the old sin he might be, but with a heavy heart. Lancelot abhors his weakness, and begins to avoid Guenevere. He is a man truly torn between two loves, love for Guenevere (a sinful, lecherous love) and love for God (a pure, uplifting love). Guenevere is appalled, she was sure that she had him once and for all once he'd returned from the quest for the Holy Grail, but now it appears that he might abandon her for God. They fight, he leaves court. Lancelot is torn, for he cannot decide who needs him the most, Guenevere . . . or God? He spends months in an agony of indecision, but then the choice is made for him. He learns that Guenevere is in trouble, and in that instant God is put aside. Guenevere needs him, and Lancelot flies back to her side.

Whatever his other failings and weaknesses, Lancelot is always Guenevere's true champion. He might agonise for months, even years, about the intellectual problem of lust versus piety, but what Lancelot *cannot* be intellectual about is the thought of Guenevere in trouble and needing him. Their relationship might be a stormy one, but Lancelot never lets Guenevere down. When no-one else will save Guenevere, Lancelot is there. Yet in one of these apparently honourable actions, there is deep dishonour.

When Guenevere is abducted by Meliagaunt, Lancelot dashes to the King's castle and, instead of effecting a rescue, sleeps with Guenevere, leaving blood from a wounded hand all over Guenevere and her bed linen in the process. Meliagaunt, on seeing the blood, accuses Guenevere of sleeping with one of her knights. Of course Lancelot fights for her, although Meliagaunt does warn him before doing so:

> 'And you be careful too, Sir Lancelot,' he said quietly. 'I know you are the best knight in the world, but be careful 'ow you fight in a wrong quarrel. God might strike a stroke for justice, Sir Lancelot, after all.'
>
> White, *The Once and Future King*, p. 547

Meliagaunt naturally thinks he is in the right. He is sure one of Guenevere's knights has slept with her, but he has no idea that it was Lancelot himself. In fighting to preserve Guenevere's honour – and her life – Lancelot perjures his own soul. Guenevere *is* guilty of the charge, although Meliagaunt did not realise the true identity of her lover. When it has come down to life and death – Guenevere will die if he does not fight for her – then Lancelot chooses her above honour and above his God. In the ensuing battle Meliagaunt is killed; his death an injustice and a dishonour.

Having once dishonoured and perjured himself to save Guenevere, Lancelot continues to do so. He and Guenevere have now been lovers for decades, and they are in their late middle-age. The discretion of court and the indecision of Arthur has been kind to them for many years, but now God, perhaps, turns against them. The lovers have stirred the resentment of several of the knights, none more so than the Orkney brothers – Gawain, Gaheris, Agravain, Mordred and, to a lesser extent, Gareth (always a far more saintly character than his brothers) – and in remaining loyal to his love, Lancelot alienates (even betrays) the Fellowship of the Round Table which he leads. Agravain pushes the issue to its bloody conclusion, informing Arthur of Guenevere and Lancelot's conduct. Arthur gives them leave to trap Lancelot, but the brothers' plans go horribly awry when they corner Lancelot in Guenevere's bedroom. Lancelot goes berserk, and kills the majority of the knights, leaving only Mordred alive. He then flees.

Arthur sentences Guenevere to the stake again (urged on by the Fellowship of the Round Table, Gawain now at their head). But just as Guenevere is being tied to the stake, Lancelot arrives and saves her.

The Queen was standing by the fire,
    All ready in her smock;
Powerful lords and barons were there,
    All knights of noble stock.
Then Lancelot, berserk, launched his charge
    And thrust apart the throng,
And after his fierce first assault
    None stood up stout and strong.

Not long they fought, and all their steel
    Stood them in little stead;

> *Many mighty barons bold*
>   *Fell on the field dead.*
> *Gaheriet and Gaheris both were slain.*[6]
>   *Then away to the forest green,*
> *Leaving the dead and wounded lying,*
>   *Lancelot took the Queen.*

Stanzaic Le Morte Arthur, Ll. 1950–1965

All of this bloodshed on Lancelot's part is sheer murder. True, he shed the blood in defence of his love, but Guenevere was guilty as charged. Is there any honour in spilling innocent blood to save the life of one justly condemned? Lancelot's actions are understandable in the light of the depth of his love and commitment to Guenevere, but they were wrong nevertheless.

It is at this point that Arthur goes to war against Lancelot; his hand has been forced. Lancelot's actions – however well intentioned – have turned a bedroom brawl into a civil war. Lancelot and Guenevere, together with a goodly host of supporters, withdraw to Lancelot's castle of Joyous Garde. Arthur lays siege, and all prepare for a wait many months long. One day Lancelot addresses Arthur over the wall of Joyous Garde in an effort to bring the war to a conclusion. He points out that he regrets the deaths, and he also reminds Arthur of the number of times he has been forced to save the Queen:

> *ofttimes, my lord, ye have consented that Guenever should be [burned] and destroyed, in your heat, and then it fortuned me to do battle for her . . . And at such times, my lord Arthur, said Sir Launcelot, ye loved me, and thanked me when I saved your queen from the fire; and then ye promised me for ever to be my good lord; and now methinketh ye reward me full ill for my good service.*

Malory, Morte Darthur, Vol. 2, Book XX, Chap. 11

---

6 Two alternative names for two of the Orkney brothers. Their deaths leave only Gawain and Mordred alive of the five Orkney boys.

Furthermore, Lancelot continues, Guenevere is a true queen to Arthur, and the king should take her back immediately. Lancelot lies, again to save the reputation of the queen, and perhaps in an effort to smooth things over. But everything has gone too far, many innocent men have died because of a supremely guilty Guenevere and Lancelot's misguided attempts to save her, and now Arthur cannot just take Guenevere and go. The war drags on (interrupted by the Pope's intervention, forcing Arthur to take Guenevere back but not stopping the campaign against Lancelot), and Mordred takes the opportunity to commit his own brand of treason while the king was away.

Lancelot loves Guenevere to the point of risking everything to continually (and continually more desperately) salvage her rapidly tarnishing reputation. At the same time he continually takes extraordinary risks that ruin her reputation utterly. Why not simply save her from Meliagaunt rather than seducing her within her chamber (a chamber filled with sleeping knights and ladies-in-waiting, any of whom could have awakened at any stage)? Why continue to see Guenevere, and even make love to her, when he was well aware that they were being watched by Agravain and Mordred (and in White's case, Arthur himself warns them about the Orkney vendetta)? In the Meliagaunt situation, as in the final confrontation, the entire disaster was Lancelot's fault: if he had *thought*, then both he and Guenevere would have remained safe, and countless men would have remained alive. Instead, Lancelot was weak and acted impulsively, and a king and a nation were ruined in part because of his actions.

As an example of the loyalty and the romance of love, Lancelot's efforts to save Guenevere are extraordinary, but they are also an example of a man who cannot think through the consequences of his actions. Lancelot is a man obsessed, and his (out of control) obsession drives Camelot into destruction. True, Mordred is the instrument by which Fate tumbled Arthur down, but if Arthur had had Lancelot by his side in his battle against Mordred, rather than still holed up in Joyous Garde, then Arthur would have won against his miscreant son.

Despite his many faults, the romance tradition loved Lancelot and this is reflected in his end. Both he and Guenevere are allowed good medieval deaths: repentant, they have made their peace with God, if not themselves. After the fall of Camelot, Lancelot retires to a religious order where he lives the life of a monk or a hermit for seven or eight years. Some of his fellow knights follow him into a life of religious contemplation: Sir Bors and six others remain with their friend, 'banded brothers', keeping watch over Lancelot and reading books and ringing bells throughout the long years of his penance. Finally Lancelot feels death approaching and takes to his bed, asking that his body be returned to Joyous Garde for burial. Sir Bors, refusing to believe that Lancelot is dying, goes to bed himself. He dreams that he sees Lancelot borne through heaven's gate by a bright angelic host, and when Bors wakes, he finds Lancelot dead. An archbishop, who shared the dream, blesses Lancelot's corpse, saying:

> 'Now I know for certain that the angels were giving this man's soul as great a welcome as I witnessed; now I know that penitence is more valuable than any other thing. I shall never leave penitence for as long as I live.'
>
> La Mort le Roi Artu, p. 234

Thus Lancelot's life ends as a moral. He was the best and most blessed knight that ever lived, the best knight in the world. But Lancelot's flesh was so tainted with the sin of lechery that he could not achieve the highest honour of all, the Holy Grail. Yet despite his failings, Lancelot was a deeply spiritual man. He constantly sought God, and constantly struggled (if as constantly failed) against sin. In the end both the romancers and God allowed Lancelot redemption. Separated from the temptress who caused him to sin so greatly, Lancelot finally achieves salvation through penance and contemplation. The heavenly hosts find a place for him, after all.

8

THE WITCHES:
Eve at the Edge of Chaos

*G*uenevere and Ygerna represent those daughters of Eve who, albeit unwillingly, tempt men into evil and ultimately cause the ruin of nations and dreams. Destructive temptresses they might be, but both women recognise their sins and failings, and both manage finally to achieve a 'good end'. Their example of Eve repentant is counter-balanced by the two women of Arthurian legend who are Eve unrepentant: Morgan le Fay and her sister Morgause. They represent female sexuality out of control, women who devote themselves to the dark arts, and who use both their sexuality and their arts in the effort to disrupt Arthur's court. Depending on the version of the legend, Morgan and Morgause share the honour of bearing Arthur's son. Neither sister seeks redemption for her sins, neither needs God's forgiveness, but both meet different fates. Morgause's rampant lust finally brings her to a gruesome death, a suitably fitting end for any unrepentant daughter of Eve, but Morgan manages to do better. Despite every Christian and patriarchal medieval attempt to blacken her character, Morgan maintains control of her own destiny. No-one ever tames her: not Arthur, not God, not any of the past millennia of Arthurian authors.

There is another woman lingering in the background of the Arthurian myth. Nimue (sometimes called Vivien), the Lady of the Lake, is a strangely ambivalent figure. Like Morgan and Morgause,

Nimue is a woman of sexuality – a dangerous sexuality, for it traps Merlin and drains him of his power and influence. But although she emasculates Merlin, and then assumes his role at court, Nimue is not a threatening figure. She uses her ill-gained position to protect Arthur, especially against the magic of Morgan le Fay. She becomes the magical protectress of Arthur and his realm – although she fails, as Merlin did, to protect him from what truly hurts him – Mordred and Guenevere's affair with Lancelot. In the earlier chronicle tradition Nimue and Morgan le Fay are one and the same character, splitting into different identities as the legend grew during the thirteenth and fourteenth centuries. Although not as malevolent as Morgan and Morgause, Nimue deserves to be discussed in the same chapter as they: she is closely identified with the Morgan character, and she, as they, knowingly uses her sexuality to bind a man and drain him of life, as Morgause and Morgan attempt to do with Arthur.

MORGAN LE FAY

Morgan le Fay is the original character from which Nimue later became a derivative. She appears briefly in Geoffrey of Monmouth's *Life of Merlin*, where she carries Arthur off to the Isle of Avalon for healing (Monmouth does not mention her in his *History of the Kings of Britain*). In Chretien de Troyes' romances Morgan becomes Arthur's sister, a healer, and, eventually, somewhat of an embarrassment when she has an affair with Guenevere's cousin, Guiomar. Ejected from court by an enraged Guenevere, Morgan bears Guiomar's son in secret, and then seeks to learn power from Merlin. As the medieval age progressed, Morgan's originally positive character was further blackened. She lost her beauty, becoming the archetypical ugly, evil witch with no redeeming characteristics. By the mid-medieval period Morgan's nurturing and healing qualities were split from her character and invested in Nimue, Lady of the Lake. It is also probable that the character of Elaine, daughter of the King of

Pelles, who seduced Lancelot away from Guenevere and bore him a child, is also a derivative of Morgan. If for no other reason than the characters of Nimue and Elaine all derive from her, Morgan le Fay is one of the most critical characters of the Arthurian myth.

Scholars have argued back and forth about the Celtic origins of Morgan. It is highly likely that she was a well-known character in oral culture before and during the development of the earlier medieval Arthurian literature. Monmouth and Chretien both doubtless borrowed her from this culture, and – prophetically – Morgan appears in twelfth-century German Arthurian literature as a witch-like character who flies through the air so efficiently she can circumnavigate the globe, lives equally well below the water as above it (a very traditional Morganic association with water), transforms men into animals and vice versa, and controls all manner of demons, devils and dragons. Many scholars associate her with ancient goddesses of the sea, with the Gaulish goddess Matrona and/or the Irish goddess Morrigan.

Whatever her pre-Christian origins, Morgan le Fay did not long survive as a benevolent healer or shape-shifter. In a patriarchal and woman-fearing medieval Europe, Morgan became the evil witch, Eve beyond control, the chaos threatening at the edge of every life. Only very recently has any attempt been made to redeem her: Marion Zimmer Bradley's *The Mists of Avalon* is a determined effort to revise our perception of Morgan le Fay to that of a fragile-yet-strong woman who does her best in a deteriorating and Christianising world to protect the old ways and to aid her brother Arthur. After some 800 years of Christian condemnation, Bradley has finally stripped Morgan of her broomstick and witch's hat and placed her back where she belongs, gliding across the lake through the mists of Avalon, at peace with nature and her power.

Morgan is Arthur's half-sister, in most tales born to Ygerna and Gorlois before Uther fathered Arthur. Her youth is shrouded in mystery, but as she is always associated with the pagan arts of Avalon, doubtless she spends her early years in training on the island. She appears at Arthur's court when he first becomes king. She (or her associate, Nimue) gives Arthur a magical sword, Excalibur, that was forged on the Island of Avalon. The sword is sheathed in a magical scabbard which protects Arthur from excessive blood loss, and thus death. In many of the Arthurian tales, Morgan takes advantage of Arthur's youth and naivety to seduce her brother (her split character and sister, Morgause, often does this, and I discuss it in more detail in the section on Morgause) and conceive his nemesis, Mordred. Whether as the mother of Arthur's son or not, Morgan then embarks on a lifetime of dark works, generally aimed at displacing Arthur from the throne so either her lover, Accolon, or her son, Mordred, can succeed him. However Morgan is not a totally evil character. Her malevolence ceases when Arthur is mortally wounded at the Battle of Camlann. She gathers him into her barge, and transports him to the Isle of Avalon in order to heal him.

As child of the Duke and Duchess of Cornwall, and as sister to the high king, Morgan is a high noble in her own right. As with all women of her era, Morgan is married, although in most accounts she remains single until mid-life. Her husband is the elderly Uriens, King of North Wales. Sometimes Morgan bears Uriens a son, Owain or Yvain, but usually she remains childless (apart from the son she gives Arthur). Trapped in an unsatisfying marriage, Morgan engages in love affairs. Her most notable lover is Accolon. In order to raise him to the throne, Morgan steals Arthur's magical sword and scabbard and gives them to Accolon. Eventually Arthur and Accolon battle it out, and despite the weapon's magical properties, Accolon is killed. Arthur regains his sword, but Morgan – furious and devastated – hides the scabbard (often in the Lake itself): Arthur has lost his magical protection against bleeding to death in battle.

Whether because Arthur kills Accolon, or because of her commitment to the dark arts, Morgan becomes the bane of Arthur's kingship. She attempts to kill him, on one occasion sending a poisoned cloak to Arthur's court; Arthur escapes death only when Nimue intervenes. Morgan also attempts to seduce Lancelot, and in at least one instance is actively involved in Elaine's successful seduction of the man. Her lovers create havoc at Arthur's court. Morgan plots against her husband, makes Guenevere's life a misery, and generally creates disharmony wherever she appears. In Christian perception, she becomes the dark witch who uses her sexuality and dark enchantments to seduce men to her cause, and then throw them against the established order.

Morgan *should* be the unreformable evil witch, yet she escapes this fate – a remarkable achievement in the woman-hating, Christian dominated culture of the high Middle Ages. Of all the characters of Arthur's household, Morgan manages to maintain control of her own destiny. She survives the frightful destruction of Camelot, and is the one who escorts Arthur's dying body and spirit away for healing on the enchanted Isle of Avalon. Of all things, this most symbolises the bond with her brother. It is a love–hate relationship, best explored in Bradley's *Mists of Avalon*, but also present in medieval literature. Despite her feuds with Arthur, they remain brother and sister, sometimes lovers, sometimes helpmeets, always bonded by ties of tragedy and love. Guenevere, Lancelot, Mordred, even Uther and Ygerna in their own way, all betray Arthur. When it matters, Morgan does not. When everyone else has failed Arthur, she is there for him.

The Enchantress

Of all the female characters in the Arthurian legend, Morgan is the most powerful, even more so than Merlin. Merlin may be a powerful prophet, Morgan is the practitioner. Merlin sees what can go wrong, Morgan accomplishes it. Morgan considers Merlin a somewhat tiresome old man, and it is fitting that it is her derivative character, Nimue, who finally divests Merlin of his power and confines him to his crystal cave.

Morgan must still be smiling through the mists.

In her earliest appearances in the Arthurian legends Morgan is a powerful but benevolent figure. She is a magical healer, and one of the ladies of Avalon. In Layamon's *Brut* she is the 'fairest of maidens, the beautiful elf Queen Argante' who will make Arthur whole again and keep him until England needs him once more.[1] Arthur's birth is witnessed by magical elves (possibly three of the ladies of Avalon) and his sword is fashioned by enchantment in Avalon. Layamon's Arthur is thus closely tied to Avalon, and to Morgan. She oversees the gateways of his life – his birth and his passage through death – and Avalon's magicians bless Arthur and his reign with his sword Caliburn (Excalibur).

Morgan never loses her capacity as a healer, even through the darkest veils of Christian condemnation. In Chretien de Troyes' late-twelfth-century *Erec et Enide*, Morgan's poultices bring instant relief from almost any wound:

> *The King . . . has a plaster brought which Morgan, his sister, had made. This plaster, which Morgan had given to Arthur, was of such sovereign virtue that no wound, whether on nerve or joint, provided it were treated with the plaster once a day, could fail to be completely cured and healed within a week.*

> *Erec et Enide*, Vv. 3931–4280

In Malory's *Morte Darthur* Morgan uses her arts to both cause wounds and then heal them, as it suits her purpose. When the hapless knight Sir Alisander finds himself under Morgan's care after receiving sixteen great wounds in a tournament, she first rubs 'such an ointment into him that he should have died', and then, when he complains about it the next day, smilingly rubs different ointments into him that take away all the pain. Then Morgan doses Alisander with yet another magical potion which puts him into a deep sleep for three days, during which time Morgan spirits him into her castle. There, having wrung from Alisander the promise that he will stay with her a year and a day, she makes him completely whole.[2] In *The Mists of Avalon* Morgan also uses her skills to brew a potion to aid in Elaine's seduction of Lancelot.

1 Layamon, p. 254.
2 Malory, Vol. 2, Book X, Chap. 37.

Healing and magic are intertwined in her character. What can one day be used to heal, may the next be used to trap.

Well might Morgan trifle with the lives of sundry knights of the Round Table, but her greatest healing arts are reserved for Arthur. In most accounts it is generally her hands that fashion the magical scabbard for Arthur's sword, Excalibur. While it is in Arthur's possession, the scabbard prevents him bleeding to death in any battle. Most importantly, Morgan is the one who spirits Arthur back to Avalon to heal the mortal blow struck by Mordred.

Morgan displays her magical abilities in many episodes. As well as the magical scabbard she gives Arthur, Morgan makes other magically endowed objects. She sends Arthur a poisoned cloak, and gives Sir Tristram a shield that aids him in tournaments and battle. Somewhat amusingly, on the shield are painted a king and a queen, with a knight standing above them with a foot on each of the crowned heads. When Tristram asks Morgan what this means, Morgan's mouth twists and she says, 'It signifieth King Arthur and Queen Guenever, and a knight who holdeth them both in bondage and in servage.' Tristram (who plays his own Lancelot-role in his affair with King Mark's queen) asks who this knight might be, but Morgan will not tell him though she is forever dropping hints to Arthur about the dangers of Lancelot and Guenevere.[3]

Morgan is also something of a shape-shifter, although this ability is usually ignored in medieval literature. In Malory she can change herself, and the score or more of knights who ride with her, into standing stones to elude capture by a vengeful Arthur. She appears and disappears at will, and can create enchanted surroundings with no apparent effort. One day Arthur, out riding in a forest, sends one of his knights to find lodging. The knight, Sagremor the Foolish, discovers a forbidding castle deep within the trees. The lady of the castle, Morgan, says she would be delighted to have Arthur stay. Once Arthur and his retinue arrive at the castle, the forbidding aspect has gone, the walls and parapets are draped with exquisite silks and a

3 Malory, Vol. 1, Book IX, Chap. 41.

thousand candles in golden sticks bathed courtyards and windows alike in light. 'In faith,' Arthur says a little dryly as he looks about the courtyard, 'if there were great wealth inside, I should not be surprised, because there is an excess of it out here.'[4]

He is not surprised to find his sister waiting inside for him. In this episode, most clearly portrayed in the French *La Mort le Roi Artu*, Morgan uses her arts in order to help Arthur. As in the shield episode, she tries to warn him against Lancelot's affair with Guenevere. She does this by housing Arthur in a splendid suite within her castle. The walls of this suite are covered with remarkable paintings, done by Lancelot himself when he'd spent several seasons trapped within the castle in Morgan's unsuccessful attempt to seduce him (or perhaps, more probably, magicked by Morgan herself). The paintings tell the story of Lancelot's love for Guenevere, and clearly show that their love is not only mutual, but consummated. Slowly walking the walls of his suite, Arthur finally understands what so many people have been trying to tell him for years, although he does not manage to use the knowledge to avoid the catastrophe hurtling towards him. It is a touching episode, if for no other reason than in these few days away from the cares and power plays of Camelot, Arthur and Morgan feel free enough to display their genuine affection each for the other.

Morgan's power is well-known – and feared – within the realms of Camelot. Her alter-ego, Nimue, has always to come to Arthur's aid whenever Morgan dares another attempt on his life, and mere mortals are terrified of her. When Arthur wakes one morning to find that Morgan has been in his chamber overnight and stolen Excalibur's magical scabbard, he furiously confronts his guards. 'Why did you not stop her?' he demands of them. The guards reply that they dared not prevent her entry into his chamber: even the thought that she might do their king to death was not enough to give them the courage to confront her.

4 *La Mort le Roi Artu*, p. 67.

The Lover

Morgan is so often perceived only as the witch that it can be surprising to discover the depth of genuine passion and love within the woman. She is a wife, to Uriens, and a lover, sometimes to Arthur, but always to Accolon and a variety of other knights. She has an unrequited passion for Lancelot, and is profoundly jealous of Guenevere's hold over him. Medieval Christian morality depicted Morgan as sexuality run rampant, but even so, she still comes through as a woman who, before and beyond all else, *loves*.

As a woman, Morgan is usually beautiful and profoundly desirable though Layamon's fairest of all ladies, his beautiful elf queen is, in Malory, as fair a lady as any might be. Other versions try to make Morgan dark, squat and ugly, attractive only through her evil enchantments. Bradley combines both traditions – her Morgan le Fay is small and dark, but is still profoundly sexually attractive if not classically beautiful. Whatever, Morgan attracts her share of lovers as much through her beauty and sexuality as through her magical arts. Her easiness with her body and sexuality can sometimes make other characters think her shameless. In *The Mists of Avalon* Morgan does not hesitate to wander naked about the chamber she shares with Elaine. Elaine is very uncomfortable with this immodest behaviour: 'had she never heard that all sin came into this world through the body of a woman?' she wonders.[5]

Morgan's husband, Uriens, sometimes a king of North Wales, sometimes of Rheged in northern Britain, is often depicted as much older than Morgan; she is variously his second, or even third, wife. This is a patently loveless marriage, although Bradley depicts it as founded on some respect and compassion. Uriens, through his very existence, is a check on Morgan's power, and she resents it deeply. Malory has her make a determined bid on Uriens' life. Here, the brisk and practical Morgan eschews her magical arts to attempt her murder.

5 Bradley, p. 600.

So on a day she espied King Uriens lay in his bed sleeping. Then she called unto her a maiden of her counsel, and said: Go fetch me my lord's sword, for I never saw a better time to slay him than now.

Malory, *Morte Darthur*, Vol. 1, Book IV, Chap. 13

The maid, more than a little disturbed by her lady's no-fuss approach to marital dispute resolution, tells Sir Uwain, Morgan and Uriens' son, before fetching the sword. She then takes the sword in with quaking hands and gives it to Morgan, who hefts it and goes boldly to her lord's bed. She stands indecisively for a moment as she wonders where best to stick it: which would be the better killing stroke – belly or breast? Just as Morgan makes up her mind, and raises the sword, Uwain grabs it from behind, swearing that the only thing that keeps him from slicing off her head is the fact that she is his mother: 'Ah,' said Sir Uwain, 'men saith that Merlin was begotten of a devil, but I may say an earthly devil bare me.' Luckily Morgan is never at a loss for speech, nor for the words that might save her, so she takes refuge in the excuse all medieval women could use without fear of disbelief: 'O fair son, Uwain, have mercy upon me, I was tempted with a devil.'[6]

Uwain hesitates, then says he hopes she'd not think to do it again. Morgan hangs her head. 'Nay son,' she says, 'And that I make you assurance.'

No doubt the moment Uwain's back was turned, Morgan smiled with all the smugness of a well-fed cat. It was just as well Uwain took the sword with him.

Morgan le Fay has many love affairs. She manipulates men as she chooses, using them for her own ends, but she invariably loves them, and is genuinely distraught if they are killed. Of her love for Arthur I speak later, but whatever she feels for her brother, and whatever her marital status, nothing stops Morgan from taking the men she chooses . . . or at least, making a determined effort for them. One of Morgan's greatest loves is Lancelot himself, but this love is unrequited. In medieval literature, Morgan kidnaps Lancelot on at least one

6 Malory, Vol. 1, Book IV, Chap. 13.

occasion, trapping him for almost a year in her castle. Despite her beauty and magical arts, Lancelot resists her, and Morgan eventually loses him. In *The Mists of Avalon*, Morgan's unrequited love for Lancelot is far more heart-wrenching. Here they are friends from a young age and, on one memorable occasion, Lancelot almost takes Morgan's virginity before they are interrupted by the child Guenevere who has lost her way onto the Island of Avalon. When Lancelot sees the beautiful white and gold girl-child, he loses any desire he has previously had for Morgan. It is an interesting moment – Lancelot, standing between the two extremes of medieval womanhood: the dark and enigmatically powerful Morgan, marked as a priestess of the forces of chaos, and the beautiful but fragile, vulnerable and already psychotically religious Guenevere. Lancelot's eyes and heart drift uncertain between both, before settling on the fragility of the golden girl, the epitome of Christian medieval womanhood. Whatever else it does, the episode sours Morgan's regard for Guenevere for the rest of their lives. Once Guenevere marries Arthur, Morgan hopes that Lancelot will turn to her. They make love, once, despondently, and Morgan senses his lack of interest and feels repulsed by his mechanical lovemaking. She never loses her love for Lancelot, but neither does she ever seek his bed again.

Morgan's tenderest affair is with Accolon. Bradley depicts Accolon as one of Uriens' sons (adding medieval incestuous overtones to the relationship, although this may have been unwitting on Bradley's part), but usually he is just one of the Knights of the Round Table. They love each other deeply, as Accolon relates: 'she loveth me out of measure as a paramour, and I her again.'[7] Love him she might, but this does not prevent Morgan from using him for her own ends. She plans to replace Arthur with Accolon; in Bradley, this is because Morgan believes Arthur has been led astray by Guenevere's persistent and weak-willed Christianity, and only a man truly bound to the ancient ways – Accolon – can preserve the realm. Malory is less kind, his Morgan is

7 Malory, Vol. 1, Book IV, Chap. 11.

driven to treason by reasons of jealousy that Arthur, her brother, is more renowned in the realm than she is.

Morgan steals Excalibur and gives it to Accolon. Accolon challenges Arthur, but despite his magical aid, Accolon is killed (in Malory Nimue comes to the aid of Arthur, knowing his peril; in Bradley it is Arthur's better battle skills which win him the day). Morgan is distraught. She mourns the loss of her lover far more than she mourns her lost chance to put her own man on the throne: 'she was so sorrowful that near her heart to-brast,' says Malory.[8] From this moment Morgan is set against Arthur. Previously, jealousy or concern for the spiritual welfare of the land may have driven her to oppose her brother; now vengeance drives her. Arthur killed her lover, thus Arthur must die.

Morgan has other lovers, and although none are as dear to her as Accolon she can still weep for their deaths. Bradley also has Morgan involved in a touching but ultimately ill-fated affair with Kevin, the Merlin of Britain,[9] and Malory gives Morgan one of the Knights of the Round Table, Sir Hemison, as a lover. Tristram fatally wounds Sir Hemison in a joust, and when Morgan sees the dead body of her lover, she again makes 'great sorrow out of reason'.[10] So, although Morgan uses her men, she loves them as well, and she grieves deeply when they literally cannot live up to her own standards and expectations.

Morgan and Arthur

Morgan and her brother spend their lives locked in a love–hate relationship. In some accounts the hate starts early: like any supplanted elder child, Morgan is profoundly jealous when her mother gives birth to a new baby. In *Sword at Sunset* it is this jealousy that drives the dark witch Morgan (called Ygerna by Sutcliff) on her

8   Malory, Vol. 1, Book IV, Chap. 14.

9   Bradley's Merlin is not the name of a man, but of an office. In *The Mists of Avalon* it is held by two men, Taliesin and Kevin.

10 Malory, Vol. 1, Book IX, Chap. 42.

quest for revenge. Uther had preferred her brother Arthur, not her, and Morgan–Ygerna waits many years before she can have her revenge: her plan is to seduce Arthur, conceive his nemesis and then curse him with impotence for the rest of his life. Alone of Arthurian authors, Sutcliff allows Morgan to revel in her hatred. Her Ygerna has no redeeming qualities at all, she is the ultimate dark witch with a ruined face and a hate-filled soul, and all this she passes on to her cunning, sly son.

In Bradley's *Mists of Avalon* Morgan initially has her jealousies of her younger brother. Her mother, whom she adores, is distracted by the child, as well as by the new duties of queenship:

> *there was this crying thing, all pink and white, at my mother's breast; and it was worse that she expected me to care as much for him as she did . . . . I hated him with all my heart, for now when I came near her she would pull away and tell me that I was a big girl, too big to be sitting in her lap, too big to bring my ribbons to her for tying, too big to come and lay my head on her knees for comfort. I would have pinched him, except that she would have hated me for it.*

> Bradley, *The Mists of Avalon*, p. 125

Not a promising start. But then Ygerna, far more devoted to Uther than to either of her children, hands baby Arthur over to her resentful daughter to mind. Morgan finds she no longer loathes the crying thing, especially not when he flings his arms about her neck and clings to her for comfort. Suddenly Morgan realises that she must be his mother, and there forms a deep bond between the little girl and her baby brother, a bond never broken through all the tumultuous years ahead. Naturally, the sister–mother bond with Arthur adds yet more interest to the incest they commit many years into the future.

Their ways part as they grow. Morgan goes to Avalon, to learn its ancient arts. Arthur is fostered at Ector's court, for his part to learn the cleaner arts of the chivalric sword thrust. Uther dies, and Arthur succeeds to the throne. Morgan always seems relatively happy at Arthur's fortune; in *The Mists of Avalon* she initiates him personally in the sexually-orientated pagan rites of king making: Mordred is the result. Either from Morgan, or by other anonymous Avalon hands, Arthur receives the magical sword and sheath that protect his body and kingship.

The initial years of Arthur's reign progress well, with no obvious friction between the brother and sister. Arthur weds Guenevere, and Morgan her aging Uriens. Arthur gives Morgan her own lands and a castle, something he later regrets as Morgan uses the castle as a base from which to launch her power-plays and attempts against his life. During the last half of Arthur's reign conflict sets in. Morgan, the enchantress, is a queen in her own right, and of the same blood as Arthur. In Malory this causes her to grow jealous of Arthur's renown: why is she not as loved and respected as Arthur? Bradley has Morgan resentful for a different reason. Morgan has never really liked Guenevere (although she professes to love her): Guenevere is a truly beautiful woman, while Morgan feels small and dark and plain beside her (Bradley's Morgan seems never to understand the potency of her sexual attraction). Guenevere has Lancelot's love, and Morgan has ever desired that herself. But, worst of all, Guenevere is the champion of the dreaded Christianity, and over many years she slowly weans Arthur away from his allegiance to Avalon. Arthur bans many of the old practices and ways of Avalon, and Morgan seethes.

Something must be done.

Although her hostility is intense, it is never underhand. Morgan sets out – very publicly – to dislodge Arthur. Interestingly, Arthur only *reacts* to Morgan, he does not initiate – at no point does he array his army against Morgan, he merely copes with whatever enchantment she sends his way. Malory's Morgan weaves her sinuous, enchanted way through his entire tale. She kidnaps and vamps Arthur's knights, sends her lovers to murder him, forms an effective 'opposition' to his rule (scores of disaffected knights join her), sends him murderous gifts, and traps Arthur in various enchantments.

Arthur metaphorically throws up his hands in despair at his sister's machinations, but does little else other than complain. 'God knoweth I have honoured her and worshipped her more than all my kin, and more have I trusted her than mine own wife and all my kin after.'[11] He rues the gifts, honours and lands he has given her, he makes half-hearted efforts to find her – where he hunts Lancelot to the ground for his betrayal of him, Morgan he leaves free. Morgan is an enemy in the 'chivalric sense': she declares outright war on him, and this Arthur can understand and even forgive. On the other hand, Guenevere, Lancelot and Mordred profess to love him, and yet they betray him with loving ease. In *The Mists of Avalon*, Arthur sometimes sides with his sister against his wife. When Guenevere, appalled, learns that Morgan has borne Arthur a son, Arthur defends his sister against his wife. In many senses Arthur and his sister have a very straightforward relationship: they feud incessantly, but they understand each other.

Their bed-rock affection is graphically demonstrated in *La Morte le Roi Artu*. Lost in a forest, Arthur seeks refuge in Morgan's castle. When Arthur finally recognises his host (Morgan has assumed a disguise), he leaps up in joy and embraces his sister. 'My Lord,' Morgan tells Arthur, 'I can tell you that there is no woman anywhere who loves you more than I do, and so I should, unless human love did not exist.' For his part, Arthur swears he will take her back to Camelot where she can be Guenevere's best friend: 'I know she will be happy and joyful when she hears the news.' Morgan sensibly refuses the offer. Whatever else has passed between them to this point, in this episode they can do nothing but profess their deepest love and affection each to the other. They spend many days talking, taking pleasure in each other's company.[12]

In the final years of his life, Arthur finds himself marooned within a sea of treachery. Lancelot and Guenevere have caused havoc within Camelot because of their affair, Mordred has seized the realm. In the final battles against his son, Arthur loses every one of his friends. His wife flees to a convent, Lancelot is lost and denied him, Gawain dies in his arms, and Mordred, in an agony of hate, strikes him a fatal

11 Malory, Vol. 1, Book IV, Chap. 11.
12 *La Mort le Roi Artu*, pp. 69–70.

wound. There is no-one left . . . save Morgan. At the last all their enmity lies as dead as Arthur's hopes; together with two other queens, Morgan comes to collect Arthur's dying body, grieving more bitterly than ever she had for her lost lovers.

> *Those beautiful and noble ladies*
> > *Gently took the King;*
> *The loveliest of them wrung her hands*
> > *And wept in her sorrowing.*
> *'Alas, dear brother!' she said, 'Too long*
> > *You have lacked good doctors' care:*
> *I know, and great is the grief to me,*
> > *Your pain is hard to bear.'*

Stanzaic Le Morte Arthur, Ll. 3502–3509

Of all the characters in the Arthurian legend, Morgan manages to thumb her nose at Christian attempts to make her the completely 'evil witch' and continues to control her own fate. The single member of Arthur's family who was so patently his foe was, paradoxically, the one who was there for him at the end of his life. Strangely, in this most Christian-controlled and influenced of legends, the dark and enigmatic Morgan le Fay is the only member of his household who does not betray Arthur.

MORGAUSE, QUEEN OF THE ORKNEYS

If Morgan le Fay thumbs her nose at Christian censure, then her sister is not so capably self-willed. Until the present century, Morgause, wife to King Lot of the Orkneys, has been a somewhat shadowy figure on the very edge of the Arthurian tragedy. Medieval literature mentions Arthur's sister, the Queen of Orkney, often the mother to his nephew/son Mordred, but they rarely give her a role to play apart from perverted motherhood. Indeed, she rarely even gets a speaking part; Morgause is merely 'there'. . . somewhere. If her character is named (rarely), then that name varies: sometimes it is Anne, sometimes a variation of Morgause, more normally just the 'Queen of Orkney'. She is a sister to Morgan le Fay, although whether they are full or half-sisters is never apparent.

Malory is the only medieval author of my key texts who gives her any role at all. She appears early in the *Morte Darthur* as Arthur's unnamed sister whose husband sends her to spy on her brother. While at court, the Queen of Orkney takes the unexpected opportunity to bed the boy-king:

> *she came richly beseen, with her four sons Gawaine, Gaheris, Agravine, and Gareth, with many other knights and ladies. For she was a passing fair lady, therfore the king cast great love unto her, and desired to lie by her; so they were agreed, and he begat upon her Mordred, and she was his sister, on the mother side, Igraine. So there she rested her a month, and at the last departed.*

Malory, Morte Darthur, Vol. 1, Book I, Chap. 19

Whether or not Morgause knew at this point that Arthur was also her brother in no way lessens her guilt. No woman could be 'innocent' in this situation. At best, Morgause was committing adultery, at worst she committed both adultery and incest – all with apparent enjoyment. Having disported herself with the boy-king for a month, Morgause then wanders back to her husband with her brother's bastard in her belly; then, when Arthur's edict orders the murder of all children born in May, she sends the infant Mordred off to be drowned with all the other babies with apparently callous indifference. To the medieval mind, there could be no penance severe enough to absolve Morgause's sins.

Medieval morality has its way with her. Morgause plays no more role in Malory's tale until it comes time for her to die. Morgause has taken a lover, Sir Lamorak, who is deeply in love with her. One night, when Lamorak is in bed with Morgause, her furious son Gaheris (or, in some accounts, Agravaine) strides into the chamber and strikes off her head. Lamorak escapes that night, but is later caught and killed. Morgause dies as she has lived, a weak, evil and adulterous woman, slaughtered by her own son.

Modern authors have been unable to resist fleshing out Morgause's character – and why not? The seductive sister of Arthur is a character no author could resist. Almost without fail (Bradley gives her some moments of kindness) most authors choose to depict her as a grasping and would-be-evil (she never commands the same degree of enchantment as does Morgan le Fay), witch-like woman who deliberately sets out to destroy Arthur, and is a bad mother to boot.

Morgause's role in the seduction of Arthur (she was the instigator) and the later infanticide of scores of children in order to try and kill Mordred is often used as a convenient means by which to absolve Arthur from blame for some of the more heinous acts of his reign, although not all authors take this easy way out. Morgause is generally older than Arthur, and very beautiful. She is a sexually experienced woman who for her own reasons (a means to bind Arthur, or a means to give her husband, Lot, a hold over Arthur) she beds the impressionable fifteen-year-old boy-king and conceives his son. At Arthur's court she comes into conflict with Merlin, who ridicules her feeble 'womanly' attempts at witchcraft, but is, nonetheless, unable to stop her seduction of his young charge. Having conceived her son, Morgause flounces home to Lot in his northern wilderness realm of the Orkneys.

What Lot thinks of his wife's behaviour varies. Lot and his wife share a love–hate relationship. They are mutually ambitious, but also equally strong-willed. Morgause flaunts her pregnancy, partly because she enjoys goading Lot and making him jealous, partly to push him into taking strong action against the child (and Arthur). Because Lot is an uncomplicated man of war incapable of thinking through the subtleties of future diplomacies, he misses the chance to nurture Arthur's nemesis at his court, and either instigates the mass slaughter of infants himself when Morgause hides the infant Mordred within the castle town (Stewart's ploy to absolve Arthur of blame) or only shrugs when Morgause sends off the child to his supposed death (generally Morgause makes sure her son survives the wreck, but does not lift a finger to save the other babies).

Morgause has Mordred raised in a foster home. In some accounts she takes him into her own home when he is a youth (it depends on whether Lot is dead or not), in others she merely arranges for him to join her four legitimate sons[13] at Arthur's court. The four Orkney boys generally accept Mordred into their strange, violent and often emotionally warped circle: because their parents are *personae non gratae* at Arthur's court (Lot because he initially made war against Arthur, Morgause for obvious reasons) the boys form a closed circle against outsiders.

Once Mordred is safely ensconced in Arthur's household, there is little left for Morgause to do save plot uselessly on the outer circle (and often trapped in a convent somewhere), so she turns her attention to Merlin. She has hated him for many years, ever since he confronted her after she'd seduced Arthur, and she is jealous of his powers. Her attempts on his life never end in Merlin's death. She might incapacitate him for a time – sometimes years – but she cannot kill him. These attempts at magic are, in the end, the defining mark of her career as a witch: she is poisonous, but not fatal.

Indeed, as a worker of magic she remains forever in the shadow of Morgan. Morgan is impressively treacherous, Morgause is spiteful and cruel. In *The Once and Future King* Morgause boils a cat alive in order to work a spell of invisibility.

In the boiling water, the cat gave some horrible convulsions and a dreadful cry. Its wet fur bobbed in the steam, gleaming like the side of a speared whale, as it tried to leap or to swim with its bound feet. Its mouth opened hideously, showing the whole of its pink gullet, and the sharp,

13 Her sons with Lot: Gawain, Gaheris, Agravain and Gareth.

white cat-teeth, like thorns. After the first shriek it was not able to
articulate, but only to stretch its paws. Later it was dead.

White, *The Once and Future King*, pp. 229–230

Morgause watches impassively. Once the cat is dead, and its skeleton boiled clean, she collects the bones and lays them in a heap. Listlessly, she stands before a mirror putting one bone at a time in her mouth in an attempt to find that single bone in a cat's body which grants invisibility. Then Morgause grows bored and throws the bones away before she finds the right one.

Apart from her womanly magics, Morgause engages in sexual affairs to while away the time. One of these, with Lamorak, is her undoing. Either Gaheris or Agravain, enraged and horribly jealous (all her sons have ever craved is the haphazard attention of their mother), kill her one night as she and Lamorak are making love. It remains one of the most appalling scenes in Arthurian legend: Morgause screaming over Lamorak's shoulder as her son (or sons) march into her bed chamber, the sudden glint of the sword, Morgause's head rolling across the floor, the blood . . . everywhere. Lamorak escapes temporarily, but it is not long before the Orkney faction hunt him down and kill him.

As a mother, Morgause is indifferent and (generally) unintentionally cruel. She bears five sons – Gawain, Gaheris, Agravain, Gareth and Mordred – but in most accounts loves none of them. They are, as is everyone about her, tools to be used in her power plays. Stewart and, particularly, T.H. White develop a touching but somehow perverted relationship between the band of boys and their mother. In White's version, they all adore her (save, perhaps, Mordred who is incapable of adoring anyone) and crave her attention. They live for months from a single careless glance she might send their way, and build their hopes on a kiss to the tops of their heads. They defend her against all those who accuse her, and thrive on the injustice of the rape of their 'granny', Ygerna, by the despicable Uther. White's Agravain has 'curious' incestuous feeling about his mother, which he keeps to himself, but all her sons love their mother intensely, and yet at the same time hate her for her coldness. They loathe her lovers, and eventually their disgust and jealousy and warped love drives one of them to kill her.

Arthur is as perturbed and as irritated by his sister as anyone else. She trapped him into her bed, and she has borne his murderer. Yet what can he do with her? Morgause knows she is relatively safe from him. His misplaced chivalric honour makes him loath to kill her (although he does not hesitate to attempt to kill their son), and finally he is reduced to placing her in a convent and hoping she repents.

NIMUE, LADY OF THE LAKE

Nimue was extracted from the original character of Morgan le Fay during the twelfth and thirteenth centuries. Rather like her mother character, she is a strangely ambivalent figure. On the one hand, she is a beautiful and mystical woman who does much good for Arthur, on the other she uses her sexual wiles to drain Merlin of his powers and confine him within a crystal cave. However, this episode should be viewed positively rather than in any negative fashion. As we shall see in the chapter on Merlin, Nimue does a vastly better job at protecting Arthur than her predecessor. Again and again during Arthur's reign Nimue comes to his aid, saving him from numerous attempts on his life from sundry dissatisfied witches.

Nimue's association with Merlin, and eventually with Arthur, begins when she, as one of the ladies of the Lake, or perhaps an apprentice of Avalon, comes to study at Merlin's feet. In several accounts she disguises herself as a boy in order to gain Merlin's trust. Merlin laps up the attention of the little acolyte, and willingly teaches the boy–girl Nimue. In time, her power begins to shine. Eventually, inevitably, Nimue's true sex is revealed and, in medieval literature, Merlin becomes as besotted with lust as an old goat. Nimue resists him for a time, until she gives herself up with a sigh, and accepts his knowledge and power along with the more mundane but inevitable emissions of the act of love (it is the sexual act which passes power from Merlin to Nimue). Except for Tennyson, who depicted Nimue as a false woman who stole Merlin's power, Nimue's role in this is treated gently. Nimue and Merlin are in love, and Merlin fully realises that, in the act of love, he will pass across to Nimue all of his power. He is old, he is tired, and he is happy enough to let Nimue take his place within Camelot. Nimue herself certainly isn't hindered by chasteness: in many versions of the legend she takes one of Arthur's knights, or a neighbouring king, as a spouse (this could be a medieval device to make her a 'good' woman, for, powerful as she is, Nimue is still controlled by a husband).

As successor to Merlin, Nimue installs herself as magical guardian of Arthur's court, but, unlike Merlin, manages to give practical help to Arthur rather than simply to warn him of danger. When Morgan sends her brother a poisoned cloak, Nimue is there to save him. When another witch, Annowre, traps Arthur inside the Forest Perilous, Nimue again springs to the rescue. Knowing that Arthur will surely die without aid, Nimue persuades Sir Tristram to ride with her to save him. As a helpless Arthur watches, Sir Tristram smites off the head of the sorceress and Nimue carries the grisly trophy home triumphantly, attached to the pommel of her saddle. In Stewart, Nimue helps Arthur in many small ways, and also (remembering Stewart's sympathetic portrayal of Mordred) eases Mordred's fear of harming his father. And in some versions of the legend, Nimue is also there as one of the queens who ride the barge with Morgan le Fay to collect the dying Arthur.

Christianity may have had its moralising way with much of the Arthurian legend, but it has never managed to entrap either Morgan le Fay, or her derivative character, Nimue. Morgan and Nimue occupy a strange place within the medieval-derived Arthurian legend. Although they are powerful and independent women, usually negative traits in medieval minds, both nevertheless meet good fates. Morgan is one of the few characters to walk unscathed through the destruction of Camelot into freedom. Nimue likewise: she is often with Morgan when she collects her brother's dying body in the barge. Morgause is the only one of the three unrepentant Eves who must succumb to a Christian sentence: her lecherous ways and bothersome magicking result in her gruesome death.

9
MORDRED:
Guilt Made Flesh

'I am your guilt made flesh, am I not, Father? You will always smell the dark birth-smell of my mother's hate on me, and hate me in turn.'

SUTCLIFF, *Sword at Sunset*, P. 419

M ordred is the most straightforward character in Arthur's household. He is Arthur's bastard son born from incest, and he is the man who kills Arthur. Thus Mordred's role is as a tool (and as a moral, if you like). He is sin made flesh, and his future treacheries are dictated from the moment of his conception. Tools tend to have little depth to their character, and so it is with Mordred; even Stewart, who gives him his own story in *The Wicked Day*, has trouble giving Mordred a personality. Yet Mordred is not *simply* the man who kills Arthur: he has a family away from the court (there are always his two sons drifting mysteriously about in the background), he is a brave and fearless knight in his own right and a war-leader to rival his father.

Like Guenevere, Mordred has a slightly ambiguous but not malicious heritage in Welsh tradition. The *Annales Cambriae* date his death at 537 when he and Arthur die in the Battle of Camlann. The entry does not specifically state that Mordred kills Arthur in that battle, but nevertheless legend has it that somehow Mordred was responsible for the battle, and may even have dealt Arthur his death blow. The

Welsh Mordred (or the variations Medraut, Medrod, Modred, Medrawd) is not Arthur's son, but an important knight or warrior at Arthur's court. Even in Welsh literature after Monmouth, Mordred often retains an honourable reputation. In the mid-fifteenth century *Gogynfeirdd* Mordred is named as one of the three Royal Knights:

> *'The peculiarity of these were that there was neither king nor emperor in the world who could refuse them, on account of their beauty and wisdom in peace; while in war no warrior or champion could withstand them, despite the excellence of his arms. And therefore they were called Royal Knights.'[1]*

Korrel, An Arthurian Triangle, p. 97

Nevertheless, there is something shadowy about the character. Not only is Mordred mentioned in connection with Arthur's death at Camlann, in one of the Welsh triads Mordred strides into Arthur's court, drags Guenevere from her throne and strikes her.

> *Medrawd came to Arthur's Court at Celliwig in Cornwall; he left neither food nor drink in the court that he did not consume. And he dragged Gwenhwyfar from her royal chair, and then he struck a blow upon her.*

'The Three Unrestrained Ravagings', cited in
Korrel, An Arthurian Triangle, p. 77

No-one knows if this was the incident that provoked Camlann, but wars have been fought over less.

From this tradition Monmouth took the ambiguous figure of Mordred and re-cast him as the treacherous villain. Mordred becomes the nephew of the king who, having been entrusted with queen and realm, then proceeds to steal both. His reputation has never recovered. Later French romances made him Arthur's son born from incest (although there has always been a faint suggestion that this was a popular tradition even in Monmouth's time), an evil worm of a man, but one nevertheless trapped in his dark destiny by the sins of his parents and grandparents. Placed into Arthur's court he cannot help but destroy it.

Both Mordred's conception and his early infancy are inextricably woven with betrayal – the betrayal of Mordred, rather than that of his father. Although Mordred eventually turns against his father, it is but a reflection of the fact that his father had attempted to murder him as an innocent child in the first instance.

Apart from a few modern novels, notably Mary Stewart's *The Wicked Day* and, to a lesser extent, Marion Zimmer Bradley's *The Mists of Avalon*, little is known of Mordred's childhood and early manhood. Having failed to kill him as an infant, Arthur's guilt then gets the better of him, and he allows the boy to grow up in peace. As a young man Mordred arrives at Arthur's court to take his place with the other Orkney boys. Arthur is well aware of who he is, but he tells relatively few people. In medieval romance Guenevere knows, but the majority of the court remains in ignorance: there is often great surprise when Guenevere reveals, at the height of Mordred's treachery, that he is also Arthur's son. In the chronicle tradition, which continued to take its cue from Monmouth until the fifteenth century, Mordred remains Arthur's nephew.

Who is the man? Mordred's role as a traitor necessarily conditions his character. He must have that one, but singularly remarkable, flaw which will drive him to treachery. At worst, the flaw is a malicious drive for power at any cost, at best it is naive political opportunism. Mordred, whatever else he might be, is supremely ambitious. He can hardly be blamed for his aspirations. Whether nephew or bastard son, Mordred is always the 'not-quite-legal' next in line for the throne. Arthur has no legitimate issue: in the chronicle tradition, Mordred is the son of his sister, and in the romance tradition, the incestuous son of both Arthur and his sister. Thus Mordred spends almost his entire life in a vague and totally unsatisfactory state of 'almost heir, but not quite'. He is unacknowledged nephew or son, never legitimate heir. Arthur may be reluctant to name anyone else heir while Guenevere might still bear him a son, but even when that hope is past, Arthur will not look to his closest blood relative to succeed him. He generally names the Duke of Cornwall (either Cador or Constantine) as heir, bypassing Mordred. One of the things a good medieval king must never do is leave close rivals bitterly disappointed; in not naming Mordred as heir sooner, Arthur won himself a vicious enemy. True, eventually Arthur leaves Mordred as regent of the realm, but after a lifetime of waiting to be acknowledged, Mordred would have every reason not to expect that single regency to extend into eventual heirdom once Arthur returns.

As a nephew Mordred has a legal right to inherit the throne, as a bastard son he has a natural right, but Arthur constantly refuses (or refrains) from naming Mordred as heir. Thus, with ambition, we must add bitterness to Mordred's character. Perhaps even hatred, as a result of his father's attempts to have him killed as an infant. Might Arthur strike again? Mordred turns into a killer himself, yet he is not only bred for the fate, but pummelled into it by his father's neglect.

Mordred is also a supremely political animal. Even before Mordred shows himself to be a more than capable king and war-leader when he does seize the throne, he is clearly adept at weaving a sinuous path through the court intrigues over many years. However, if he has ambition when he first arrives at Arthur's court, then he generally does not show it. Mordred appears to be popular with most knights – either the product of an extremely sly character, or of a genuinely likeable man. He is certainly trusted enough for the knights to recommend to Arthur that he be given the regency, and trusted enough by Arthur to grant it. Yet in most accounts (save Mary Stewart's), Mordred is sly. In the chronicle tradition Mordred often seduces the queen right under Arthur's nose. In the romances he supports Agravain in his plan to expose Guenevere and Lancelot's adultery, then in a cowardly fashion leaves Agravain to the vengeance of Lancelot's sword when the plan goes awry.

Nineteenth- and twentieth-century literature (again, apart from Stewart) has deepened Mordred's slyness. Someone must be blamed for Arthur's demise, and who better than the man who so closely resembles Judas that there can be no discernible difference.[1]

---

1 The names are linked on several occasions. In the stanzaic *Le Morte Arthur* Mordred swears 'by Judas who sold Jesus', L. 3250.

Tennyson, unsurprisingly, loathed Mordred. In *The Idylls of the King* Mordred is a 'subtle beast' who creeps about spying on Guenevere and Lancelot, and lurks in shadows for the moment when he can 'spring'. He has a narrow foxy face, and a 'heart-hiding smile'.[2] Following from Tennyson (and from Malory, for that matter), T.H. White cannot condemn Mordred's character enough: he is a 'cold wisp' of a man, and a 'sniveller' to boot. Furthermore, he is compared to the I.R.A. in being the kind of man who murders landlords, then blames them for being murdered.[3] Nonetheless, inasmuch as White is sympathetic to almost everyone's plight he is also sympathetic to Mordred's. His Mordred is the unloved boy who has been raised in the cold north by a woman, his 'carnivorous' mother Morgause, who alternately loved and forgot him. Mordred is confused by this, but finds a kind of refuge in hating his father . . . only to find that when Arthur finally meets his son, he is prepared to love him as best he can.[4] Sutcliff also plays on the fact that Mordred was raised in a home of implacable hatred, a hatred which warps and destroys his character: his mother's hatred of Arthur reaches out from the grave through Mordred. But, unlike White, Sutcliff does not allow her reader to ever like, or even sympathise with, Mordred. In *Sword at Sunset* he remains the cold traitor, slinking throughout the pages of the book as a hateful man who freely admits his loathing of his father, but who uses his father's guilt to maintain his place in Arthur's band of warriors.

As can be imagined, Mordred and Arthur share an uncertain and extremely uncomfortable relationship. What can Arthur make of this man who arrives at his court a competent knight, yet who is at the same time known to him as his bastard son of incest who is fore-ordained to murder him? And what does Mordred make of the man, his father, who has tried once in the past to murder him, and who refuses to acknowledge him to the court as his son? At best they share an uneasy truce that slides inevitably into treachery, at worst

2 Mordred is depicted in Tennyson's *Guinevere* (1898), p. 457.

3 White, p. 562.

4 White, p. 568.

Mordred takes every opportunity to remind his father that he is guilt made flesh. White's Arthur knows that Mordred will be the death of him, but he tolerates his presence because he feels so guilty about his attempt on Mordred's infant life. Mordred never loses a chance to reinforce that guilt. Sutcliff's Mordred is desperate for love from his father, but Arthur cannot give it, and Mordred cannot reach out for it.

Only in *The Wicked Day* is Mordred given a genuinely sympathetic portrayal. Mary Stewart does not seek to excuse his actions, but she does try to make them understandable: 'I have not made a "hero" out of Mordred, but in my tale he is at least a man who is consistent in his faults and virtues, and has some kind of reason for the action with which the legend has credited him.'[5] Stewart's Mordred is an ambitious prince who, while he did not mean to do harm, is overly impatient in seizing power when he thinks Arthur might be dead. But he is not an impatient heir: in *The Wicked Day* Mordred and Arthur share their most peaceful relationship. They respect and trust each other deeply, but there is no love between them: Mordred appears incapable of it. The wicked day, then, where both kill each other, is a tragedy that becomes more poignant at the turn of every page.

Stewart also gives us a face – albeit a shadowy one – to Mordred's family. In Monmouth's account Mordred has two nameless grown sons, knights, who attempt to seize control of the realm after their father's death and Arthur's passing into Avalon. Arthur's heir, Constantine, slays both men at different times and in different cities, but always before the altar of a church. These two anonymous sons, it appears, were also a sacrifice to their father's treachery. Later chronicles and romances briefly mention the sons, generally in relation to Guenevere who sometimes bears Mordred two children. These boys are also murdered in a reflection of the way Arthur initially tried to murder the infant Mordred. As Arthur lies dying he instructs Constantine in their fate:

5 Cited in Raymond H. Thompson, *The Return from Avalon* (Greenwood Press: Westport, 1985), p. 52.

Then be stern and see that the offspring of Mordred
Are secretly slain and slung into the sea:
Let no wicked weed wax twisting on this earth!

Alliterative *Morte Arthure*, Ll. 4320–4322

In *The Wicked Day* these two boys are the offspring of two of Mordred's casual relationships; one to a woman he marries in the north, the other to a woman who keeps his bed warm in Camelot. Neither relationship means a thing to Mordred. He marries one of the women, but does not feel bound by the vows. His feeling is that if it makes her happy, he does not object to mumbling a few words and sharing a cake with neighbours, and with that he shrugs it off and leaves the woman to fend for herself and their son when the opportunity for advancement at court again presents itself to him.

Mordred seems incapable of forming a genuine bond with another human being. Perhaps this is as a result of his conception and upbringing: one parent loathed and feared him as his future doom, the other coldly manipulated him to achieve a revenge on his father. But his inability to love is also necessary to the purpose of the story. The Arthurian legend needs an anti-hero, a traitor, a trickster, a man on whom the blame can be loaded.

Mordred spends years at Arthur's court before he makes his move against him. During these years Mordred makes little obvious impression, but it is nonetheless clear that he is an excellent knight. His prowess as a knight, war-leader and king come into full view only when he seizes power and then wars against Arthur. No author, however strongly they might denounce Mordred's actions, is able to prove him anything but an excellent knight who has the makings of an outstanding king. He is also an excellent tactician, capable of building a massive alliance against Arthur which not only includes sundry pagan kings and chieftains whom Arthur has never been able to bring under his sway, but also the people of Arthur's kingdom itself. Heinous Mordred's actions might ultimately be, but they bespeak enormous skill and charisma. Here Mordred is not some slinking upstart, but a man who brings the entire realm, including many of Arthur's enemies, behind him. Arthur is isolated from all support, loyalty and love, save that of the army he has with him, by Mordred's actions.

In the English chronicle tradition, Mordred is able to win Guenevere's love and loyalty away from Arthur, no mean feat in itself. He may love her, or he may not, but her support is vitally important to him. They become lovers well before Arthur departs to fight abroad (warring on Rome in the chronicles, Lancelot in the romances). Having gained the queen, Mordred is then given the realm to govern while Arthur is away. His actions in gaining the realm vary: sometimes he demurs, pretending indifference or even dismay that he should be given such a weighty responsibility:

'I beg you, Sire, my blood brother and lord,
Choose another for this charge, for charity's sake!
If you appoint me to this post your people will be deceived;
I am too feeble to fulfil the function of a prince.'

Alliterative Morte Arthure, Ll. 681–684

Mordred speaks nothing but truth, everyone *will* be deceived if Arthur leaves him in charge! In the alliterative *Morte Arthure* Guenevere is so deep in treachery by this point that she has given her lover the state regalia; she stands by Mordred as he makes this pretty speech, no doubt smiling sweetly, and knowing exactly how Arthur will react. Arthur does precisely what Guenevere wants him to do, he dismisses Mordred's fears and leaves him as regent.

In the romances Mordred either leaps forward at the last moment to suggest himself as regent, or he wins over the entire corps of the Knights of the Round Table as he has won over Guenevere in the chronicles. Whatever the scenario, Arthur himself trusts Mordred enough to leave him as regent: Mordred is, after all, his own flesh and blood, whether as son or as nephew. In modern literature Arthur tends to lean on Mordred as he feels himself aging. The king has no legitimate son, he is growing old, and he must think seriously about a possible heir. Mordred is the obvious choice, and he needs to be given the chance to prove himself a capable king. Mordred does exactly this, but at Arthur's expense.

Having waved Arthur farewell, Mordred then moves swiftly to consolidate his position within England. He woos the nobles with gifts and promises of favour; wealth Mordred has aplenty, for either Arthur or Guenevere has given him the keys to the treasury. Soon Mordred has the nobles almost eating out of his hand; *La Mort le Roi Artu* relates that there was nothing the nobles would have denied him. The English commoners also adore him – even when King Arthur returns. Malory, in recounting the tale of Mordred's treachery, can hardly understand this:

> *Lo ye all Englishmen, see ye not what a mischief here was! For he that was the most king and knight of the world, and most loved the fellowship of noble knights, and by him they were all upholden, now might not these Englishmen hold them content with him . . . . Alas, this is a great default of us Englishmen, for there may no thing please us no term. And so fared the people at that time, they were better pleased with Sir Mordred than they were with King Arthur; and much people drew unto Sir Mordred, and said they would abide with him for better and for worse.*
>
> Malory, *Morte Darthur*, Vol. 2, Book XXI, Chap. 1

Having won the backing of both nobles and commoners, Mordred then declares himself king and vows to wed Guenevere in order to consolidate his grasp on power. In the chronicles, Guenevere needs no persuading to leap into Mordred's bed. Often she is soon pregnant by him, and, given that Arthur's lengthy overseas campaign keeps him away for a prolonged period of time (never defined, but at least two years), she sometimes has time to bear Mordred two sons.

In the romances, Guenevere puts up a spirited fight against Mordred's advances. Although she agrees to marry Mordred, she begs a few days leave to shop for a trousseau in London. Once there, she locks herself and a band of determined archers and knights within the Tower of London. Mordred is forced to lay fruitless siege to the Tower, bombarding it with various missiles, and, doubtless, having to endure the quiet sniggers of the Londoners as his amorous adventures leave him literally out in the cold. Guenevere is not the only one to frustrate his claim to her bed. The Archbishop of Canterbury supports her cause by loudly proclaiming that Mordred plans incest in marrying his father's wife, and excommunicates him. Further embarrassed, Mordred sends for the archbishop but, foiled by the elderly gentleman's quick escape, has to content himself with the seizure of Canterbury's treasure instead.

Mordred claims the title of king in one of two ways. Either he simply seizes the crown and hopes that Arthur does not have the military strength to seize it back, or he deceives England's nobles and people. He has a letter written, purporting to be from a dying Arthur, somewhere on the continent. The letter begs England's nobles to take Mordred as their king:

> 'I greet you as one who has been mortally wounded at Lancelot's hand; all my men have been killed and slaughtered. I feel more pity for you than for any other people, because of the great loyalty I have found in you. For the sake of peace I beg you to appoint Mordred king of the land of Logres.[6] (I have always treated him as my nephew, but he is not.) You will certainly never see me again, because Lancelot has mortally wounded me and killed Gawain. Moreover, I request you on the oath you swore to me that you marry the queen to Mordred. If you do not do this you might suffer as a result, because if Lancelot knew she was not married, he would attack you and take her as his wife. That is the thing my soul would most regret.'
>
> La Mort le Roi Artu, pp. 160–161

Note how Mordred has also cleverly removed Lancelot from contention: Arthur is dying by a traitor's hand, and Mordred makes sure the nobles know it by making mention of it twice. He also 'kills off' Gawain, Arthur's nephew and most trusted knight, who might also have had some claim to the throne. Whatever the means and deceptions used, Mordred manages to gain the backing of the nobles of England.

---

6 Often the name given to Arthur's kingdom in medieval literature.

Having won (or failed to win) Guenevere's hand, Mordred must then guard against the possibility (and soon to be reality) that Arthur will try to regain throne, queen and kingdom. Arthur has drained the land of fighting men in order to battle Lancelot (or Rome), and thus Mordred must look elsewhere for battle-hardened men. He conducts alliances with Arthur's traditional enemies, men who have the most cause to hate Arthur: the Saxons, Scots, Irish and Picts. Some tales have Mordred buy this foreign support as he had bought the support of the nobles at home, others have him play on their hatred of Arthur, but by whatever means, Mordred concludes enough alliances to build himself a massive army – larger than anything Arthur has ever commanded – against Arthur's possible return. Monmouth puts the army at 60,000, Layamon increases it to 100,000, while the romances generally put Mordred's strength at twice that of Arthur's.

Having heard of Mordred's treachery, Arthur breaks off his battle with either Lancelot or Rome and returns home. In most versions Mordred is shaken, even frightened, when he hears that Arthur is about to land on the south-east coast of England, but he recovers swiftly. Even though he is the consummate traitor, this is Mordred's finest hour. Generally Arthur and Mordred meet in two battles. The first is fought on the coast itself. Both sides suffer heavy casualties, and Mordred eventually flees to again face Arthur a few days later. Despite the fact Mordred loses both encounters, he is a brilliant war-leader. He rallies his army at critical moments, is always in the thick of the fighting and is able to continually command his army's loyalty: they swear they will die for him, and, of course, in the end they do. In battle Mordred fights with the best of them (even though the alliterative *Morte Arthure* calls him a 'churlish chicken' for using deceptive tactics). And even though a traitor, Mordred is still capable of chivalric behaviour. At one point he kills Gawain, the most senior of Arthur's knights and Mordred's own half-brother. Mordred is appalled, and can hardly contain his grief. At the behest of King Frederick of Friesland (whom Mordred addresses), Mordred makes an impressive battle-field memorial speech in Gawain's memory.

'He was unmatched on middle-earth, I must affirm, Sire.
This was Sir Gawain the Good, the greatest of all
Of men who go under God, the most gracious knight,
Hardiest of hand-stroke, highest-fortuned in war,
Most courteous in court under the kingdom of heaven,
And the lordliest leader as long as he lived.
In many lands his lion-like lustre was praised.'

Alliterative *Morte Arthure*, Ll. 3875–3881

Having farewelled his brother, Mordred then breaks down, 'weeping and bewailing the hour his destiny doomed him to deal such woe'. Gawain's death makes him recall the honours of the Fellowship of the Round Table. Now that fellowship lies broken, and Mordred can barely stand it, and hastens away.

But he does not back down. There is one more battle to be fought, and one gets the sense that Mordred knows that he will not live through it. In the chronicles where Mordred and Guenevere are willing lovers, this is the point at which he tells her to flee to save herself and their children. Arthur also spends the days (sometimes only a night) preceding the fatal battle in contemplation. Both men are somehow aware of their impending doom.

The final battle, at Camlann in Welsh tradition, is one of sheer frightfulness. The day is long, bloody and fuelled by anger and displaced love:

never was there seen a more dolefuller battle in no Christian land; for there was but rushing and riding, foining and striking, and many a grim word was there spoken either to other, and many a deadly stroke . . . . And thus they fought all the long day, and never stinted till the noble knights were laid to the cold earth; and ever they fought still till it was near night, and by that time there was an hundred thousand laid dead upon the down.

Malory, *Morte Darthur*, Vol. 2, Book XXI, Chap. 4

Arthur and Mordred fight their way towards one another through a shifting sea of the dead and dying. Both their worlds are disintegrating amid that sea: now their only thought, their only need, is to kill the other. Both are exhausted, both wounded, but neither wounds nor exhaustion make them hesitate. Finally Arthur nears Mordred. He readies his lance, or sometimes Excalibur itself, and charges his son as a madman.

There is a stillness. The entire world seems to cease turning, waiting for the point to drive home. Even Mordred hesitates, almost deliberately, as if he seeks the forgiveness the fatal blow will bring.

Sometimes he flings his arms wide, as if presenting his father with a clear target.

Arthur has no second thoughts. He drives his sword through Mordred's body, the entire weight of his charging horse behind the blade.

With the mortal wound, and despite the agony, Mordred now loses his own hesitation. He wriggles down the shaft of either sword or lance and, raising his own sword one last time, strikes Arthur a great blow through his helmet.

The pretender is dead, the king lies dying.

The dream is ended.

Mordred is a tool, the necessary Judas to explain his horrifying betrayal of Arthur. But Mordred should not be vilified for his role. He is a bastard son, conceived in incest, he has no choice but to betray, for he was bred, as his father was, amid the tangled sheets of betrayal. As a man and a knight, he was strong and charismatic enough to win the support of the entire realm (queen, nobles and commoners) against Arthur – enough in itself, in the medieval mind, to justify seizing the throne.

And never let it be forgotten the ultimate sin that shaped the man: his father's attempt to drown the defenceless infant Mordred. Who is the betrayer? Mordred . . . or Arthur?

10

MERLIN:
The Inept Shepherd

Come back Merlin, we need you right now,
And bring forth Arthur – only you know how.
Our country is bleeding; we need a man who is true,
So come back Merlin, and bring Arthur with you.

KEN WHITEHOUSE, 'STAND UP FOR ENGLAND!'

IN *This England*, SPRING 1998, P. 41[1]

Merlin is a highly ambiguous character within the Arthurian legend, and one of the most misunderstood. He is more a prophet than a master wizard; he foresees and warns, but does relatively little in the way of spell-making. His task is to oversee Arthur's conception, and then to ensure the boy's accession to the throne. Essentially, Merlin's role is to shepherd Arthur into what he hopes will be a golden and glorious reign. However, whatever his task and hopes, Merlin is so inept at his duties he almost certainly ensures Arthur's doom. He mishandles critical events, he finds it difficult to cope with the enchantments of more powerful magic workers (Morgan le Fay is the prime example), and he spends most of his time standing behind Arthur's throne, metaphorically wringing his hands, and impotently mumbling, 'Oh,

---

1 Reproduced by permission of *This England* magazine.

you really shouldn't do that, sire!'. Merlin's reputation has always been far greater than his deeds. A competent Merlin is a modern myth.

Merlin is, essentially, an invention of Geoffrey of Monmouth's imagination, although aspects of Merlin's character appear in earlier literature. The ninth-century *History of the Britons* relates how a boy with no father was brought before King Guorthigirn (later Vortigern) as a sacrifice in order to ensure the success of the fortifications the king was building. The boy, called Ambrosius by the *History*, stuns the king by revealing that the foundations of the citadel continually fall down because of a pool deep within the earth. Ambrosius then begins to prophesy, using the metaphor of the two dragons to depict the fate of Britain.[2] Monmouth took this episode, renamed the character as Merlin, and expanded his role in Britain's fate a hundredfold in his *History of the Kings of Britain*. Merlin is now a powerful wizard who plays a role in the reigns of three kings. He relates great but ambiguous prophecies for Britain (necessarily ambiguous, for Monmouth did not want to upset either the Church or his Norman masters), and plays a major role in Arthur's early life. Monmouth was as much responsible for the medieval and modern legend of Merlin as he was for Arthur's legend. The author later expanded Merlin's life in his *Life of Merlin*, somewhat poorly based around the life of a sixth-century prophet and bard, Myrddin. However, the *Life of Merlin* has never been very influential and, as far as the story of Arthur is concerned, it is the Merlin of Monmouth's *History of the Kings of Britain* which interests us here.

Most people are reasonably familiar with Merlin's role in Arthur's life. During King Vortigern's reign, Merlin foretells the demise of Vortigern, the reigns of two kings, Ambrosius and Uther, and the eventual rise of Arthur. During Uther's reign, Merlin stage manages Arthur's conception. When Arthur is born, Merlin usually spirits the

2 The prophet, later called Merlin, used the metaphor of two dragons, one red, one white, bathing in a pool under the foundations of the tower. (In Monmouth's *History* people actually see the dragons.) The Red Dragon represented the people of England, the White Dragon the Saxons who would eventually overrun the island of Britain. Merlin's prophecies form a chapter in Monmouth's *History*.

boy away to Sir Ector's wardship and oversees his education until he is fifteen. At that point Uther dies and Merlin manages to ensure Arthur succeeds to the throne. After Arthur takes the throne, Merlin plays a relatively minor part in the king's life. He attempts to warn Arthur against various dangers, but does little to prevent them. He wars against Morgan le Fay and, sometimes, Queen Morgause, but is relatively ineffective against both of them. Finally, Merlin falls in love with the beautiful and talented Nimue, sleeps with her, and, as a result, is trapped in the crystal cave. Thus, Merlin's part in the Arthurian tragedy occurs very early on in the king's life, principally at Arthur's conception, and then in the events surrounding Arthur's coronation. Merlin mishandles events badly at both of these critical junctures in Arthur's life, the wizard's actions at Arthur's conception virtually ensuring the Arthurian tragedy.

Merlin's prophecies before Vortigern are astounding and, as far as they relate to the events leading to Arthur's reign, completely accurate (after that the prophecies become hopelessly vague and open to any interpretation). But his role as prophet fails him completely when it comes to the most critical moment of Arthur's life: his conception. Uther asks for (or accepts) Merlin's aid in order to accomplish Ygerna's seduction. Merlin transforms Uther into the likeness of Gorlois, Uther enters Tintagel and seduces Ygerna, while outside his men attack Gorlois' camp and kill the Duke. Arthur is conceived within a bed of betrayal, and his future reign is compromised beyond hope of redemption.

In many versions of the Arthurian legend Merlin actively plots Ygerna's rape, bargaining with Uther that his reward will be the charge of any child that might result from the night's activities. That in itself is bad enough, but worse is the fact that as a supposedly accomplished prophet, Merlin should have realised that Uther's forces would attack the duke's camp and kill Gorlois. If Merlin had realised what was going to transpire that night, he could have advised Uther that he had only one more night to wait before he could have Ygerna legitimately. If Merlin *had* foreseen events, Arthur would have been conceived legitimately, and would have had none of the problems surrounding his accession. As well, there would have been no sexual sin surrounding Arthur's conception to rebound through the king's life and finally result in his doom. But Merlin failed to see any of this. Instead, he manipulated the events in a manner which ensured Arthur's death, as well as the failure of everything that Arthur would strive for.

There can be only two ways of understanding Merlin's handling of the events surrounding Arthur's conception. Firstly, that he failed to foresee that Uther need wait only twenty-four hours in order to conceive Arthur legitimately. Alternatively, Merlin knew perfectly well that Gorlois would die that night but needed, for his own purposes, to have Arthur conceived amid betrayal. If the second scenario is correct, then it could be reasonably argued that Merlin is the primary traitor of the Arthurian legend.

Merlin disappears once Arthur has been conceived. Once Arthur has been born, Merlin generally reappears and spirits the boy away from Uther's court to grow up in peace in Sir Ector's household. Fifteen years pass and Arthur grows. In modern versions of the tale he is educated by a disguised Merlin during this period. Uther sickens, and Merlin must bring the youthful Arthur to Uther's court in order to be named heir, or to claim the throne if Uther has died in the meantime. Arthur faces a struggle to claim the throne. Many of Uther's barons distrust Arthur, and are suspicious of the circumstances surrounding his conception: Gorlois' son, or Uther's? Legitimate claimant to the realm, or to the lesser dukedom of Cornwall? If Merlin had handled Arthur's conception better, there would have been little fuss made but now he has to struggle to gain recognition (whether by the removal of Excalibur from the stone, or by winning his barons' trust in war).

Having managed to place Arthur on the throne, Merlin then makes his second error as prophet. It is in the immediate aftermath of the coronation and Arthur's first successful foray into war, that his sister seduces him and conceives his nemesis, Mordred. Merlin should have realised the dangers surrounding Arthur that night. Instead, Merlin bids the king a sweet night's rest, and heads off to his own bed totally unaware of the doom about to be enacted.

Medieval accounts do not have Merlin accomplish even a vague guess at the catastrophe about to be accomplished that night, but modern revisionist accounts of Merlin's life, determined to find some small excuse for his behaviour, sometimes have him manage a glimpse of disaster. Stewart's Merlin has a vision of the doom unfolding in Arthur's bed . . . but is too late to prevent it.

> *The woman lay, naked and wide-legged, across the covers of the bed. The boy, brown against her whiteness, lay sprawled over her in the heavy abandonment of pleasure . . . . She held his head cradled . . . but her face showed none of the tenderness that the gesture seemed to express. And none of the pleasure. It held a secret exultation as fierce as I have ever seen on a warrior's face in battle; the gilt-green eyes were wide and fixed on something invisible beyond the dark; and the small mouth smiled, a smile somewhere between triumph and contempt.*
>
> Stewart, *The Hollow Hills*, p. 527

Is it not the case throughout history that the most powerful prophets are always those who manage to foretell an event *after* it has occurred?

His prophetic powers finally spluttering into life again, Merlin realises that Arthur's sister has conceived of a son who will eventually kill Arthur. But Merlin is not one to blame himself for his literal lack of foresight. Having caught Arthur with his pants down, a self-righteous Merlin cannot resist the opportunity to berate him for it.

> *Ye have done a thing late that God is displeased with you, for ye have lain by your sister, and on her ye have gotten a child that shall destroy you and all the knights of your realm . . . it is God's will that your body to be punished for your foul deeds.*
>
> Malory, *Morte Darthur*, Vol. 1, Book I, Chap. 20

The boy-king is naturally ashamed of himself and, sometimes on Merlin's advice, sometimes at his own instigation, he attempts to have his son murdered soon after birth.

As prophet and as shepherd to Arthur's early life, Merlin makes a reappearance when Arthur determines to marry Guenevere. Depending on the version of the legend, Merlin has long had vague and unsettling fears about Guenevere:

> *And across the room, thrown by the lamplight, the shadow of a bird floating – the white owl that lived in the roof –* guenhwyvar *– the white shadow, at whose name I had felt a creeping of the flesh, a moment of troubled prevision which now I could scarcely recall, except for the fear that the name Guenever was somehow a doom for him.*
>
> Stewart, *The Last Enchantment*, p. 197

Presentiments of doom, indeed, but in *The Last Enchantment* Merlin keeps his silence. Generally, however, Merlin does make some attempt to dissuade Arthur from the match. In Malory's *Morte Darthur*,

> *Merlin warned the king covertly that Guenever was not wholesome for him to take to wife, for he warned him that Launcelot should love her, and she him again.*
>
> Malory, *Morte Darthur*, Vol. 1, Book III, Chap. 1

White also has Merlin (somewhat vaguely) warn Arthur about Guenevere and Lancelot, but Arthur, friendly, stupid man that he is, hates knowing about the future and manages to forget about the warning.[3] Always, Arthur refuses to take Merlin's advice, preferring the warmth of Guenevere's body to the chill of his adviser's prophecy.

If Merlin does warn Arthur before the event, then Arthur must bear his share of responsibility for ignoring some sound advice (given, for once, in the nick of time). However, in Bradley's *The Mists of Avalon* Merlin is held more accountable. Here, it is Ygerna who can see the disaster unfolding as Guenevere gazes entranced into Lancelot's eyes. She confides her fears about the marriage to Merlin

3 White, p. 361.

and wonders if there is any honourable means by which the marriage can be stopped: 'Can anything come of it but misery, when the bride is besotted with another, and that the groom's best friend?'[4] But Merlin refuses to even consider trying to prevent the marriage. He admits there might be a love between Guenevere and Lancelot, but believes that the girl will forget it when she's been wedded and bedded. And even if the love is a genuine one, Merlin feels it would be a political disaster to try and stop the marriage. Better the king be betrayed perhaps, than to endure the ignominy of a diplomatic shambles. Whatever he does, Merlin's behaviour is hardly justifiable. The wizard either fails to press the issue and make Arthur listen, or he keeps silent about his fears when he suspects that Guenevere is likely to bring down everything that he and Arthur have worked for.

Having organised Arthur's conception within the tangled sheets of betrayal, missed the opportunity to warn him not to sleep with his own sister, and failed to pursue his warning that Guenevere will also be the death of Arthur, Merlin then finds himself with little left to do at Arthur's court. He remains as one of Arthur's chief advisers, but he generally has little advice to give. He tries to protect Arthur – in Malory, Merlin manages to save him on two occasions from being killed by more competent fighters than himself – but fails against the king's major adversary, Morgan le Fay. Only Nimue manages to deflect Morgan's more virulent enchantments against her brother. Even Morgause's 'girl magics' defeat Merlin: in modern Arthurian tales he cannot stop her conceiving Mordred, and Morgause continues to niggle at Merlin's equanimity throughout her life, often using what Merlin calls her 'girlish' vials of poison to put him into states resembling deep comas for lengthy periods of time.

Morgan and Morgause confound Merlin, but the wizard–prophet meets his ultimate fate in Nimue, Lady of the Lake. Merlin has remained chaste all his life (possibly an excuse for mishandling every event in Arthur's life which involves the sexual act), but when the disguised Nimue arrives at his den to study the arts of prophecy and

4 Bradley, p. 321.

magic, Merlin is lost. At first he is flattered, thinking to see his own power reflected in that of his boy apprentice . . . but then Merlin realises that Nimue is no boy.

Merlin is smitten with love . . . or, in the medieval legends, with pure and unfeigned lust. Malory depicts him as a lecherous old goat:

> *Merlin showed her many wonders, and came into Cornwall. And always Merlin lay about the lady to have her maidenhood, and she was ever passing weary of him, and fain would have been delivered of him, for she was afeard of him because he was a devil's son, and she could not beskift of him by no mean.*
>
> Malory, *Morte Darthur*, Vol. 1, Book IV, Chap. 1

Nimue finally allows Merlin his way with her and, in doing so, drains Merlin of his powers. She traps Merlin into a magical undead existence in a crystal cave, and Merlin departs once and for all from the Arthurian legend. As with so many other events, Merlin had long foreknown the means of his demise, but did nothing to prevent it. Perhaps even prophets grow weary with chastity after too many years.

Along with so many other aspects of the Arthurian legend, Merlin has been extensively revised in the post-World War Two period (writing just before the war, T.H. White depicts Merlin as a magician of astounding skill and humour). In these versions Merlin is no longer the all-powerful prophet and wizard – it would be too hard to justify, considering his failings – but a warm human being who manages a few visions, and tries his best to shepherd the boy-king onto the pathway to glory. If he fails, then they are only the failings of every human being. Mary Stewart has done the most plausible revision of Merlin, making of him a human being with few powers apart from the occasional vision which he cannot control. Bradley's Merlin (an office, rather than a person) is little more than a bard and adviser to the Lady of Avalon, although the final occupant of the office of Merlin, Kevin, manages a brutal betrayal of all Avalon stands for.

Sometimes he is dropped completely: Sutcliff's *Sword at Sunset* has no Merlin character at all.

The recent television series *Merlin* has tried to reconcile the medieval character with the modern. Here, Merlin is a creation of Queen Mab (who has no place in the Arthurian legend at all!), meant to drive back the forces of Christianity and restore paganism to the land. Merlin has amazing magical powers (his constantly waving hands are a sight to behold), but he is also a warm and likeable fellow. *Merlin* is meant to appeal to the rising tide of neo-paganism, but this bland revisionist account of his life disguises what was, after all, his utter failure.

Merlin is not totally accountable for what went wrong: Uther and Arthur are both headstrong and proud men, determined to take what they want and damn the consequences. But as prophet, adviser and wizard, Merlin is close to useless. As a prophet he cannot prophesy doom until too late to prevent the action that ensures it; as an adviser he is totally unable to persuade others to accept his advice; and as a wizard he is out-magicked both by Morgan le Fay and by Nimue. Camelot was never better off than when he was put to rest in his crystal cave: it was to Arthur's misfortune that he wasn't incarcerated earlier.

Part III

ARTHUR
the KING

Arthur and his companions ride forth again and again, full of hope and promise. Eternally they are destroyed, their achievements cast down.

THOMPSON, The Return from Avalon, P. 172

'My house hath been my doom.'

ARTHUR, IN TENNYSON, The Passing of Arthur (1898), P. 469

The figure of Arthur is, not surprisingly, the most complex of all the characters within the Arthurian tragedy. He must fill many roles, some public, some private – but even the private roles intrude into his public persona, as do the British royal family's today. In a sense, this is one of his greatest tragedies: Arthur can never be just a *man*, a private individual. Like all kings, he must weigh and judge his every action, whether in the bed chamber or the throne room, to assess its likely impact on not only his public persona, but on the nation as a whole.

Arthur is a man foremost, but it is convenient to divide discussion of this man into two aspects: public and private. In public Arthur is a king, a war-leader and a Christian icon in a world threatened with pagan bleakness: he is the living representation of the nation. Arthur is also a family man – a son and a brother, a lover, a husband and a father. He has a family with whom he interacts, on whom he leans, and which he must uphold.

In the end, his family betray and destroy him, but no-one can be blamed exclusively for his ruin. In whatever aspect you choose to consider Arthur, as a king or war hero or consummate lover, he is a blemished icon: as a king he is too often weak and indecisive, as a war-leader he can be cruel and unjust, and as a Christian icon he is deeply ambivalent. All of these flaws contribute to his destruction. But it is the sins of his private life – the sins of the son, brother, lover, husband and father – that ensure his downfall. Arthur was stained from birth, the sins of his parents, especially that of his father, reverberating through his life.

11

THE PUBLIC ARTHUR:
King, War-leader and Christian Icon

Hear now the wonder of Arthur's reign. As king, the excellent brave knight
Arthur was generous to all, a father to the young and a comfort to the old,
though with fools he was most stern. He held justice very dear and loathed
wrongdoing . . . . He held his people with great joy, overcoming all kings by
fierce strength and treasure. Such were Arthur's virtues known to all his folk;
loved by his subjects, he was a good king and famous throughout the land.

LAYAMON, Brut, BZDYL TRANSL., P. 194

*L*ayamon's panegyric depicts the king as we would all like to
perceive him. But is too easy – and way too false – to believe
in Arthur as a glorious hero and valiant king. All the legends
make superficial gestures towards this image, but the image
is a lie, and in all the versions of the legend (save Tennyson and most
of the glittering Hollywood spectacles) Arthur's actions belie the
popular perception. Arthur as king, war-leader and as a Christian is
largely a failure. Arthur may be a man caught in Fate, betrayed by
friends and family and the machinations of sly invaders and
treacherous sons, but Arthur himself is the main contributor to his own

downfall. Depending on the version of the tale, he might be weak and malleable, too open to the wrong influence, hesitant, tactless and, in his dealings as king and war-leader, cruel and inflexible: remember the seed that planted him. This is doubtless an unpopular view – everyone wants (or needs) to believe in Arthur the hero, but the fact is, Arthur himself cannot sustain the tag: ironically it is the 'traitors' surrounding him who tend to be the true heroes of the legend. Arthur succeeds in only one thing: providing an effective foil to the nobler individuals of his household and kingdom. The central theme of the Arthurian legend is tragedy, and Arthur is the greatest tragedy of all.

Although history places Arthur in the Dark Ages, as a legendary hero he is the product of the feudal age (roughly the twelfth to the fourteenth centuries). The historical Arthur of the fifth or sixth centuries is a very different man, as we will see in Chapter 13. In each of the categories in this chapter I judge Arthur by the standards of medieval Europe: this is the world which forged him, and their standards are the only ones by which we can understand him.

THE MONARCH

Despite popular conceptions of the medieval king, monarchs were constrained not only by military considerations (powerful nobles) but also by theological and ideological constraints. The Church was an immensely powerful organization that controlled many aspects of medieval life. One of the aspects that it tried to control – with varying degrees of success – was the behaviour of the secular rulers of Europe. According to Church theory, kings rested on the rung *below* popes in the hierarchy of earthly importance. Popes had the ear of God, and kings should listen to what the popes had to say. The Church believed this gave them the right to interfere in secular affairs. Not unnaturally, kings tended to resent deeply this interference.

What made the good medieval king? First of all, he should be a good Christian. A king's morals must be spotless, for he was an exemplar to the entire realm. Indeed, the king was the physical manifestation of his realm; if he sickened, then inevitably the realm would sicken. However, if the king sinned, then whatever sin stained his character and soul eventually would stain the soul of his realm.

> *You should, with all your strength, shun everything which you believe to be displeasing to Him. And you ought especially be resolved not to commit mortal sin . . . and should permit all your limbs to be hewn off, and suffer every manner of torment, rather than fall knowingly into mortal sin.*
>
> Louis IX's advice to his son, thirteenth century

A king was anointed by God, or at least by the Church as God's representatives on earth. Thus the king ruled on behalf of God and for God, and as part of his duties the king should protect the Church, and advance its cause, at every available opportunity. As well, as a Christian king, the king was responsible for the morals of his subjects, for which he would make account to God on his death. If a king failed in his duties to protect the morals of his subjects, if he became manifestly corrupt himself, or if he failed to protect or further the cause of the Church, then the pope (as God's voice on earth) had the power to remove God's will from a king. At this point it became the duty of every subject in the realm to rise in rebellion against the king. Excommunication was the ultimate threat a pope could use against a king, and it was not unknown for a pope to wield it.

Having taken care of his soul and the Church, the king should uphold the law with all his might, giving rich and poor equal justice. He should protect his kingdom, and maintain peace at home. He should be impartial and incorruptible. The king was not above the law, but must remain within it. He should not become a tyrant, and should strive to be loved rather than feared. Kings should not rule by force, but must consult with their subjects (in reality, this meant consulting with the higher nobles) and strengthen the institutions of government if they were to rule as well as reign. The medieval English kings swore at their coronations that they would protect the Church, do justice and suppress evil laws and customs. A king had to serve, as well as rule.

The king should defend his realm from both internal and from external threats (internal threats could not only mean rebellion, or criminal activities, but also heresy and moral lapses among his subjects). He must be an effective war-leader in order to sate his nobles' ambitions and needs with the acquisition of land. This was a vital aspect of medieval kingship, and I discuss it in more detail below.

Moreover, a king should look the part. In medieval Europe majesty was very much a visual statement. The population of any given realm was generally illiterate, and not subject to the kind of mass media we are now. They were therefore highly susceptible to pomp and pagaentry. The power of any noble, whether king, prince or local knight, rested as much on visual display as on actual deed. To impress his subjects, a king wore a crown, he carried the insignia of office (sceptre, orb and sword), he dressed in the robes and furs of a monarch. About his person he gathered his royal household: his family, personal guard, knights and courtiers, clergy, bureaucrats, administrators, and the courts and peoples of justice. No medieval king lived a stationary life. If he was not making justifiable war upon a rebellious baron or a recalcitrant neighbour, then he made stately progress about his realm. Eventually the importance of power through visual display also manifested itself through the construction of massive and stunning palace complexes in the main cities of the realm. Paris and London (or more specifically, Westminster) are excellent examples of the construction of cities to house court complexes to magnify the glory and power of their monarchs.[1]

A good and careful king also had a legitimate claim to the throne. In practical terms, a 'legitimate' claim to a throne more often than not meant 'the most powerful' claim to the throne, but most usurpers spent considerable time and energy proving their claim to a throne by extensive (and often imaginary) family pedigrees. The

---

1 And they had practical as well as aesthetic value – the avenues and boulevards leading to monarchical residences are not only excellent for the display of monarchical progress, they are also needed to give cannon straight and clear shot when subjects prove a trifle too rebellious.

Tudors at best only had a tenuous claim to the English throne (they were descended from a bastard son of the fourth son of Edward III) so when Henry Tudor defeated Richard III at Bosworth in 1485, they hastily produced a family pedigree that not only traced their bloodlines back to the Pendragons, but also to the biblical King David and the classical Brutus, great-grandson of Aeneas.[2] The Tudors then spent most of their dynasty executing the heads of the ancient English noble families so that at least there would be no-one else who could produce a better pedigree.

Having secured the throne (by whatever means, peaceful succession or violent overthrow), a good and careful king then secured his dynasty by producing an heir. If the king had come to the throne by means less than savoury, getting the heir on the previous king's wife or daughter was usually an excellent means of breeding some legitimate blood into the new dynasty (and the careful Henry Tudor did this as well, taking Richard III's niece, the elder daughter of Edward IV, as wife). It was disastrous if a king died without an heir (or even with an infant heir), for it meant that both internal and external contenders subsequently would tear the realm apart to gain control of the throne. Tragic civil wars instigated by the lack of a viable heir litter European history. The spectre of a barren queen also caused tragic consequences: witness the struggle of Henry VIII of England to get a legitimate son.

Having claimed his throne, engendered his son and led an upright life protecting the interests of the Church and defending the morals and laws of his kingdom, the king also had to maintain the respect of his subjects. Bluntly, this meant maintaining the respect and loyalty of his barons, any one of whom might control more land, wealth and knights than the king did himself. In any kingdom, the combined might of the barons had the potential to bring down the king (especially if the Church backed the barons, and announced that God had withdrawn his goodwill from the king – then not only would the barons have might on their side, they would also have right). In

2 The legendary founder of Britain. 'Britain' derives from his name.

order to maintain the respect, love and loyalty of his barons, the medieval king had to be an effective war-leader. He had to fight, and he had to win.

Arthur fills many of these criteria. He most certainly looks the part: no version of the myth ever has him looking frail or ugly. Arthur is a splendid man, the physical manifestation of a hero. He surrounds himself with the accoutrements of power: the crown (or golden helm), the splendid and sometimes magical armour, the supernatural sword and the splendour of his court. As far as sheer physical presence goes, Arthur is the epitome of chivalric monarchy. He wears sumptuous clothes, and his brow and fingers glitter with gems.

Depending on the origin or date of an Arthurian myth, Arthur variously holds court at the City of Legions, Caerleon, Camelot or Winchester but, whatever the location, all agree that this city cannot be bettered by any other in Europe.

Never among any people has there been born a man, whether layman or cleric, who could tell half the wealth of Caerleon, of the silver, gold and fine garments; of the horses, hawks, and hunting hounds; of the noble men in the court, or of all the splendours among the people.

Layamon, *Brut*, Bzdyl transl., p. 226

Arthur's city is inhabited by the handsomest men and the most winsome women in all of Europe, his court is peopled by the wisest and bravest: Arthur's fame pulls them from far and wide. There is wondrous music, singing and entertainment. And there is feasting day and night. Arthur's table is well laden: in one feast Arthur, his knights and their ladies consume peacocks, plovers, hedgehogs, herons, swans, beef pies, wild boar shoulders, barnacle geese, young hawks, brisket of pork, a variety of stews, cranes, curlews, roasted rabbits, pheasants and sundry pies. All this they wash down with clarets and Cretan wines, as well as wines from Osay and Algrave, Rhineland, Rochelle and Venice in goblets of silver and gilt. This is, by medieval standards, a reasonably conservative feast – some menus boasted at least thirty different kinds of meat and poultry, often culminating in the all-time favourite of live blackbird pie. Nevertheless, the aromas rising from the golden platters of Arthur's table were enough to impress one senator from Rome:

> *'Sire,' said the senator, 'So save me Christ,*
> *Such royalty never reigned within Rome's walls!*
> *No prelate or Pope or prince of this world*
> *But would be pleased to partake of this priceless feast!'*

Alliterative Morte Arthure, Ll. 227–230

Arthur could afford to smile, knowing he'd made such a fabulous impression on an emissary from Rome.

Unfortunately, as in many a medieval and modern feast, the wine could sometimes get the better of chivalric manners. Layamon describes one incident where, having eaten and drunk to excess, the diners 'grew angry and blows were numerous. First they threw their bread while it lasted and then their silver bowls filled with wine; afterward, fists struck necks.' The brawl worsened, Arthur and Guenevere seeking refuge in their private apartments as drunken earls grabbed knives: 'great was the bloodshed as calamity reigned in the court.' Finally, Arthur returns to the hall with a hundred warriors in helmets and armour, threatening everyone with gruesome deaths, and thus managing to restore peace. Thereupon the feast continued for another seven days and nights in good humour and gracious manners.[3]

After the feasting it is time for sport and tournaments. The court retires to the meadows outside beyond the city walls; the knights to engage in mock combats, the ladies to stand atop the walls and cry encouragement . . . and flirt with whichever knight takes their fancy. According to Monmouth, the knights engage in archery, hurling of weighty stones, wrestling and the playing of dice. Tournaments are rife in Arthur's realm: Malory has King Arthur and his knights joust at every opportunity. Medieval tournaments were practise wars: they

3 Layamon, p. 213.

were not only an opportunity for knights to keep their battle skills sharp, but were also a chance to release grudges and resentments in a controlled environment rather then resorting to murder in the shadows of night. Knights generally fought in a melee (or incoherent jumble) rather than in one-on-one combat: the entire force of knights would divide into two, ride to opposite ends of the field, then each side would charge towards the other, finally meeting in a great clash of steel and bruising. The fighting would last all day, no quarter given: more knights died on the tournament field than ever died in battle. Malory describes one incident where a field of 700 knights 'so fought that their shields fell to pieces, and horse and man fell to the earth'.[4]

In medieval literature there is no court which can compare to Arthur's. Modern authors, in placing Arthur back into his historical Dark Age milieu, have necessarily toned down the high-medieval splendour. White, of all my twentieth-century key texts, persists in placing Arthur into the high-medieval stage of Camelot:

> *On the battlements of their castle at Camelot . . . the young king of England was standing with [Merlin], looking across the purple wastes of evening. A soft light flooded the land below them, and the slow river wound between venerable abbey and stately castle, while the flaming water of sunset reflected spires and turrets and pennoncells hanging motionless in the calm air . . .*
>
> White, *The Once and Future King*, p. 232

A beautiful image, but White gives this Camelot a distinctly uncomfortable undertone.

> *Then, outside the curtain wall, there was the distant noise of old wives bargaining, and brats bawling, and corporals quaffing, and a few goats mixed with it, and two or three lepers in white hoods ringing bells as they walked . . . On the other side of the river, which ran directly beneath the*

4 Malory, Vol. 1, Book I, Chap. 2.

castle wall, there was a man ploughing in the fields, with his plough tied
to the horse's tail.

White, The Once and Future King, p. 233

Sutcliff, Stewart and Bradley resist the soaring stone spires and place their king into wooden forts and halls, but even within the necessary respect for historicity, they give Arthur as much splendour as the age will allow him. As a roving war-captain within the chaos of northern Britain, Sutcliff's Arthur necessarily lives a frugal existence, although when he finally comes to the throne (a royal throne of men's shoulders, the only kind this Arthur would treasure) in mid-life he lives in the comfort any king of that age could expect: a smallish, smoky palace. Writing in the decade after the excavations on the flat-topped hill of South Cadbury, only an enchantment's distance from Glastonbury (the historical site of Avalon), Stewart allows her Arthur to build a Camelot atop that windswept and barren hill. It is a place of battlements and great gates, a place marvellous yet comfortingly homely, a city,

> *gay with gilding and the fluttering of banners, and fresh with gardens and orchard trees . . . . [its] streets crowded with folk, and full of talk and laughter, the chaffering of the market-place, the quick hooves of Arthur's fleet and glossy horses, the shouts of the young men, and the clamour of the church bells. It [is] grown rich with peaceful commerce, and splendid with the arts of peace. Camelot is a marvellous sight . . .*

Stewart, The Last Enchantment, p. 187

In *The Mists of Avalon* Arthur begins his reign in the Roman fort of Caerleon but ends it in the awe-inspiring Camelot. Thus every author gives Arthur his architectural and courtly setting. But buildings are one thing, actions another. Majesty is as much actions as it is soaring stonework and fine gold brocade. Is Arthur king enough to warrant the gilded stage?

As king, Arthur is responsible for the well-being of hundreds of thousands of people. He must uphold the law, dispense justice to all while remaining impartial and incorruptible, maintain peace and protect his realm. He must be a king worth the love and admiration of his subjects, he cannot rule absolutely or without recourse to the advice of his nobles. Largely, Arthur does all this, although his reliance on advice sometimes goes too far.

The English chronicles, not unnaturally, stress Arthur's magnanimous kingship. His people love and respect him for his championship of the law of the land and their own personal rights (such as they were in medieval England). In Monmouth, Arthur is exceedingly generous, his inborn goodness making him beloved of all. Having driven out the Saxons, Arthur establishes his kingdom in a state of lasting peace. When Arthur conquers Gaul he also spends time making sure the peoples of that land are governed peacefully and legally. Similarly in Layamon, Arthur is generous to all, whether old or young. He holds justice dear and loathes wrongdoing. For his virtues, Arthur is loved by all in the land. Again, once the Saxons have been subdued, Arthur takes care to reinstate and then to maintain all the good laws of his ancestors: 'he set his peace and then established rights and privileges.'[5] Arthur is consumed with love during the first months of his marriage to Guenevere, but even the passion of early marriage cannot keep him from his kingly duties as he constantly wonders what he could do to keep his good folk from languishing away from the boredom of peace. In the twelve years before his campaign of European conquest, all people within Britain prospered, and 'all people who saw Arthur, men rich and poor, bowed to him as hail falls'.[6] No wonder Arthur introduces himself about as 'Arthur, Britain's darling'! As a dispenser of justice and peace and prosperity, he is unparalleled.

Similarly, Arthur is always careful to consult with his barons. He is in every sense a warrior's man. Indeed, as we shall see, he holds his warriors' lives more dear than he ever does his wife's. Before each major campaign Arthur consults with his highest nobles and knights,

5 Layamon, p. 209.
6 Layamon, p. 212.

listening carefully to what they have to say. While this is a commendable trait, the truly wise king carefully weighs the advice he receives, and acts only on that which is good. Arthur, unfortunately, tends to accept and act on every bit of advice he receives, good or bad. The French romances, as one might expect, make the most of this, but even the English chroniclers dwell on it. In Monmouth, Arthur nods as he listens to Cador, Duke of Cornwall, advise him that it would be a good idea to wage all-out war on Rome in order to keep his men from idleness. Keeping warriors from idleness is a necessary and desirable thing, but it is not the best reason to wage war on a powerful enemy. In Layamon, on the other hand, Arthur does not take kindly to advice. Here, the admittedly youthful Arthur is capable of making some truly bad decisions – and apparently his nobles fear to advise him differently. Arthur allows the Saxon chief Childric to withdraw after Arthur has had him at his mercy: 'In this Arthur was deprived of honor,' Layamon writes, 'but no man dared advise him that he would repent of it sorely thereafter.'[7] In this instance, a bad decision on Arthur's part results in a frightful massacre of innocent Britons as Childric returns to ravage the countryside. In Monmouth, Arthur allows the Saxons to leave, then is 'greatly astonished' when they actually take advantage of their freedom to resume their ravages.[8] It is naive of Arthur to assume that even if he kept some Saxon hostages, their released comrades would not resume hostilities the moment they were able.

The French romance tradition makes much more of Arthur's habit of taking bad advice without thinking through the consequences, or even of Arthur's tendency to be weak, indecisive and impotent in an emergency. Because the romance tradition concentrates so much more on the 'relationship' side of the Arthurian legend – Guenevere, Arthur, Lancelot and Mordred – rather than the detailed campaign analyses of the English chronicle tradition, Arthur's weakness and bad decisions tend to be those

7 Layamon, p. 200.
8 Monmouth, p. 216.

which affect his relationships more than his army (save in the instance where Arthur wages war on Lancelot). And, as far as kingly relationships are concerned, one of the stupidest Arthur ever indulged in was bedding his most potent political rival's wife. What was the youthful and self-indulgent Arthur thinking of, taking the Queen of Orkney to his bed? Forgetting for the moment that she was his sister, a king simply does not bed the wife of his strongest rival. But then again, Arthur *is* his father's son.

But Arthur's indecision and weakness (as a king and as a man) is most apparent in his handling of his wife's adulterous affair with Lancelot: if a man cannot rule his own household, how can he rule a kingdom? In most versions of the legend, even modern ones, Arthur is aware of the affair for years before he is forced to do something about it (either that, or he is almost criminally blind in not seeing it when the rest of the court is well aware of what is going on). Guenevere is not only a wife, she is also a queen, and her affair affects the entire country, not just her marriage. Arthur has a duty as a king to resolve the situation, but somehow he never does, not until his hand is forced by either Agravain or Mordred (the foster-son and son of Morgause of Orkney). A queen's primary responsibility to her husband the king, and to her country, is to bear an heir. It was, and technically remains, treason if an English queen, or the wife to the heir of a throne, engages in an adulterous affair because then it would put in doubt the paternity of any child she bore. No matter that Guenevere bore no child to Lancelot (in the chronicles where she has an affair with Mordred she sometimes does bear children), no queen should engage in adultery. In doing so she betrays her nation as much as her husband.

In modern novels, which tend to use Malory (and thus, to a significant extent, the French romance tradition) as a base, authors must somehow excuse or justify Arthur's behaviour. White explains that Arthur simply refused to admit to himself that Jenny and Lance were having an affair:

He had never actually found them together or unearthed proofs of their guilt. It was in the nature of his bold mind to hope, in these circumstances, that he would not find them together – rather than to lay a trap by which to wreck the situation. That is not to say that he was a conniving husband. It is simply that he was hoping to weather the trouble by refusing to become conscious of it. Unconsciously, of course, he knew perfectly well that they were sleeping together – knew too, unconsciously, that if he were to ask his wife, she would admit it.

White, The Once and Future King, p. 421

And thus Arthur wanders the hallways of Camelot with his eyes firmly screwed shut until someone *else* lays the trap and throws open the door to admit the ultimate wreckage. Bradley has Arthur actively connive in the affair, even to the point of orchestrating a *ménage à trois* one night in an effort to get Guenevere with child. An admirably open-minded way to treat a respected wife and beloved friend, perhaps, but a dismal way to try to beget an heir to the throne. Sutcliff has Arthur blind to a situation he should have known about, while Stewart's Arthur, when confronted with the situation by Merlin, admits to a long knowledge of Guenevere's affair with Bedwyr (the Lancelot figure).

'But if it is not to destroy our faith in one another, what would you have me do? I must give Bedwyr the trust and freedom to which he is entitled. Am I a cottager, with nothing in my life but a woman and a bed I am to be jealous of, like a cock on his dunghill? I am a king, and so my life is a king's; she is a queen, and childless, so her life must be less than a woman's. Is she to wait year by year in an empty bed?'

Stewart, The Last Enchantment, p. 370

Again, a wonderful exhibition of selfless blindness in a husband, but an abysmal line of reasoning for a king. A husband may be willing to sacrifice his marriage for a bit of quiet on the domestic front, but a king his kingdom?

Arthur's hand is finally forced when either Mordred or Agravain, or, more generally, both, force Arthur to confront the situation.

Sir Agravain told Arthur all
  With innocent-seeming cheer:
'Sir Lancelot lies with the Queen,
  And has done many a year.'

Stanzaic *Le Morte Arthur*, Ll. 1728–1731

Instead of confronting Guenevere and Lancelot privately, Arthur allows Agravain and Mordred to catch the lovers in bed, an action that has terrible results. Sometimes it is in this fight that Gareth (and occasionally Agravain) is killed, sometimes in a later one. Bad decision follows bad decision as Arthur then allows Gawain to persuade him to wage war on Lancelot to avenge his brother Gareth's death. Tact, diplomacy and common sense are absent from Arthur's dealing with the entire matter.

Guenevere acts as a catalyst for Arthur's poor decision-making on at least one other occasion, the banquet at which a knight dies after eating a poisoned apple. Although there is no evidence that Guenevere is to blame, Arthur agrees to put her on trial. He is a king, and he must uphold the law of the land. Again, fine words, and true to a point, but Arthur appears to meekly accept Guenevere's guilt even though there is no evidence at all.

The worst example of Arthur's bad judgement is when he leaves Mordred in charge of the realm. All chronicles and romances agree he should never have done this, especially as in many of them Mordred is portrayed as potential trouble-maker for years beforehand. Sometimes the decision to leave Mordred as regent is Arthur's alone, sometimes it is the advice of his nobles.

The knights at length advised the King
  They being of one mind,
Sir Mordred was the trustiest man
  That any of them could find
To rule the realm and keep the peace.

Stanzaic *Le Morte Arthur*, Ll. 2516–2520

This of the man who had not only taken part in the raid on the Queen's bedroom, but had then fled when the fighting turned nasty, leaving Agravain to die.

Arthur consults, as every good king should, but he depends too greatly on the consultative process. He is loath to act on his own – he lets the Guenevere and Lancelot affair drift until he is pushed into creating a needless crisis. Arthur is naive, allowing Saxons to escape, thus causing great harm to his innocent subjects. Arthur is too grateful for well-meaning but poor advice, leaving Mordred in charge of realm and queen. Arthur is weak, allowing Gawain to push him into war with Lancelot and he ignores sound advice when it *is* given – having made peace with Lancelot, Arthur ignores pleas that he should wait for Lancelot and his army to join him before waging war on Mordred. He is also, as we shall see when considering his attributes as war-leader, too full of pride and confidence. Arthur begins his reign in a burst of glory, but that burst is not enough to see him through a lengthy reign that is fraught with crises. Arthur is a magnificent spectacle, a Sun King in a blazing-bright glorious court, but to a marked degree, it is the Sun King's failings that eventually light the conflagration which consumes man and realm.

Finally, although this is an issue that affects Arthur's reign from his succession, does he have a legitimate claim to the throne? As I remarked earlier, this was not actually a vital ingredient of a successful kingship – any noble who had the greatest military strength often seemed to have the greatest legitimate right – but it was important, and particularly so in Arthur's case, given the nature of his conception. Arthur was born in marriage to the rightful king, but there were shadows and rumours surrounding his true paternity. Uther, or Gorlois? Was he conceived in adulterous sin, or true wedlock? There were too many questionmarks surrounding his paternity for Arthur to succeed without some trouble from his barons. It made no difference that he could pull the magical Excalibur from the stone – 'Pulling swords out of stones is not a legal proof of paternity, I admit,' says White's Merlin – although, having got his hands on the official state regalia Arthur does slightly improve his claim to the throne. Whatever the case, the story of Arthur pulling Excalibur (itself a fairly late medieval addition to the legend) from the stone appears very little in modern versions, apart from a few films which have popularised the appeal of combined muscle and magic.

There is a shadow from the very beginning of Arthur's reign. Is he the true, legitimate heir? Malory has Ulfin accuse both Ygerna and Merlin of treason in the suspicious manner Arthur was conceived; Ygerna should have been more careful, or Merlin should not have shrouded the night in so much magic.[9] Arthur has a difficult time at first trying to convince sundry rebellious barons and minor kings that he has a legitimate claim to Uther's crown: often war results as ambitious barons try to seize control of the throne themselves. At first Arthur wins glory for both himself and his land, a sure sign of God's favour. But then both Arthur and his grip on household and realm begin to fall apart as war consumes the nation.

One of Arthur's greatest failings as a king is his inability to sire a son within marriage. It was every king's duty to sire an heir who had no blemish on the certificate of legitimacy he waved in his hand when he marched up to take the throne. Arthur was married to Guenevere for many years. A good and careful king would, at some point, have put her away in order to take a wife who *could* give him an heir. But Arthur does not do this. He cannot claim love as an excuse (and as a king he should never claim it), for Arthur rarely loves Guenevere with abandoned passion. He is a distant and cool husband. But as in so many other things, Arthur does nothing. He might conquer distant realms, but he cannot rule his own household. Arthur fails in the primary duty of every careful medieval king: making sure that the succession to the throne is assured.

9 Malory, *Morte Darthur*, Vol. 1, Book XXI, Chap. 21.

THE WAR-LEADER

The reliance of a king on the image (and reality) of being a good war-leader largely rested on the necessities, and culture, of feudal society. Medieval society was divided into three estates, the divisions being based on labour. The first estate was composed of the clergy, the nobles made up the second estate and the third estate was composed of everyone else, mainly the peasants. The clergy prayed for the souls of mankind and guarded the road to salvation, the nobles fought to protect society and the peasants worked in order to feed society. This system, often loosely referred to as feudalism, had emerged out of the chaos and invasions of the Dark Ages and as such, however it may appear to us now, was a reasonably fair and equitable system for the needs of society at that time. Medieval Europe was founded on war and the concomitant need for protection, and the second most powerful rank of society was based entirely on a culture of war. War was the noble's reason for existence, and often his only means of existence. Via war, a king won land for his nobles, and from their land the nobles raised the monies needed to fund their life of war: the expenses of war horses, armour and retainers were enormous. Via war, a king could also lose land for his nobles. A landless noble was a restless noble, and unjustly or not, nobles often judged the effectiveness of a king on his skill as a war-leader. So what made a good war-leader?

Firstly, and most obviously, success. Success at winning wars (or at least seizing land from a neighbouring kingdom), and at making a profit from them. Profit not only came from the acquisition of land and sundry items of booty, but from the acquisition of large numbers of knights from the opposing force. In a medieval battle, knights did not set out to kill each other; rather, it was more lucrative to capture their opponents for ransom (foot soldiers – peasants – they happily slaughtered as utterly ransomless). As well as the captive himself (and the higher rank he was, the more he would fetch), the victorious knight also obtained his captive's armour and war horse. Because of this emphasis on ransom rather than slaughter, lengthy campaigns could go by without the death of a single knight. During a year-long campaign in Flanders in 1127, a force of 1,000 knights lost only five of their number: one fell from a horse, one slipped while climbing a wall, one was crushed under a collapsing ceiling, a fourth died after blowing a horn too enthusiastically and only one was killed in conflict.[10] Of course, Christian knights never rejoiced in spilling the blood of their fellow Christian and noble brothers, but the monetary rewards of capturing rather than slaughtering also had a great deal to do with the low death rate of knights on the field of war.

A king who led his armies to victory won the admiration and loyalty of his barons. The Norman barons and knights who followed William the Conqueror into England gave their king and his successors decades of undivided loyalty for the rich rewards they gained during the campaign of 1066. Contrariwise, King John, who lost much of the Norman land-holdings in France to the French king in the thirteenth century, came home to face the combined might of his discontented barons clutching the Magna Carta (a charter that severely restricted the powers of the king) in their mailed fists.

Although it is true that success was the prime factor in maintaining status as a war-leader, it mattered very much *how* a king achieved that success. War could only be fought for a just cause: to avenge a wrong, to regain wealth or land or goods unjustly stolen, to protect the Church, to protect lands and people. This meant that some ambitious kings (or kings with ambitious nobles) tied themselves in knots to find that single just cause to justify and promote the war they wanted to fight. War was declared and waged on the authority of a king or prince, but if that war was unjust, then the sin was the king's alone. When was a war unjust? Naturally, those attacked always cried 'unjust', but there were several signs that could demonstrate that a war had been fought for unjust reasons: an army that engaged in

10 Philippe Contamine, *War in the Middle Ages* (Guild, 1985), p. 255. The drinking parties held after battles or tournaments were also excellent opportunities for seizing fallen comrades. It was not unknown for drunken knights who fell over while urinating to be seized for ransom.

atrocities or undue violence, or an army that engaged in desecration of Church property. These acts indicated God's displeasure, and pointed the divine finger of wrath at a sinful king.

The successful warrior-king was also brave (bravery produced a commendable boldness and fearlessness in war) and proud, but never rash or cruel (which was a sign of 'unjustness'). The medieval warrior-king inspired his army by leading from the front and engaging in individual outstanding acts of prowess. He adhered to the 'rules' for the conduct of warfare. He shed blood blamelessly without becoming a man of blood: that is, he did not wage war for the sake of it, nor for the enjoyment of it (yet another sign of the unjust war). Finally, the warrior-king was magnanimous to those he defeated . . . within reason. Foot soldiers received a knife in the throat, nobles were banqueted, entertained and measured for their ransom potential.

Sutcliff's work is the only one which depicts Arthur as a war-leader, a *dux bellorum* (a leader of battles) rather than as a king. As one of the very few modern novels which places Arthur back into his historical setting, and the only one which does it convincingly (Bradley is the least historically convincing of the trio of post-sixties authors I use), *Sword at Sunset* follows the ninth-century *History of the Britons* in portraying Arthur in this manner. Here, his force is but some 300 men, and he spends most of his fighting life in the north of the country. There are no bright battles, no massed displays: Arthur is left to fight a dirty, guerilla-style war against the invaders.

Sutcliff aside, the vast majority of Arthurian tales over the past 1,000 years depict him as a mighty king and glorious war-leader. Or do they? On the surface, the legendary Arthur appears the perfect war-leader, and yet most medieval and modern authors depict him with serious flaws. Broadly speaking, Arthur waged just wars, and fought them well, during the early part of his reign, but during his latter years Arthur waged unjust wars – and paid the price. Monmouth's *History of the Kings of Britain* demonstrates this perfectly. Monmouth wrote that Arthur embarked on four major military campaigns during his reign:

1) The campaign Arthur fought against the invading Saxons and sundry pagans when he first came to the throne. Once he has successfully driven the pagans out, Arthur marries Guenevere, then conquers Ireland and Iceland, and accepts the homage and fealty of the kings of Gotland and the Orkneys. Arthur then sails home and rules Britain in peace for twelve years.

2) Having heard that all fear him, Arthur decides to campaign abroad, conquering large portions of Europe, including Gaul. He remains abroad for nine years, then sails home.

3) Arthur cannot rest on his laurels for long, because almost immediately he is challenged by the emperor of Rome, and thus begins Arthur's campaign against Rome which results in tragedy when Mordred seizes queen and throne while he is away.

4) The civil war against Mordred in which both die, and Arthur's realm is fatally weakened to fall apart under his successors.

These four campaigns appear in most later versions of the legend, although in the romance-inspired versions there is a fifth campaign – that against Lancelot, which is sandwiched between the campaign against Rome and the final war against Mordred. The crucial question is: were these just wars? To answer this, we should briefly weigh Arthur's capabilities against the other criteria on which all medieval war-leaders were judged.

As we have seen all good war-leaders had to succeed, and make a profit, at war. In the first two campaigns Arthur does this. In the third, although he wins swathes of new territory across Europe in his march on Rome, he is called home to battle Mordred's treachery before he can consolidate his gains. The first two campaigns, however, are gloriously successful and profitable: his barons, nobles and sundry knights must have been ecstatic. Having secured Britain itself, Arthur then adds Ireland and Iceland to his personal territory, and accepts the homage of two further areas, Gotland and Iceland. Arthur stays at home consolidating his court and reputation for twelve years, but then mounts another campaign and conquers large portions of northern and western Europe: Norway, Denmark and, most notably, Gaul (a

Dark Age empire that covered all of modern day France, as well as extending deep into central Europe: it was a rich and wondrous acquisition to Arthur's lands). By the time Arthur embarked on his third campaign – to conquer Rome – he could brag to his men that Britain was the 'mistress of thirty kingdoms'[11] and could soon lay claim to Rome's riches: 'What rewards you will win, if only you obey my will and my orders, as loyal soldiers ought to do . . . . yours shall be the gold, silver, palaces, towers, castles, cities and all the other riches of the vanquished!'[12] But Arthur never reached Rome, and his loyal soldiers never had the chance to avail themselves of its riches. At the moment when he had defeated the Roman army, and was preparing to march on Rome itself, word reached him that Mordred (his nephew, in this version) had usurped both throne and queen.

The final war against Mordred (or final two wars, if we count the romance-inspired war against Lancelot) was disastrous. Arthur lost not only his life, but his entire empire. Eventually Britain itself was lost to renewed Saxon invasions. Ultimately then, despite his stupendously successful initial campaigns, Arthur loses it all in civil war.

The English chronicles are the sources which focus the most on Arthur's stupendous feats of conquest. No doubt the English wished that they were, indeed, the rulers of thirty foreign kingdoms (although neither the Angevin nor the Plantagenet kings did badly, as well-planned royal marriages brought them extensive European territories). Unsurprisingly, the French romances place Arthur into an almost exclusively British setting: the romance tradition thrived

11 The alliterative *Morte Arthure* names thirty-two, although it comments that there were a 'host of other lands' besides these named: Argyll, Orkney, Ireland, Scotland, Wales, Flanders, France, Holland, Hainault, Burgundy, Brabant, Brittany (Britain the Less), Guienne, Gotland, Grasse, Bayonne, Bordeaux, Touraine, Toulouse, Poitiers, Provence, Valence, Vienne, Auvergne, Anjou, Navarre, Norway, Normandy, Austria, Germany, Denmark and Sweden. Some of these areas are now only provinces of greater nations, but in medieval Europe they were independent states in their own right; L1.33–47.

12 Monmouth, p. 249.

during a period when the English and French fought viciously over English land-holdings in France, and no Frenchman wanted to give the English even the mythological satisfaction of an all-out Gallic conquest. Twentieth-century novels also tend to place Arthur into a more historical Dark Age setting. In Stewart and Bradley, Arthur might sally forth on numerous and successful campaigns but he holds nowhere near the territories that Monmouth gave him, while Sutcliff's Arthur is fortunate if he can hold on to a small British village during a rain squall, let alone even think about a foreign campaign of conquest. Thus it is primarily the medieval English chronicles which have bequeathed us the all-conquering Arthur, but their vision of grandeur was so sweeping, and so pervasive within English-speaking cultures, that we still remember Arthur as a world conqueror.

As well as being successful, a good war-leader has to be bold and active in his leadership: no medieval king watched a battle from a command tent on a safe hill. Arthur is a brilliant and courageous battle leader. Monmouth depicts him almost as a Viking berserker, rushing forward at full speed into the thickest ranks of the enemy with no thought of his own safety. He kills with a single blow, and in one of his early battles against the Saxons manages to kill over 470 men in the one day (Monmouth is almost modest in this number, considering the source he worked from, the ninth-century *History of the Britons*, claimed that Arthur personally slew some 960 men at the Battle of Badon).[13] Arthur's courage inspires his men, often being the factor that saves the day for the Britons when they are close to losing. Like Monmouth, Layamon describes Arthur's bravery and inspiring leadership in glowing terms, but with considerably more poetry:

---

13 These numbers must never be taken literally. The medieval mind had difficulty with large numbers (witness Monmouth's own problems with addition), and chroniclers and scribes often merely meant 'lots' when they gave what they felt was an impressively large number. No-one was in the least interested in a careful kill-count.

Arthur raised his shield in front of his breast and rushed forward like a
mad wolf who comes from the woods, hung with snow, thinking to ravage
the flocks at will. Calling to his beloved knights, Arthur shouted:
'Onward quickly, bold thanes, then all will be well.' His men surged
forward like the tall trees of the forest swept by the wild, mighty wind.
Thirty thousand warriors flew over the field and struck Colgrim's knights
so that the earth shook.

Layamon, *Brut*, Bzdyl transl., p. 195

Further, Arthur singly defends a ford with his spear, denying the fearful Saxons a retreat to safety: 7,000 of the enemy drown, increasing Arthur's personal tally considerably. Monmouth's and Layamon's descriptions of Arthur as a berserker, or a 'mad wolf' are not necessarily critical: great feats of bravery could be accomplished when the single warrior temporarily became maddened with anger and a desire to kill. Layamon also describes Arthur as an 'enraged boar' who roars towards the enemy 'like a lion'. Again and again, in these earlier campaigns, Arthur leads from the front, inspiring his men into victory after victory against the hated Saxon invaders.

The late fourteenth-century alliterative *Morte Arthure* concentrates on the final years of Arthur's reign. This work was based on the chronicle tradition and thus, although it deals only with the battles against the Romans and Mordred, continues to describe Arthur's battle prowess in glowing terms:

Arthur shot through the shield-wall with his sharp weapon,
Shearing through the chivalry, shattering their armour,
Bearing down their banners and battering to bits their shields,
And wreaking his wrath on their ranks with his sword.
He twisted and turned in his towering strength,
Angrily harming the adversaries he attacked.

Alliterative *Morte Arthure*, Ll. 2210–2215

The French romances also depict Arthur as a great war-leader, although not with quite the same enthusiasm as the English chroniclers. In these, he may display great courage and battle-madness in combat, but he rarely leads from the front (and, in true French tradition, the greatest feats of chivalric might are performed by Lancelot). In the early thirteenth-century *La Mort le Roi Artu*, Arthur performs marvellous feats of chivalry in his battle against the Roman army, although he is among the *last* to join in the fight: forgivable (perhaps) if we consider that the author of this work made Arthur ninety-two at this time.[14] In the same passage, the author remarks that Arthur kills the Roman emperor, 'which was a great shame, because he was a very fine knight and only a young man.'[15] When Arthur sails back home to meet Mordred, he again leads the last battalion, as does his son in his own force. In the French-inspired but English-composed stanzaic *Le Morte Arthur* of the mid-fourteenth century, Arthur is depicted as a brave knight, but only in his battles with Mordred.

> *King Arthur fought so fiercely then*
> *That none against him stood;*
> *He hacked their hauberks[16] and their helms*
> *Until their breasts ran with blood.*
> *So some were killed, some ran away,*
> *And some of the treacherous horde*
> *Fled to Canterbury to warn,*
> *Mordred, their traitorous lord.*

Stanzaic *Le Morte Arthur*, Ll. 3082–3089

To be fair to the French, or the French-inspired, romances, they only deal with the later campaigns of Arthur's life. Even the English chronicles tend to gloss over Arthur's bravery and leadership skills for the final few campaigns. There is a good reason for this, and I discuss it below in examining whether or not Arthur's wars were fought for just reasons.

14 *La Mort le Roi Artu*, p. 189.
15 *La Mort le Roi Artu*, p. 190.
16 Armour for a knight's neck and shoulders.

But while on war-courage and skills, it is appropriate to look at Arthur's fighting skills. At first glance he seems to be the epitome of the splendid, skilled knight, but there are problems with this depiction. Yes, Arthur has courage and he is among the most skilled warriors in his kingdom, but rarely is he the best and often he is only mediocre. His anger does seem too 'hot', even out of control, and as intimated above, he sometimes kills without thinking. Arthur's short-comings as a knight appear most obvious in the French romances. This is not surprising, given that in all these romances Lancelot is the true hero, and no-one is allowed to outshine him.

Firstly, in both the Welsh and English chronicle traditions, Arthur bears the accoutrements of the heroic warrior. In *Culhwch and Olwen*, Arthur has a sword named Caledfwlch, a spear called Rhongomyniad, a shield called Wynebgwrthucher and Carnwennan, his dagger. Monmouth changed the names slightly, making the sword Caliburn (which it stayed until the French re-named it Excalibur) which had been forged on the island of Avalon, his shield was Pridwen (bearing an image of the Virgin Mary), and his spear was the now much abbreviated Ron. Layamon added the elvin-wrought armour, Wygar. Thus armoured, and fitted out with his golden helm, Arthur surely looked the part of the perfect knight.

But did he act it? Looking splendid is all very fine, and having an armoury of lengthy-named and magical weapons is even better, but a knight still must prove himself in battle. This Arthur does, even the French grudgingly allowing him a few heroic moments in battle, but it is in one-on-one combat, often a duel or a tournament joust, where Arthur literally comes undone. In Malory, Arthur takes a tumble time and time again. Well might he do 'marvellous deeds of arms' in war, but King Lot is still able to smite him down.[17] Merlin has to save Arthur from having his head hacked in two by a mightier knight, Pellinor,[18] and again has to keep King Lot away from Arthur

17 Malory, Vol. 1, Book I, Chap. 9.
18 Malory, Vol. 1, Book I, Chaps 23–24.

for Arthur's sake.[19] Nimue also assumes responsibility for rescuing Arthur. She uses her magic to save Arthur in his battle with Accolon,[20] and must beg Lancelot and Tristram to save Arthur from the Forest Perilous where she knows he will be slain without someone riding to his aid.[21] Tristram's goodwill fades slightly as he later de-horses Arthur in a tournament (although to be fair, once Arthur has been dusted off and re-horsed he then sets about Tristram with great gusto),[22] and then in a subsequent tournament Tristram again de-horses the king and so severely wounds him that Sir Uwain must save Arthur from a certain death;[23] further in the book Tristram *again* smites down King Arthur: 'And therewith Sir Tristram mounted upon his horse, and there he met with King Arthur, and he gave him such a buffet upon the helm with his sword that King Arthur had no power to keep to his saddle'.[24] No doubt inspired by Tristram's efforts, Palomides[25] then downs Arthur with a spear for daring to stare at Queen Iseud,[26] and shortly afterwards compounds the king's indignity by unhorsing him in a tournament.[27] Thus, in Malory's *Morte Darthur*, supposedly one of the legends which most extols Arthur's virtues, the heroic king must be picked up and dusted off by so many different people, and saved from a certain death by sundry others, that it is remarkable Arthur survives past the clarion announcing the first tournament of the book.

Thus we must question Arthur's greatness as a knight to some degree, if only because he displays such ineptitude in tournaments,

19 Malory, Vol. 1, Book II, Chap. 10.

20 Malory, Vol. 1, Book IV, Chap. 10.

21 Malory, Vol. 1, Book IX, Chap. 15.

22 Malory, Vol. 1, Book IX, Chap. 32.

23 Malory, Vol. 2, Book X, Chap. 1.

24 Malory, Vol. 2, Book X, Chap. 69.

25 Palomides is a knight closely associated with the romance of Tristram and Isolte (Tristram and Iseud in Malory).

26 Malory, Vol. 2, Book X, Chap. 73.

27 Malory, Vol. 2, Book X, Chap. 79.

jousts, and in retrieving himself from potentially fatal calamities. But there are other problems with Arthur's skill as a warrior and war-leader, and far more serious ones. In medieval thought, no king, knight or war-leader should ever display wanton cruelty. War is war, but there have always been rules. A king, it was felt, should be magnanimous to those he has defeated (with, perhaps, the exception of the common foot soldier), and he certainly should not raze and destroy for the sheer joy of doing so. And yet time and again we are presented with images of a cruel Arthur, even among the English chroniclers (who are kinder to Arthur than most).

It begins in Monmouth (and for very good reason, which I shall return to shortly). In his second campaign, when Arthur sets out to conquer much of western Europe, he defeats the Norwegians, then:

> *Once they were sure of victory, they invested [sic] the cities of Norway and set fire to them everywhere. They scattered the rural population and continued to give full licence to their savagery until they forced all Norway and all Denmark, too, to accept Arthur's rule.*
>
> Monmouth, *The History of the Kings of Britain*, p. 223

Having slaughtered the northerners, Arthur then rides south into Gaul where 'he drew his troops up in companies and began to lay waste the countryside in all directions'.[28] This is pointless savagery, and it foreshadows Arthur's slaughter of newborn children in the romances in his attempts to kill his son. In Layamon, Arthur does not so much indulge in cruelty, as threaten it: 'I will send sixteen thousand bold warriors to your great misfortune,' he tells King Doldanim of Gotland, who stubbornly refuses to swear allegiance to Arthur. 'They will plunder your land, slay your people, dispose of your realm as seems best, bind you and bring you to me.' Doldanim capitulates, as does King Rumareth of Winetland who Arthur similarly threatens.[29] In the stanzaic *Le Morte*

[28] Monmouth, p. 223.
[29] Layamon, pp. 211–212.

Arthur Arthur's troops attack, burn and slaughter through Lancelot's territory when the foolish king moves against his best friend and staunchest ally.[30]

These are the acts of a rash man out of control, burdened with the lust for power. This is someone who does not wage war justly, but only to feed his over-weening ambition. Even if the acts of cruelty are committed by Arthur's troops, then Arthur should still be king enough to either forbid such behaviour, or put a stop to it. There are versions of the legend that do present Arthur in a better light: the alliterative *Morte Arthure* has Arthur order his troops not to rape or mistreat the townsfolk of a captive town, while Robert Mannyng of Brunne, in his version of Monmouth, carefully pointed out how well Arthur behaved while moving through Gaul:

> *His folk so wisely again he lead,*
> *He destroyed no land where he went,*
> *He took nothing from no hand,*
> *But meat and drink and horse provend;*
> *Yet took they none with mastery,*
> *But bought it where it was to buy.*

> Mannyng, *The Chronicle*, Douglass transl.

But Arthur the magnanimous, Arthur the forgiving, is rarely seen, especially not in the later parts of his reign. Cruelty, whether towards his opponents or their hapless families, or to his wife, constantly darkens his face and clouds his actions.

There is good reason for showing Arthur as cruel, especially in the English chronicles where one would have expected him to have been portrayed with a little more humanity: after the early years of Arthur's reign, God withdraws his goodwill and grace from the king as Arthur wages increasingly unjust wars. Of the four campaigns he fights, only the first is fought for good and just cause. Having assumed the

---

30 Stanzaic *Le Morte Arthur*, Ll. 2536–2537.

throne, consolidated his position and then repelled the Saxon invaders, Arthur then goes off the rails.

In fact, Arthur 'goes bad' immediately after marrying Guenevere. This may be just coincidence, or it may have far deeper implications.

Let's examine these campaigns one by one. When Arthur comes to the throne at the age of fifteen, he has to contend with the ravaging Saxon pagans who threaten Britain. His people live under constant terror, the Saxons pillage at will – something must be done. Yet even with the obvious 'justness' of this war (which is a foreign and non-Christian invasion), Monmouth gives Arthur a somewhat strange reason for sallying forth: 'The justness of his cause encouraged him, for he had a claim by rightful inheritance to the kingship of the entire island.'[31] In Monmouth, Mordred actually had better claim to the throne than Arthur did, thus clouding the statement that Arthur had rightful inheritance, but this sentence implies that Arthur fought back the pagans not to save his people, but merely to reclaim his inheritance. In other words, he did the right thing for the wrong reason. Whatever Arthur's reasons, everyone else approved. The Church approved, particularly since Arthur had asked their advice about the campaign, and the 'saintly' Dubricius, Archbishop of the City of Legions, gave the assembled troops a rousing speech, blessed them and promised that anyone who died in the conflict would achieve instant absolution from all their sins (thereby gaining salvation). The nobles approved, and brought their men in their tens of thousands. Eventually, after several trials, the Saxons were routed, and Arthur, flushed with success, then conquered Ireland and Iceland for good measure. He certainly had just cause to attack Ireland, for Gilmaurius, King of Ireland, had supported the Saxons against the Britons, although there are less clear reasons to justify Arthur's attack on Iceland (save that it was peopled by pagans, and Arthur could be seen merely as doing his duty as a good Christian king to conquer it for the Church).

Essentially, this first campaign was eminently just. Every king's duty is to fight back invaders, and Arthur does this admirably. Monmouth

31 Monmouth, p. 212.

further shows how just this war is by having Arthur consult with the clergy beforehand; Arthur's army and campaign is blessed by the Church, Arthur shows mercy to his conquered foe and rebuilds churches and restores possessions to those of his people who had been ravaged by the Saxons. And finally, when 'Arthur had restored the whole country to its earlier dignity, he himself married a woman called Guinevere.'[32] He establishes his realm in a state of lasting peace and lives a blameless life for twelve years, developing a code of courtliness in his household, and inspiring many men of nobility to join him: the fame of his generosity and bravery spread to the very ends of the earth.

To this point Arthur has done everything right. But then he hears that many foreign kings tremble at the thought that they might be invaded by him. 'The fact that he was dreaded by all encouraged him to conceive of the idea of conquering the whole of Europe.'[33] Thus Arthur fits out his ships, readies his armies and sails forth to conquer Norway, Denmark and Gaul. Even though Arthur demonstrates some personal bravery (especially in his duel with Frolle, the tribune who rules Gaul on behalf of the Romans), this campaign is marked by cruelty and savagery. Arthur spends nine years in Gaul, pacifying all of its provinces before he finally rides home to wife and country 'quite overjoyed by his great success.'[34]

There is no manner in which this campaign can even remotely be called 'just'. Arthur invades, slaughters and burns simply because he can. Notably, he seeks no advice for this campaign, not from the Church nor from his nobles – although, as they won great lands from the campaign, the nobles doubtless were in no hurry to denounce it. Through northern Europe as well as Gaul, Arthur shows little mercy. He no longer calls on God in battles as he did when fighting the pagans.

Once home in Britain, however, Arthur apparently slips effortlessly back into the role of model king. He builds more churches, further enhances the reputation of his court and holds a magnificent feast in

32 Monmouth, p. 221.
33 Monmouth, p. 222.
34 Monmouth, p. 226.

his City of the Legions (Monmouth situates this city on the River Usk in Monmouthshire, not far from the Severn Sea). During the occasion of this feast Arthur is again crowned by the several archbishops (the Church has yet to withdraw its goodwill). There are games and much bright chivalric behaviour. But then the saintly Archbishop Dubricius resigns, saying only that he wishes to live as a hermit.

Arthur crowns his uncle, David, as the new Archbishop of the City of Legions, and bestows various other dioceses on his favoured friends. He replaces the 'holy' Samson, Archbishop of Dol, with Tebaus, priest of Llandaff (King Hoel of Brittany supports this action), and sundry other clerics are given rich positions.

As this is happening twelve men walk in carrying olive branches. They deliver a message to Arthur from Lucius Hiberius, Procurator of the Republic of Rome. Among other things the letter informs Arthur that Lucius is 'amazed at the insolent way you continue your tyrannical behaviour. I am even more amazed at the damage you have done to Rome'. Further, he continues, Arthur has the 'presumption' to withhold tribute from Rome. Arthur must appear before the Senate to explain himself, and if he doesn't come, then Lucius will invade Britain and set things to rights personally.[35]

On the face of it there seems no justification for this letter – in fact, it seems all the more odd seeing there had been no Roman Empire for 100 years at least when a historical Arthur would have existed, and certainly not for almost 700 years by the time Monmouth wrote this passage. But the letter, and the timing of its arrival, are highly significant when considering the political to-ing and fro-ing between the monarchs of Europe and the papacy in the twelfth century.

Relations between many of the monarchs of Europe and the papacy were sliding to an all-time low in the twelfth century. The papacy claimed the exclusive right to nominate, and invest, holders of high clerical office. Just as stubbornly, monarchs insisted they had the right to invest their own men into these offices. The Investiture Crisis, as it came to be known, was a battle for political power waged between the

35 Monmouth, pp. 230–231.

secular monarchs and the papacy. The Church owned vast amounts of wealth and land across Europe, as well as vigorously defending its right to remain outside state law and taxation systems. Monarchs naturally wanted to place their own men in the powerful Church positions within their own realms (how many younger sons of English kings ended up as the archbishop of something or the other?), while popes just as naturally wanted to prevent them doing it.

There is nothing more significant in Monmouth's Arthurian story than when the 'Senate of Rome' (the papacy) challenges Arthur's power at the very moment he is happily investing his own men (including his uncle) into high Church office, displacing at least one 'holy' archbishop in the process. The tribute that Lucius demands to be paid could easily be read as the tithes (taxes) which the Church collected from every person in every land, and then sent to Rome. Many nationalities, the English among them, resented this outpouring of national wealth to what most perceived as a foreign power.

After receiving Rome's challenge, Arthur retires with his nobles to discuss the situation. Cador, Duke of Cornwall, speaks for all the nobles when he states that the Britons are turning to sloth without a good war to fight. Peace is all very well, he says, but too much peace tarnishes every good soldier's reputation with the taint of cowardice. This support vindicates Arthur's need to wage war on Rome. He states that Lucius' demand for tribute is a 'trumped up case':

> *'He says that he ought to be given it because it used to be paid to Julius Caesar and those who succeeded him. When these men landed with their armed band and conquered our fatherland by force and violence at a time when it was weakened by civil dissensions, they had been encouraged to come here by the disunity of our ancestors. Seeing that they seized the country in this way, it was wrong of them to exact tribute from it. Nothing that is acquired by force and violence can ever be held legally by anyone.'*
>
> Monmouth, *History of the Kings of Britain*, p. 232

Nothing that is acquired by force and violence can ever be held legally by anyone. What an extraordinary statement to issue from Arthur's lips –

and no wonder he now proceeds to lose everything he has ever gained. Arthur not only loses his external empire (gained through force and violence) but, in doing so, he creates within his own realm the disunity and civil dissensions that originally allowed the Romans to conquer the island, and would now allow the Saxons to do the same. There is prophecy in that speech, and doom.

Arthur now proceeds to wage war on Rome (again, to be read as the papacy) – the most unjust cause for war in medieval culture! All monarchs were sworn to uphold the Church, and to defend it; here, Arthur makes every attempt to storm the citadel of Rome itself and make himself its master. As a sop to English pride, perhaps, Monmouth allows Arthur the defeat of Lucius' armies, but as a cleric, Monmouth cannot allow Arthur to conquer Rome. On the morning before he is to march south to the fortress of the Christian faith, Arthur receives word of Mordred's foul treachery back home. At this point no medieval audience could have possibly been surprised at Arthur's ultimate failure. Although Monmouth's Mordred is Arthur's nephew rather than his son and there is no shadow of incest (unless you count the fact that even a husband's nephew commits incest by sleeping with his uncle's wife), Mordred is the sum total of all of Arthur's unjustness and cruelty. God will not be mocked, Arthur must be cast down from his pride and vaunting ambition.

It is worthwhile here to consider whether the campaign against Lancelot was just, even though this campaign does not appear in the original English chronicles. When Lancelot is trapped in Guenevere's bedchamber, he fights his way free, killing Gareth – one of the Orkney boys – in the process. Gawain, Gareth's eldest brother, is distraught when he discovers his brother's body:

Sir Gawain went at once . . .
  To where the dead men lay
In pools of gore on the chamber floor
  And cloth of gold array

Stanzaic Le Morte Arthur, Ll. 1994–1997

He faints, and cries, and then swears revenge:

> '. . . *By God, between*
> *Sir Lancelot du Lake*
> *And me, there is no man on earth*
> *Could peace or fair truce make*
> *Till one of us has killed the other.'*

Stanzaic Le Morte Arthur, Ll. 2008–2012

A furious Gawain, one of Arthur's most senior knights and closest friends, persuades a hesitant Arthur to make war on Lancelot in order to avenge Gareth's death.[36]

Was this war just? On the face of it, yes. Lancelot, noble though he is, is nevertheless committing adultery (and treason, in English law) by sleeping with Guenevere: almost all versions of the legend make clear that the relationship was a hotly sexual one. Lancelot has also killed Gareth, although whether or not this was 'murder' or an action of self-defence is a moot legal point. Lancelot clearly deserves some kind of punishment for his misdeeds . . . but all-out war? Is this in the best interests of the realm? In some versions of the legend Arthur is initially reluctant to make war on Lancelot, but is persuaded by Gawain who is driven by an all-consuming need for revenge; in other versions Arthur cannot wait to don armour and mount horse and wage war on his once best friend.

The war on Lancelot is not in the best interests of the realm at all (what would have been in the best interests of the realm was a decisive king putting a halt to the affair years beforehand). Instead, this war is waged for reasons of personal revenge, or even as an outlet for years of frustration. Gawain is certainly driven by a need for revenge – eventually struck down by Lancelot, Gawain admits he was wrong to push Arthur into this destructive war. Whatever the motivation, Arthur generally has a change of heart at some point

---

36 Gawain also probably wants to avenge Elaine's suicide. He was in love with her, and jealous of her love for Lancelot.

during the war (usually about the time he realises he cannot win against the mighty skills of Lancelot).

> *The King, when mounted in his saddle,*
> *   On Lancelot fixed his gaze,*
> *And knew there was never another knight*
> *   Who had such courteous ways.*
> *He thought how things had used to be,*
> *   And tears from his eyes ran;*
> *Sighing and groaning, he cried, 'Alas!*
> *   That ever this war began!'*

Stanzaic Le Morte Arthur, Ll. 2198–2205

And yet Arthur does nothing to stop the fighting:

> *The two sides slowly separated,*
> *   So many knights were slain,*
> *And on the following day the fight*
> *   Was set to start again.*
> *Yes, the armies drew apart*
> *   In noble style, I swear:*
> *Was he not a sinner who started*
> *   This miserable affair?*

Stanzaic Le Morte Arthur, Ll. 2206–2213

Was he not a sinner who started this miserable affair? It matters not who this sentence refers to, Lancelot, Gawain or Arthur: they are all equally sinners, and this war is equally tragic, from whichever side it is viewed. There can be no happy outcome. Sometimes there is a hiatus in the war when the pope personally intervenes and tells Arthur and Lancelot to make peace. However, the peace they make cannot last, and soon Arthur is preparing to 'burn, kill and lay waste again'.[37] Arthur unleashes his considerable streak of cruelty, allowing

---

37 Stanzaic *Le Morte Arthur*, L. 2507.

his armies to slaughter at will, and the war – however it began – has now become unjust.

Civil war now destroys Arthur's court, setting knight against knight, and the Fellowship of the Round Table is shattered:

This realm will be now no quiet, but ever strife and debate, now the Fellowship of the Round Table is broken; for by the noble Fellowship of the Round Table was King Arthur upborne, and by their noblesse the king and all his realm was in quiet and rest, and a great part . . . was because of [Lancelot's] noblesse.

Malory, *Morte Darthur*, Vol. 2, Book XX, Chap. 17

In the romance tradition, this is the war during which Mordred makes his play for power. Arthur's actions have handed him his chance on a golden platter: not only is the unity of the Round Table broken, but Arthur has left Mordred in charge of the realm. United, Arthur and Lancelot could have defeated Mordred. At odds each with the other, they are destroyed.

Why did Arthur 'go bad'? Why did he fight such disastrous wars, wars that common sense alone should have prevented? In part, it is because there needs to be some mechanical means by which Arthur's reign and realm are torn apart, some excuse, if you like, for the unthinkable. But largely Arthur initiates and fights these wars because his character is already severely faulted. His unjust wars are the physical manifestation of his sin.

THE CHRISTIAN

As well as glorious king, war-leader and knight, Arthur is also the face of Christianity in his kingdom. It was part of his duties as king to not only protect the Church, but to promote its interests. All medieval kings had to administer the law of the land, not only to keep the peace, but to check their subjects' propensity to sin.

Arthur is the Christian king *only* in the medieval legends; in modern times he has become something of a closet pagan. Medieval authors could depict Arthur in no other way than as a Christian. The Church, and Church-promoted thought dominated European society, and to depict Arthur as a non-Christian, or pagan, would have brought suspicion at best, a charge of heresy at worst, upon whatever author or troubadour chose to depict him as such. Nevertheless, even as a medieval Christian Arthur occasionally has his lapses.

In Monmouth the lapses are plain, and closely tied to his slide into unjust wars for reasons of pride and personal ambition. For the initial twelve years of his reign, Arthur is the perfect Christian and Christian king: at fifteen, his accession to the throne is supported by the Church. As a Christian king, Arthur then sets about ridding his land of pagans; any slaughter or cruelty shown in this initial campaign is justified, because nothing but slaughter and cruelty can be shown to those who stubbornly refuse to accept the word of God. Arthur fights in the name of God, he carries a shield with the likeness of the Virgin Mary on it (Monmouth follows the *History of the Britons* in this), and calls on both God and the Virgin Mary in the midst of battle. When Arthur attacks the Scots and Picts in the north of Britain, he does so with 'unparalleled severity, sparing no one who fell into his hands'.

As a result, all the bishops of this pitiful country [Scotland], with all the clergy under their command, their feet bare and in their hands the relics of their saints and the treasures of their churches, assembled to beg pity of the King for the relief of their people . . . they fell on their knees and besought him to have mercy.

Monmouth, *History of the Kings of Britain*, p. 219

Arthur is moved by their appeals, and grants them mercy – another sign of a good Christian king. He then moves back south, re-building churches and restoring benefices to clerics. In Mannyng's version of this scene, the Scottish clerics also bring a number of Scottish noble women with them for added effect: the women tear out their hair in despair, and drag their crying toddlers behind them – a truly pitiful scene. Nevertheless, Arthur stands there, listening to their appeals and excuses, with (one assumes) a stern face. Nothing moves him to pity and forgiveness until the women say to him:

> 'For we are Christian as are ye,
> 'And if we die in such distress,
> 'Christendom is much the less;
> 'Then is thy peril much the more,
> 'If thou wrathest Christ so sore.

Mannyng, *The Chronicle*, Douglass transl.

At this single threat – that Christ would be angry if Arthur doesn't forgive the Christians, however treasonably they had acted by allying themselves with the Saxons – Arthur shows his fear and respect of God and Christ by instantly seeing reason and magnanimously forgiving them! Even though he must be prodded into it, Arthur still acts as a good Christian king should at this point. He has the people at his mercy, they have sworn their fealty and begged forgiveness, he has let them grovel in the dust for a suitable length of time (good for their souls), and now he forgives them and restores their lands to them . . . even if he does keep them in servitude.

However, once Arthur begins to wage war for unjust reasons, and to wrongly assert his control over the Church in Britain, then Monmouth strips Arthur of the accoutrements of a good Christian. Arthur no longer calls on either the Virgin or God, and he begins to act in an ungodly manner, causing slaughter and havoc in good Christian lands. God withdraws his grace, and Arthur fails.

Layamon depicts Arthur as more godly. The first words Layamon has Arthur speak – when knights have come to fetch him to the throne after Uther's death – are those of a good Christian king: 'Lord Christ, help us now that while I live I may keep God's laws.'[38] In battle

38 Layamon, p. 193.

he calls on the Virgin and Christ, 'Now Mary, merciful mother of God, help us! I pray that your Son aid us!',[39] he has the Virgin's image engraved in red-gold tracings on his shield, and rides with the Lord's goodwill and aid to destroy the invading pagans. Layamon moderates Monmouth's clear depiction of Arthur's unjust second and third campaigns (by the time Layamon wrote, England was not only far more deeply embroiled in the power struggle with the papacy, but nationalistic sentiment was on the increase), giving Arthur semi-justifiable reasons for embarking on the campaign to conquer Europe, and omitting any reference to cruelty. When Arthur invades Gaul, Layamon has Arthur again call on God the night before he is due to meet the Tribune Frolle in single combat:

> *'Let the trumpets blow, let all my good men to keep a vigil tonight praying that the Lord Who rules all judgements will shield me against the fierce Frolle and protect me with His right hand against disgrace. If I can win this kingdom for my own hand, every poor man will be comforted and I will work God's will. Now may He Who can do all things help me, the Heavenly King assist me, for I will love Him as long as I live.' All the night long there were hymns and candle light.*

Layamon, Brut, Bzdyl transl., pp. 219–220

A more godly king cannot be imagined: not only does Arthur invoke God's aid, he also promises that should he win, he will rule Gaul under God's law. Layamon has considerably toned down the 'unjust' war theme that Monmouth chose to use. Arthur continues to call on God, pray to him, invoke his aid, and if he finally fails, then it certainly is not for want of piety and outspoken devotion on his part.

In most chronicles there is an episode at the start of Arthur's Roman campaign which can be interpreted as portraying Arthur as a champion of the Christian faith in a world threatened by bleakness and chaos. Landing in France near Mont Saint Michael, Arthur

---

39 Layamon, p. 198.

learns that a giant has taken the niece of one of his supporters, Duke (sometimes King) Hoel. This giant is of monstrous size and aspect, so fearsome and strong none can best him, and he eats his victims while they are still half-alive. He inhabits the 'untamed' landscape of hills and forests[40] and causes grief and destruction throughout the local regions. The giant is a symbol of anti-Christianity, a demon who ranges down from his shadowy haunts and ravages good Christian folk at will. Arthur sets off to rescue the girl, accompanied only by Bedwyr and Kay. Arthur engages the giant in single combat and slays him (sometimes it is Bedwyr who actually lops off the demon's head); but it is all too late. The noble girl has been raped and killed, her nurse likewise ravished but left alive. The symbolism of this episode is somewhat hazy. It does show Arthur in a good light but on the other hand he is too late to save Hoel's niece. He has done all the right things, but he has still failed.

Later medieval, early modern and nineteenth-century works continued to portray Arthur as the epitome of godliness and Christian virtue, but Arthur's holiness has undergone a remarkable change in the later twentieth century. Sutcliff, Stewart and Bradley have all chosen to portray Arthur as more pagan than Christian. These three novelists have chosen to depict a historical Arthur in a Dark Age world rather than the chivalric glory of the medieval legends. After the Roman withdrawal from Britain in the early 400s, the Christian Church suffered terribly under the pagan invasions. Christianity survived in Britain, but only in pockets, and never strongly. It is quite possible that the historical Arthur was a Christian, but more likely that he was not. Having driven the pagans from his lands, Arthur's realm basks in years of peace. Then the Christian Church enjoys a resurgence, and Arthur necessarily has to arrive at a compromise: if he mouths Christian piety and values, then it is only to avoid distancing himself from the growing power of the Christian Church in his land.

---

40 Landscape that refused to come under man's dominion was always perceived as evil and the haunt of demons and sprites in medieval thought.

Stewart's Arthur is a somewhat indifferent Christian. He uses the Church to grant his own reign more authority, but is never overly pious. Sutcliff's Arthur is often at odds with the Church. He is a man who is the ultimate warrior, his religion the welfare of his men, not some abstract god obsessed with sin:

> *I also have loved God in my way, but there are more ways than one. I have never seen the flame on the altar nor heard the voice in the sanctuary; I love my men who follow me, and the thing that we are prepared to die for. For me, that is the way.*

Sutcliff, Sword at Sunset, p. 72

But it is Bradley who truly turns the ideal-Christian king image on its head. For Bradley, anyone who turns their back on the old ways and on the power of Avalon is doomed to failure. The old religion and the old gods anointed and initiated Arthur, and when he eventually listens to Guenevere's pleadings and whisperings and turns to the Christian Church, then Arthur betrays both gods and land. In medieval literature, Arthur fails when he turns his back on Christian values, in *The Mists of Avalon* he fails when he embraces them. Bradley not only relates the story of Arthur, she relates a battle between two Britains: that under the One God and Christ, and the other under the benevolence of the Great Mother. Arthur, and Britain, fall when the One God assumes such power and primacy that it will allow no other, and the Great Mother and the Isle of Apples, Avalon, must needs retreat into the mists.

12

THE PRIVATE
ARTHUR:
Son, Lover, Husband, Friend
and Father

THE SON

'How does one meet the mother, who gave one away at birth?'

STEWART, *The Last Enchantment*, P. 35

Arthur is never allowed to be a son. Uther and Ygerna send him away either at birth or as a toddler. This scenario, as so much of Arthur's life, has resonances of Christ's life. There is a period of peace until the Christ-figure is thrown into the spotlight to do his best, yet is finally betrayed by the one he loves most. The quiet of Arthur's early life is the only period of tranquillity he ever enjoys; it is significant that while with his foster-parents he does not know his true identity.

On Uther's death Arthur is thrust into the public sphere: in T.H. White's words, it is his 'glorious doom to take up the burden and to enjoy the nobility of [his] proper title.'[1] Suddenly Arthur has to

1 White, p. 222.

become king, war-leader and the living representative of the hopes of a nation – falter, and the nation falters with you. There is no time to think or to draw breath, for Saxon invaders batter from the east, the Scots from the west and the Picts from the north while ambitious and rebellious barons at home question his legitimacy. Arthur must to work, and at once, or risk losing it all. But as well as being so precipitously thrust into public attention, Arthur also finds himself with a ready-made family and, soon enough, with a beautiful wife and a company of loyal knights as friends. As an anonymous boy he ran the forests with Ector's hounds. Now, thrust into the battle of invader and family alike, he must sometimes wish again for that anonymity.

Few versions of the legend have Arthur meet either of his parents. Medieval legends merely have Uther die, Ygerna fade from view and Arthur succeed to the throne without ever meeting them. Modern authors sometimes feel the need for Arthur to have at least a brief interview with either mother or father, or, rarely, both. T.H. White spent no time on Arthur's parents at all, and his 'Wart' succeeds and is crowned without a single thought as to his true parents. Sutcliff does not care about either Uther or the serving girl he wrestled under a hedge one night to get Arthur; neither make an appearance, although it is clear Arthur has known his father. Nevertheless, Sutcliff's Arthur is an unsentimental man, and he shrugs off his years spent at Uther's knee with no more than a passing thought.

Stewart carefully engineers a meeting between Arthur and both Uther and Ygerna. Subsequently, although Uther dies within days, Ygerna lingers in a convent for some time, eventually – symbolically – introducing Arthur to Guenevere. Merlin brings Arthur back to Uther's side when it is clear that Uther is dying. It is important that Uther publicly acknowledges Arthur as his heir: to this point Uther has refused to do so, heavy with guilt about the way he had taken Ygerna on the night Gorlois died. We never see Arthur meet Uther as his son – the meeting takes place behind closed doors – but we do witness the meeting of Ygerna with her son. Arthur greets her, stumbling over the word, 'Mother', then retreating back to the safer,

'Madam'. She will never be more than a wise matron, respected but not loved, and a woman that Arthur will never be entirely comfortable with: 'behind the courtly exchanges could be felt all the turmoil of what lay between them unspoken'.[2]

Alone of all chroniclers, troubadours, writers, poets and sundry tale-tellers, Marion Zimmer Bradley has Arthur raised at Uther's and Ygerna's court. They largely ignore him – in a vague, kind way – and it is left to Morgan, here Arthur's older step-sister, to raise him (this compounds the incest as Morgan is both mother and sister to Arthur). When Arthur is some seven years old he is sent away to be fostered at a vassal's house – a common enough medieval custom – and when he returns Uther is dead and there is only his mother. As with Stewart, the relationship is an indifferent one. In 1,000 years of legend Arthur has never been allowed to be the son, nurtured, protected and loved by his birth parents. Uther and Ygerna ever had love for each other, and little left for the son of that night of betrayal.

Arthur's true parental bonding must have been with Ector and his wife, and with Kay, their son. Kay remained with Arthur as one of his most loyal knights, if a slightly clumsy one, and was probably as close a brother as Arthur was ever likely to get. From Ector's household Arthur received love and guidance in his formative years. From his birth parents he received a legacy of legend and betrayal.

THE LOVER

The liking of unlawfull lust, whereto this worthie was inclined,
Deprived him by judgment just, from life and kingdome (as I find)
And threw him down most sodainlie, amid his fame and victorie.

Lloyd, *A Brief Discourse*

2 Stewart, *The Last Enchantment*, p. 37.

Uther is generally portrayed as a man of lusts, and Arthur inherits some of this from his father although it is rarely as pronounced or remarked upon. Arthur has love affairs, but rarely are we allowed to see him as a lover. His lovers exist in a darkness, many times we do not know their names, more often we are never permitted to see them. His most notorious lover is his sister Morgan (or Morgause, or Anne, depending on the version). He does, however, have a number of other lovers before his marriage, and in some early legends these liaisons produce sons.

Both medieval and modern readers expect some degree of lustiness in their military heroes: it may not be considered entirely 'proper', but there is a belief that the male aggressiveness that produces the great warrior must also produce – in moments of rare peace – an energetic lover. Unlike Lancelot, whose deep spirituality keeps him relatively chaste, Arthur does take the occasional opportunity as an unmarried man to indulge in the delights of love. In Welsh poetry Arthur has a son named Llacheu, although little information is given on him. In the Welsh *Life of Saint Cadog*, Arthur engages in some energetic daydreaming about the delights of a rape, but is prevented from carrying wish through into action by Kay and Bedwyr. In the French *Livre d'Arthus* Arthur has an affair with Lisanor, Loth's wife, and has a son by her called Artus le Petit. There is also another lover in the romance tradition, Camille, and sometimes a 'false' Guenevere. In modern literature he has the occasional lover (apart from his sister) before his marriage, but relatively little is made of them; Arthur is a man who has to have some sexual experience to make him believable (and perhaps even attractive) to the modern reader. None of Arthur's pre-marital affairs are grand romances, or appear to mean very much to him. In the recent *The Character of King Arthur in Medieval Literature* Rosemary Morris writes that Arthur is 'about as subtle and considerate as a tank' in his role as a lover; moreover, that 'Arthur's affairs are, indeed, the least pleasant aspect of his personal relationships, contrasting sharply with the delicacy, warmth and devotion with which he treats his knights.'[3] Poor press, indeed.

3 Rosemary Morris, *The Character of King Arthur in Medieval Literature* (Brewer, 1982), p. 105.

In Arthur's pre-marital love life there is only one affair that counts, even though it was but a one night stand: the bedding of his sister. Arthur is superficially innocent of the seduction of his sister. In most versions of the legend it is Morgan who seduces him, and Arthur has no idea he lies with his sister. He is a young man, flushed with the success of his first battle win when an unknown (or at least, unknowingly related) beautiful woman tempts him, and Arthur leaps. Medieval romances (it was the romance tradition that contributed this particular variation) do not dwell at any length on the actual night of love – it has been left to modern authors to fill in the hours. The sense of impending doom as Arthur falls into Morgan's bed has become stronger the closer we move to our own age.

The Elizabethans were the first to take a very public, very horrified breath at the thought that the noble Arthur had slept with his sister. In 1584 Richard Lloyd made it perfectly plain that Arthur caused his own downfall by sleeping with his sister:

> *For Mordred, his fatall son, he did beget incestuously,*
> *Unto his utter overthrow, on his own sister wickedly:*
> *And thus the father was forlorne, through his sons force in incest borne . . . .*
> *Thus may you see, of lecherie the punishment and due reward,*
> *. . . death is the reward of sin.*
>
> Lloyd, *A Brief Discourse*

Four years after Lloyd was published, Thomas Hughes had Arthur 'delight' in his sister Anne, who then presented him with Mordred. In Hughes' scenario, it would have been very difficult for Arthur *not* to have known who Anne was – she was his twin.

Twentieth-century novelists have generally preferred to keep Arthur innocent of his sister's identity and – with the exception of Bradley – have placed most of the blame on his sister's shoulders. The majority, but not all. Stewart's Arthur is asked by Merlin to stay within his chambers on the night of the seduction, but Arthur goes wandering anyway – with grievous results. White's Arthur simply goes to sleep after a hard day in battle and wakes to find a complacent sister smiling at him, winding up the enchantment she had used to seduce him. In *Sword at Sunset* Arthur is drugged, but there is still some small part of him that thrills in the seduction, knowing that this bedding will be like no other. Bradley has Arthur and Morgan couple as part of an ancient pagan ritual. Her version places the sin not in the initial bout of love-making, which was done under the protection of sacred ritual, but in their second coupling on the morning after when they make love purely for pleasure:

> *It did not matter when we were priest and priestess, God and Goddess joining under the power of ritual. But in the morning, when we wakened and were man and woman together . . . that was real, that was sin . . .*
>
> Bradley, *The Mists of Avalon*, p. 219

Yet if Morgan is generally held entirely to blame for the seduction, no author allows Arthur to escape the consequences. He had indulged in 'unlawful lust', and thus he must pay the price.

Arthur's major sexual relationship outside marriage is with his sister, and this is problematic when we try to examine Arthur in his role as lover. A love affair, even if it is but one night of passion, with one's sister is hardly a normal template on which to judge any man as a lover. Arthur is a lover, but in this case he is also a brother, and it is sometimes difficult to determine when Arthur reacts to Morgan as a lover, and when as a brother. In medieval literature he largely reacts to her as a king: Morgan tries to undermine his royal authority, she tries to kill him, she tries to place her lover Accolon on the throne. To these determined efforts to undo him Arthur fights back, but he does so as king rather than as a brother or lover.

In modern literature Arthur reacts variously to the news he has unwittingly slept with his sister: in *Sword at Sunset* Arthur is repulsed, in *The Mists of Avalon* he is sympathetic to Morgan's distress. Bradley is the only author seriously to examine the welter of confusing emotions between Arthur and his sister, and she is the only author to give them a chance to remain in a lover's relationship beyond that single night which produced Mordred. They never sleep together again, but one can see it crossing Arthur's mind from time to time. When Arthur marries Guenevere, his eyes remain on Morgan during the ceremony. When Guenevere, not unnaturally, is horrified to find that Arthur and Morgan have not only enjoyed a sexual relationship, but have produced a son out of it, Arthur defends Morgan against his wife (displaying a salutary loyalty to a sister and a lover, but hardly conducive to maintaining a good conjugal relationship with Guenevere). He grabs Morgan to him, holding her close, weeping to think of the burden she has had to bear alone for so many years. Morgan is touched, Guenevere is appalled.

Apart from Morgan, Arthur's lovers largely remain anonymous. To be able to truly understand Arthur as a lover, however, we must look to his marriage: to his relationship with Guenevere. Arthur may have been a somewhat cool lover, but he was an even worse husband.

THE HUSBAND

'Much more I am sorrier for my good knights' loss than for the loss of my fair queen; for queens I might have enow, but such a fellowship of good knights shall never be together in no company.'

Arthur, in Malory, *Morte Darthur*, Vol. 2, Book XX, Chap. 9

Arthur is always an indifferent husband; his marriage to Guenevere never becomes a love affair fed by heated passions. Although indifference in a husband might affront modern attitudes, it was not so frightful to medieval sensibilities and expectations. Marriage was there to engender children, to provide an outlet for lust and to keep women under some form of control lest they explode in unreliability and cause universal grief and despair. Marriage was certainly not an institution to provide a framework for love. No-one believed love was an essential requirement for marriage; it might even be disastrous, if it made people act without thought. For a king, marriage was an essential step in providing his dynasty and realm with an heir: and an heir meant stability. The king who died with no heir bequeathed his realm chaos and civil war.

Medieval Church and society imposed many expectations on the husband and wife. A husband was in every respect a wife's feudal lord. This was reflected in the law: under medieval English law, if a man killed his wife he was tried for murder, but if a woman killed her husband she was tried for petty treason. A husband should impose his authority over his wife, and take responsibility for her moral lapses. He could chastise his wife within reason, and 'within reason' included a certain degree of physical violence; a broken arm or nose was not going too far. A wife should obey her husband in all things, she should never speak back to him, never question his orders and defer to him at all times. In return, the husband provided for his wife in all things, kept her safe, warm and fed. If all this seems distasteful to our modern minds, then it should be remembered that the medieval marriage was generally a partnership where a woman was highly valued for her capacity to work, her capacity to bear children and for the goods and livestock she brought into a marriage as her dowry. Romantic love held no place in the medieval marriage. Marriage meant a chance to increase land and livestock, the keys to survival. It meant a chance to have children, and in a world where there was no state welfare and no pension schemes, children were literally a couple's old-age insurance policy (it was not only kings who prayed for heirs – everyone wanted them). A romantic liaison which resulted in unsuitable marriage, again whether for rich or poor, could result in disaster. To marry for reasons of 'love' was simply unacceptable. Love weakened, it did not bind.

A husband who failed in his duties to his wife, especially if he failed to keep his wife under control, earned the contempt of his community. Medieval society was a deeply patriarchal society governed by an obsessively misogynist Church which continually reinforced the evils of the daughters of Eve. Women could not be trusted to remain sinless, their husbands were there to control and chastise them. The cuckolded husband was a joke, an emasculated man and the focus of village contempt – even more so than his wife.

Like the majority of medieval marriages, Arthur's marriage with Guenevere is generally arranged. It is a diplomatic settlement, not an affair of the heart. If there is a courtship, it is perfunctory and hardly necessary: who would refuse the greatest king Britain has ever seen? Arthur marries Guenevere for a variety of reasons: she is of noble lineage (in Monmouth, Guenevere is descended from the Romans, although in other accounts she is King Leodegan's daughter), she is beautiful (so she will make an impressive addition to Arthur's aura of royalty) and she brings a marvellous dowry – the circular table around which Arthur later forms his Fellowship of the Round Table. Guenevere is also beautifully mannered and spoken. She will make an impressive queen.

Despite Guenevere's overall suitability, however, there is always a little discomfort about the nuptial arrangement. In *Sword at Sunset* Guenevere virtually embarrasses Arthur into taking her as a bride. She pushes her father to offer her to Arthur (only a war-captain at this stage, rather than king); Arthur, somewhat taken aback and not sure he wants a wife at all, finally gives in to her desperate pleading. In later years, when Arthur continues his lifelong preference for the thrill of war before the delights of marital comradeship, Guenevere finds the missing companionship with Lancelot.

Bradley takes great pains to let us know that Guenevere is a highly strung, unstable and neurotic woman well before Arthur chooses her for a wife, and yet she is the person who, with Arthur, must create the 'symbol of the central strength behind all the armies and the wars – the home and the centre for which the men rallied their strength'.[4] Having made this point as strongly as she can, Bradley then has Ygerna watch Guenevere and Lancelot's behaviour immediately preceding the wedding.

> *And again Igraine saw that hopeless, transfixed look in [Lancelot's] eyes when he looked at Gwenhwyfar, and the brilliance of the girl's smile as she looked up to him. She could not hear now what they were saying to*

4 Bradley, p. 318.

each other – she had no doubt it was innocent enough. But they needed no words. Igraine felt again the despairing awareness that this would come to no good, but only to misery.

Bradley, The Mists of Avalon, p. 319

Ygerna confides her fears to Merlin, but she cannot stop the marriage. Neither can Merlin. In most versions of the legend Merlin tries to warn Arthur about taking Guenevere to wife, but Arthur will not listen. He will have Guenevere or no-one: his refusal to listen to other people's doubts about the marriage foreshadows his later refusal to see, or do anything about, Guenevere's adultery with Lancelot.

Arthur marries Guenevere amid much spectacle and grandeur. A king must always make a splendid marriage, and Arthur accomplishes this with much aplomb (even if Bradley has him fix his eyes on Morgan during the entire mass). The young couple wed, bed and embark upon their married life not only as husband and wife, but as king and queen. Arthur fails in many aspects of his character, and his role as husband is no different. Superficially, however, he appears the perfect husband.

As we have seen, the medieval husband must first of all protect his wife and provide her with a safe haven, adequate shelter and food and all that life needs to sustain itself. As king, and with an income and influence that most husbands only dream of, Arthur provides the essentials: his wife lives in splendid station as befits her dignity, and she lacks for nothing (save for genuine love, but to that we will turn shortly) in physical comforts. Guenevere has fine clothes, servants and the respect a wife who is also a queen expects. Yet Guenevere is never entirely 'safe'. There are a number of occasions when she is exposed to danger – physical and emotional. The first of these occasions is when Arthur allows Lancelot to escort Guenevere to Camelot, a disastrous decision, even if made in innocence. Having failed her in this first instance, Arthur continues to fail to provide Guenevere with a safe environment during the course of their marriage. She is kidnapped and raped by a rival king, Melwas, and later Arthur leaves her in the care of Mordred who also attempts (and accomplishes, in some versions) a ravishment of the queen.

The first of these cases – Guenevere's kidnapping by Melwas – is not entirely Arthur's fault. In some accounts, Guenevere is head-strong either in insisting on riding out when she shouldn't, or in outstripping her escort and thus enabling Melwas to capture her.

Arthur cannot be blamed for this episode (save in the sense that he was not able, as good medieval husbands should be, to curb his wife's impulsiveness), but he does not come out of it well. As in many other incidents, it is Lancelot who must rescue her when Arthur, for sundry reasons, finds himself unable to do so. A husband's duty to protect his wife must surely extend to rescuing her when she has got herself into trouble, but Arthur is never the one to do so.

Arthur may not be entirely blamed for the Melwas episode, but he can be for directly placing Guenevere into Mordred's hands (in both figurative and literal senses) when waging war overseas.

> *The king took her by the hand and gave her to Mordred, telling him to care for her as loyally as a liege man should care for his lord's wife. In that way Mordred received her. The queen was very angry that she had been given over to his charge because she knew such wickedness and disloyalty in him that she was sure that suffering and ill would come of it.*
>
> La Mort le Roi Artu, p. 156

No doubt Guenevere had words to say to Arthur about it, but Arthur ignored her concerns as he ignored so much good advice given to him throughout his reign. He handed Mordred both Queen and keys to the treasure chamber, and rode off into his swift-approaching oblivion.

Arthur's worst offence in his marriage lies, though, not so much in failing to offer Guenevere the protection due to her as his wife, but, more importantly (from a medieval point of view), in failing to keep her under due restraint both morally and physically. Guenevere betrays him, yes, but Arthur should never have given her the opportunity to sin in the first instance, and he should have stepped in to stop her affair with Lancelot as soon as he became aware of it.

The romances (which make it plain Arthur did not know about the affair) blame him as much for being a cuckold as other versions of the legend blame him for turning a blind eye to the affair. Too late does Arthur realise the mistake of his tolerance:

> I hold that man the worst of public foes
> Who either for his own or children's sake,
> To save his blood from scandal, lets the wife
> Whom he knows false, abide and rule the house:
> For being thro' his cowardice allow'd
> Her station, taken everywhere for pure,
> She like a new disease, unknown to man,
> Creeps, no precaution used, among the crowd.

Tennyson, Guinevere (1898), p. 464

Tennyson depicts Guenevere as a cancer, or some virulent sexual disease, that Arthur should have had treated at the outset. Instead, he allows his wife, with the 'wicked lightening of her eyes', to destroy his entire kingdom and all he has worked for. T.H. White is slightly more sympathetic, but says much the same thing as Tennyson: the king should have acted, and because he hasn't, the entire realm is in disarray. 'I was a fool,' Arthur says to Gawain. 'I didn't want to be conscious of it. I hoped that if only I was not quite conscious of everything, it would come straight in the end. Do you think it was my fault?'[5] The French and French-inspired romances make a great deal of Arthur's failure to keep his wife in line, mostly in order to compare Arthur's weakness with Lancelot's splendour and strength. In the romance tradition Arthur is very much the weak, cuckolded husband.

As a husband, Arthur's worst failing is in his supreme indifference to his wife. Guenevere turns to Lancelot because of inherent failings in Arthur as both husband and man. Admittedly, she falls in love with Lancelot prior to her marriage, but if Arthur was half the man Lancelot proved to be, then he should have had no trouble in

5 White, pp. 629–630.

turning Guenevere's heart from Lancelot to him. In the medieval world, few people would have expected Arthur to love his wife in the romantic sense we know and expect now, but they surely would have expected him to treat her lovingly, and with respect and honour. Arthur makes passing attempts at the respect and honour, and makes an utter hash of the loving.

As Malory points out (in the quote on p. 224), Arthur is married to his kingdom and to the Fellowship of the Round Table more than he is ever married to Guenevere. As both wife and Queen Guenevere has every right to expect honour, respect, loyalty and affection from her husband. The medieval French romances, as the modern core Arthurian legend, allow Arthur every chance to give his wife all of these: he fails at every test. It is no wonder that Guenevere turns to Lancelot in emotional desperation, and it is no wonder that the legend gives both lovers a good end as opposed to Arthur's brutal one.

A good example of Arthur's indifference to his wife is the episode where Guenevere unwittingly poisons a knight at a banquet. The other knights present immediately blame Guenevere, inscribing on the dead knight's tomb the epitaph: HERE LIES GAHERIS[6] LE BLANC OF KARAHEU, THE BROTHER OF MADOR DE LA PORTE, WHOM THE QUEEN KILLED WITH POISON. Filled with the desire for revenge, Sir Mador demands justice of Arthur:

> *'My Lord, now I request you as a king to grant me justice concerning the queen who killed my brother; if she wishes to deny and disavow that she has acted treacherously and dishonourably, I shall be pleased to prove my case against the finest knight she wishes to represent her.'*
>
> La Mort le Roi Artu, p. 90

Trial by ordeal, or battle between champions, was an accepted (if rarely used) means by which to determine someone's guilt: God would be on the side of the innocent.

6 Normally named Patrise.

Malory's Arthur is very sad to hear of the poisoning but he will not act as Guenevere's champion.

> [*'Fair lords,' said King Arthur,] 'me repenteth of this trouble, but the case is so I may not have ado in this matter, for I must be a rightful judge; and that repenteth me that I may not do battle for my wife, for as I deem this deed came never by her.'*

Malory, Morte Darthur, Vol. 2, Book XVIII, Chap. 4

T.H. White's Arthur acts in the same way: 'Arthur could not fight in his wife's quarrel, just as married people are not allowed to give evidence against each other today.'[7] Guenevere believes that her husband could possibly be slightly more flexible on the matter: remember, there is no proof of guilt against her. 'My Lord,' she says in *La Mort le Roi Artu*, 'can I not expect any other attitude from you?' Arthur shakes his head. 'No, my Lady, because I should not wish to act unjustly for you or for anyone else.'[8] Arthur retreats into royal impartiality rather than bend the law to save – or even merely to verbally defend – his wife.

Arthur repeats this behaviour – better the queen be burned at the stake than allow his royal impartiality to be questioned – towards the end of their marriage when he discovers (or has been forced into admitting) his wife's adultery with Lancelot. Again, we see no compassion on Arthur's part as he allows himself to agree to a frightful death for the queen. 'That very day, without delay,' demand the massed knights, 'she must be burned.'[9] Arthur concurs, bewailing the destruction of the Fellowship of the Round Table. This is the crux

---

7 White, p. 520.

8 *La Mort le Roi Artu*, p. 91.

9 In medieval England, and even in more recent times, treason has always been punished by death. What is unusual is that all the legends have Guenevere sentenced to death by burning. Burning was normally the fate of heretics, all other criminals being put to death either by hanging or beheading. Why is the legend so insistent that Guenevere die the death of a heretic?

of the matter: Arthur cares not so much that his wife is sleeping with his best friend, but that the affair has driven a sword into the Fellowship. The law stated that anyone caught in treason must die, and thus the queen must suffer death by burning.

Again Lancelot rescues her, and carries Guenevere off to Joyous Garde. After some months of Arthur laying siege to Joyous Garde, the Pope hears that Arthur has promised to kill his wife (with no evidence of guilt at all, according to *La Mort le Roi Artu*) and intervenes, forcing Arthur to take Guenevere back.

Since the nineteenth century western society has grown to expect romantic love between a husband and wife; it is the primary, if not the mandatory, prerequisite for marriage. Yet in twentieth-century literature Arthur continues his indifference towards Guenevere, if not his medieval cruelty. The twentieth-century Arthur feels many things for Guenevere: guilt, desire, paternal (and sometimes patronising) affection and some considerable exasperation. Arthur may love her, but he remains an indifferent husband: he must be so, in order that Guenevere be driven time and time again to turn to Lancelot's compassion. Guenevere is a royal wife, therefore she is largely an attachment, an accessory, and whatever he feels for her, Arthur rarely treats her as anything else. Above all, Arthur is a king, not a husband, and his failure to attend to the most intimate relationship within his household contributes in no small manner to the destruction of his realm.

THE FRIEND

When the king saw the body of the man he had loved so much, there was no grief that a man can suffer for another that Arthur did not feel. He ran up to him as fast as he could and embraced him very closely. He swooned again and all the barons were frightened that he might die in front of them . . . . the king kissed [Gaheris'] eyes and his mouth, bloody as they were, and grieved so much that all those watching were astonished.

La Mort Le Roi Artu, p. 127

Arthur's most intimate emotional relationship has always been with the knights of the Round Table. Select knights among them, such as Gaheris, whose corpse Arthur swoons over in the quote above, are far more beloved to the king than is his wife. He is a lacklustre lover, an indifferent husband but as 'one of the boys' he is superb. This is hardly surprising. Arthur is forged in the furnace of war, his life is spent at war, and his entire purpose is spent in the pursuit of war. He is bred and trained to be a warrior and, like all medieval kings, he puts that first, before the irksome problems of marital relations.

In the later medieval legends Arthur uses the circular table that Guenevere brings as her dowry to form the Fellowship of the Round Table. In the very early, English-based legends Arthur has a war-band of warriors but no table; the Round Table was introduced by English chroniclers in the century after Monmouth, while the concept of the Fellowship of the Round Table was promoted by the French romances . . . only the French could take a piece of furniture and make of it a legend. The circularity of the table is significant because it implies that all knights who sit around it are equal (there is no head or foot to the table), although there is clearly a hierarchy of rank, strength and importance (and thus of access to Arthur) among the knights. Arthur has several close friends among the knights of the Round Table: Kay, his foster-brother, son of Ector; Gawain, eldest son of Lot and Morgause; Gareth, boyish and charming youngest son of Lot; and Lancelot (or Bedwyr, in the English chronicle tradition). Just beyond this charmed inner circle and before the host of the Round Table are Cador, Duke of Cornwall, Hoel, sometime king of Brittany, Bors, and even Mordred in some accounts. These men are not only his closest friends, but they are his deepest loves. They share with him the sweat and blood of battle, they joust and jest as a team and they are all as perplexed and frustrated as each other by the (to them) bizarre emotions and demands of the women in their lives.

Everywhere in the past 1,000 years of literature are examples of Arthur's love for his friends and his knightly companions. In Welsh literature Kay and Bedwyr are constantly with him and, on the odd occasion when Arthur's lusts threaten to rise beyond control, they are the better part of his nature. In the English chronicle tradition Kay and Bedwyr fight by Arthur's side, ride with him through the night on crazy adventures to rescue ravished maidens and advise and support him against sundry invaders. Arthur leans on them as he leans on no-one else. In the French romance tradition the relationship between Arthur and his knights (and the relationship between all of the knights) becomes a far more intense emotional experience. Arthur grieves more for the death of his friends than he ever does for the loss of Guenevere; he feels more deeply betrayed by Lancelot's 'adultery' than he does by Guenevere's. In the nineteenth century Tennyson has Arthur blame Guenevere, and other beautiful women attached to the court, for the collapse of the Round Table, that 'glorious company', that 'flower of men'. Before Arthur married Guenevere the Fellowship thrived, but the introduction of temptation and lust into Camelot (as represented by Guenevere) destroys everything Arthur has worked for. As Arthur prepares to meet Mordred, he tells Guenevere (talking of himself in the third person) in no uncertain terms that she is the cause of all the misery in his realm.

> How sad it were for Arthur, should he live,
> To sit once more within his lonely hall,
> And miss the wonted number of my knights,
> And miss to hear high talk of noble deeds
> As in the golden days before thy sin.

Tennyson, Guinevere (1898), p. 463

He pauses, and stares at her grovelling on the floor. 'Thy lord has wholly lost his love for thee,' he says, and leaves Guenevere to her shame. His queen should have provided the inspiration for the knights: instead, she proved the cancer that killed the Round Table.

Time and again Arthur mourns more for the loss of the Round Table than he does for the loss of his wife's faithfulness:

> Alas that ever I bore crown upon my head! For now I have lost the fairest
> fellowship of noble knights that ever held Christian king together . . . .

much more am I sorrier for my good knights' loss than for the loss of my
fair queen; for queens I might have enow, but such a fellowship of good
knights shall never be together in no company.

Malory, Morte Darthur, Vol. 2, Book XX, Chap. 9

The relationships between Arthur and his wife, and Arthur and his knights are complex. When Guenevere and Lancelot commit adultery the larger number of the knights of the Round Table revile Guenevere for removing Lancelot physically and emotionally from their Fellowship. Arthur can hardly bear the fact that Lancelot has betrayed him: but he blames Guenevere more. She was the one who had tempted Lancelot, she is the one who must bear the stain of original sin.

THE FATHER

Not every king would care to start his reign with the wholesale massacre
of children.

Stewart, The Last Enchantment, p. 3

Arthur's single son is the child of trickery and incest: we can hardly expect him to love the boy. But neither do we expect the youthful Arthur to besmear his early reign with the Herod-like attempt to murder his newborn son. No wonder, perhaps, that Mordred later repays the favour.

If Arthur tries his best to ignore Merlin's warning about his marriage with Guenevere, then he does at least listen to Merlin's warning that if the boy is allowed to live, he will prove Arthur's nemesis. Having sinned, Arthur then decides to compound his sin. Nine months later, he attempts to have all newborn male infants in his realm put to death. They are gathered together, put to sea in a leaky and unmanned vessel, and left to their fate. Fate, however, will not be mocked, and when the vessel is dashed to pieces on rocks, the infant Mordred is the only survivor. Thus Arthur begins his reign with two foul deeds: incest with his sister, and then the murder of scores of children.

Sundry authors, depending on their depiction of Arthur, deal with this episode differently. Mary Stewart has King Lot, at Morgause's (Morgan's) prompting, instigate the action to destroy the child of his wife's adultery. Sometimes it is Merlin who suggests and then plots the murder, sometimes it is all Arthur's doing, but whoever instigates the murder, Arthur's character remains stained. T.H. White has Arthur say that he wanted to do Mordred to death 'for his own sake'[10] which is an ambiguous statement at best, horrifyingly despotic at worst. The episode is so appalling that a number of authors prefer to forget about it entirely as it is too hard to excuse Arthur's part in the mass infanticide.

Why kill so *many* children? If Arthur had only been aware of some unformed threat from an unnamed and unknowable newborn infant, then perhaps we could understand (if not excuse) the widespread net of murder. But Arthur *did* know who both mother and child were. Merlin informed Arthur of the threat the unborn infant posed virtually the morning after the coupling. At this very point Arthur's course of action should have been clear. Detain Morgan until the child was born and then quietly dispose of it (or at least remove the infant from her keeping and influence). But no. Both Arthur and Merlin let Morgan wander smugly off to bear her child in comfort and quiet, and then they (or one of them) panic and order a mass infanticide.

Not unnaturally, then, the father–son relationship between Arthur and Mordred gets off to a shaky start. Having failed in the original attempt to do away with Mordred, Arthur then lets him be (again, the action is the product of flawed logic, surely). Mordred grows into young manhood, in most legends suitably corrupted by the hatreds of his mother, and then joins his four elder stepbrothers at Arthur's court. Mordred's arrival coincides with the breakdown of Arthur and Guenevere's relationship. Guenevere is patently unable to bear an

10 White, p. 595.

heir by this stage, and she is deep into her adultery with Lancelot, an adultery that Arthur is doing his best to ignore.

Suddenly, here is a son. A possible heir. Arthur sits back on his throne, considers the new arrival, and thinks. No doubt he is now grateful that his earlier attempt to murder Mordred failed. Mordred is the only son of his body. Mordred is standing before him with courtly manners and a smile on his face. Mordred can now possibly be loved, or, at the least, trained and watched carefully.

Arthur turns to his wife. 'Guenevere,' he says, 'I think there is something I should tell you.'

It is an extraordinary moment, and a further betrayal of Guenevere. In all their years of marriage, Arthur has never told her of his incest, nor of the fruit of that incest. Until this moment, Guenevere has managed to find some small comfort in the fact that if she was childless, then so too was Arthur. Now here before her, smiling and nodding, stands the lie to that belief. It can do nothing but drive her further from Arthur.

Oblivious to his wife's distress, Arthur, in utter contrast to his earlier attempt to kill Mordred, decides that he will accept his son into the bosom of his family. Again, as with the concerns about his marriage, Arthur decides to ignore all warnings and prophecies about the doom that Mordred represents. Mordred will be his heir, and Arthur will love him.

The relationship, of course, is not quite that simple. The English chronicle tradition always has Mordred as Arthur's nephew, not his son. The French romance tradition, while depicting Mordred as the fruit of Arthur's incest, generally glosses over the years Mordred spent at court before the final year or so when Guenevere and Lancelot are discovered, and Arthur goes to fight his final wars. In the nineteenth century, Tennyson ignored the entire incest theme: his 'stainless' Arthur never slept with anyone he shouldn't have. It is left to twentieth-century authors to develop the fascinating possibilities of a relationship between a man and a nephew who is also his son and who has been the victim of attempted murder by his father. Stewart is the only one who treats Mordred and his motives and actions sympathetically; White, Bradley and Sutcliff continue the broad medieval theme of depicting Mordred as a slimy, treacherous man who pulls the wool over a naive Arthur's eyes.

White and Sutcliff both play on the guilt that Arthur feels now that Mordred stands before him. In Sutcliff's case (where there is no attempted infanticide) Arthur defends his patently malevolent son to Guenevere: 'whatever he is, it is my fault, mine and my father's who unleashed the evil.'[11] Arthur refuses to hate Mordred, as he refuses to hate any man who has done nothing to earn it: he is instead sickened by the wrongs done to Mordred.[12] If there is a doom waiting in that attitude, then Sutcliff's Arthur simply lowers his head and waits for the axe to fall.

White's Arthur merely continues on in his well-meaning, plodding, stupid way when it comes to the matter of what to do with his newly arrived son. He carefully explains the incest to Lancelot and Guenevere, and, like Sutcliff's Arthur, explains how guilty he has been feeling. Not so much about the incest, but because he'd tried so hard to have Mordred murdered as an infant. The scheme did not succeed, Arthur declares, because 'God saved Mordred, and sent him back to shame me.'[13] Meanwhile he has spent decades suffering nightmares about the infants who drowned. Now he won't touch a hair on Mordred's head because he can't afford to have any more murders on his conscience. Mordred might be an unhappy young man (a vast understatement, given that White depicts him as a 'cold wisp of a man', a resurrected Richard III without the hump, and further compares him to a member of the I.R.A.!), but Arthur decides that he is, after all, rather fond of the boy.

Aghast, Guenevere and Lancelot sit and squint, almost as if they can see the gleam of the blade whistling through the air.

Even Mary Stewart keeps a distance between Arthur and his son. Her Merlin trilogy and her novel, *The Wicked Day*, are viewed through

11 Sutcliff, p. 342.
12 Sutcliff, p. 419.
13 White, p. 595.

the eyes of Merlin and Mordred respectively, and Arthur's innermost thoughts are generally veiled from us. The relationship between the father and the son, however, is the most positive in modern novels. Arthur and Mordred share a mutual respect, a deep trust, and a friendship that almost, but never quite, verges on love.

In all cases, Mordred still goes on to betray Arthur – for whatever reason, misguided ambition or sheer malice. In dealing with his son, Arthur should have done the same thing he did so often to Guenevere, retreat into his kingship and unthinkingly remove the threat from his court – he never hesitates to condemn his wife to the flames. But with Mordred, Arthur lets his guilt and his blindness drive him into his grave. He would have been better served by his more youthful murderous impulses.

HERO OR BETRAYER?

What can we make of the Arthur in all these different accounts? He is a human being above all else, and that means he has his flaws, as do we all. Conceived in sin, Arthur as king and as man has little chance to escape sin. Almost as soon as he gains his heritage, Arthur repeats the sin of his father: he beds the wife of a political rival. But this rival's wife is also Arthur's sister, and so Arthur not only repeats, but compounds his father's sin. The resultant son eventually proves to be the deliverer of Arthur's mortal wound.

But Mordred is not the one who destroys Camelot. Arthur does that well enough by himself. Arthur builds the dream – a strong and glorious Britain, as represented in the splendid chivalric court of Camelot – but he is also the one who betrays it. Although the early years of his reign go well, Arthur then succumbs to pride and a consuming ambition. He wages war for unjust reasons, and is viciously cruel in the warring. He is a distant and cool husband, giving his loyalty and love to the Fellowship of the Round Table rather than his wife. He allows corruption to infiltrate his court, as epitomised in his weakness and reluctance to put a stop to Guenevere and Lancelot's affair. He follows the most appalling advice, and leads his nation into a destructive civil war that could have been averted with the smallest modicum of common sense.

Arthur achieves far more in a single, tumultuous lifetime than most kings. Yet he also loses it all and that is what damns him. Nothing remains of any value except a name handed down through the generations. Compared to the true heroes of the Dark Ages – Alfred the Great and Charlemagne – what has Arthur left posterity? A legacy of failure, the legacy of a man who did not have the strength of character or will to consolidate his initial successes. Arthur destroys his own legend, no-one else. The legendary Arthur is the betrayer, rather than the betrayed.

There can be only one redemption for the legendary Arthur: that the historical Arthur did not share the failings of the legend.

Part IV

The QUEST
for ARTHUR

13

DID ARTHUR EXIST?

It is as well to say outright that Camelot has no historical authenticity: it is a place that never was.

ALCOCK, 'By South Cadbury is that Camelot . . .', P. 14

Arthur owes his place in our history books to a 'no smoke without fire' school of thought: 'We must reject him from our histories and, above all, from the titles of our books.'

DUMVILLE, IN KORREL, An Arthurian Triangle, P. 15

*V*arious ages have believed – or not – in a real, flesh-and-blood Arthur as they needed. Today, after a period of believing in Arthur only as a grand myth, there is a renewed surge in the need to believe in his actual existence. If Troy can be found, then why not Camelot? As the millennium dawns, many people have begun to search for a millennium hero: a Christ-like figure who will return to 'save' them from . . . well, from whatever. The modern age is becoming more and more determined to believe that there *was* an Arthur: is it possible he existed, or have we only fallen in love with a myth?

There are several problems in the search for Arthur's existence. First, we need to realise that if Arthur did once exist, then his life, desires, needs and ambitions would have been nothing like those ascribed to him by legend. The Arthur we know now is the product of legend, imagination and medieval needs. In order to find the historical Arthur we have two main sources available to us: historical record and archaeological investigation. To these two may be added a third, oral and traditional culture, taking what we know of the oral culture of the late Dark Ages and early medieval period and trying to discover what truth if any underpins it.

First to the historical records. If Arthur existed, then everyone agrees he lived during the late fifth century or early to mid-sixth century. But for twentieth-century people, whether scholars or interested observers, there is a problem: by our standards there were no accurate records kept during the Dark Ages. By Dark Age standards oral culture was an accurate means of preserving the knowledge of events and people. However, oral culture does not satisfy today's need for sound documentary evidence. For 'proof', we would prefer an eyewitness report, a photograph and the odd sixth-century newspaper article or two about Arthur's victory at Badon Hill certainly would not go astray. The problem in the Dark Ages was that the skills of literacy were generally available only in the Church, and in that age of chaos and invasion the Church was in sad disarray. Those monks and priests who survived rarely wrote down what they experienced (or, more pertinently, their records have not survived), or simply were not in the 'right place at the right time'. Nonetheless, several Dark Age chronicles have survived: what do they say of Arthur?

All were written by clerics. The first, by Gildas, always excites the most interest and attention if only because Gildas wrote *The Ruin of Britain* in the immediate period after a historical Arthur would have lived. He also probably wrote in southern Wales, which, assuming Arthur was associated with the south of England (and there is growing debate about this now), would place him physically close to the events he described. *The Ruin of Britain*, written about AD 540, is not a 'straight' historical account as we would understand it. Gildas meant his chronicle as a moral lesson: he used every bit of British history since the pullout of the Roman forces to demonstrate the moral decay of the society in which he lived. So *The Ruin of Britain* is difficult for the modern reader, if only because we have to somehow glean the historical fact from Gildas' outraged moral invective.

What does he say about Arthur? Nothing. There is no Arthur for Gildas. However, there is an Arthur-like figure – Ambrosius Aurelianus. He appears as the Saxon hordes – foolishly invited in, like wolves to the fold, by Britons desperate for help against the Scots and Picts – are laying waste to the land:

> *After a time, when the cruel plunderers had gone home, God gave strength to the survivors. Wretched people fled to them from all directions, as eagerly as bees to the beehive when a storm threatens, and begged whole-heartedly, 'burdening heaven with unnumbered prayers', that they should not be altogether destroyed. Their leader was Ambrosius Aurelianus, a gentleman who, perhaps alone of the Romans, had survived the shock of this notable storm: certainly his parents, who had worn the purple, were slain in it . . . . Under him our people regained their strength, and challenged the victors to battle. The Lord assented, and battle went their way.*

> Gildas, The Ruin of Britain, Winterbottom transl., p. 28

From this point the Britons, presumably under Ambrosius (although Gildas does not make this clear), went on to claim victory after victory until the siege of Badon Hill which was 'pretty well the last defeat of the villains' and, Gildas notes, the year of his own birth.

Was Ambrosius Arthur? Some scholars have argued vehemently for this interpretation. Although Gildas says little about this great leader, the mere fact that Ambrosius (a war-leader rather than a king) united the Britons to lead them successfully against the invading Saxons, finally defeating them at Badon Hill, indicates that this is the man who gave rise to the legend of Arthur. The difference in name is a problem, although in *An Arthurian Triangle* Peter Korrel presents an intriguing explanation for the gradual change from Ambrosius Aurelianus to Arthur.[1] Korrel argues that the double name of Ambrosius Aurelianus (and a Latin one at that, difficult for peoples now reasonably distant from their Roman past), gradually became two separate names and two separate people in Welsh oral tradition.

1 Peter Korrel, *An Arthurian Triangle* (E.J. Brill, 1984), pp. 24–27.

One came to be known as Embreis (and eventually took on a different role), the other, who remained the hero of Badon Hill, Aurelianus. The Welsh, who preserved the victory of Badon Hill in their oral traditions, were uncomfortable with the name Aurelianus and eventually (and very gradually) altered it to Arthur, which was British in appearance, but Roman in origin. As Korrel is careful to point out, this theory can only ever remain conjecture, but it does serve to explain very neatly the Ambrosius–Arthur mystery.

Thus, the one surviving chronicle record we have from the sixth century does not mention Arthur, but it *does* mention an Arthur-like figure which, with some imagination and argument, can be re-figured to fit the existence of Arthur.

From Gildas there is a gap of some 200 years before another chronicle emerges. This is the *History of the English Church and People* written by a cleric named Bede, living and working in the north of England. In his chronicle, written about AD 731, Bede repeated virtually word for word Gildas' account of Ambrosius Aurelianus, adding only that the man was of 'good character'. Patently Bede worked from a copy of Gildas on the desk before him. Like Gildas, he makes no mention of Arthur. This should not be surprising (unless you subscribe to the school of thought that places Arthur's life and activities in the north of Britain) – Bede used Gildas as his source on the events of the Anglo-Saxon invasions, and he had no reason to doubt Gildas' word. Bede was also a northerner, and far removed from the traditions and oral cultures of the south. Although Arthur was a well-known figure in Welsh tradition by this time, there is no reason Bede should have known of this.

And then comes *The History of the Britons* (the *Historia Brittonum*), sometimes ascribed to a man called Nennius, although scholars now believe the chronicle was a compilation over time and by many different scribes. The date of its composition is vague (particularly as it was likely compiled over a lengthy period), but probably dates from the late eighth or early ninth centuries. Here, for the first time in Church chronicle record, is specific mention of Arthur. The chronicle reports of the Saxons who waxed strong in Britain, and then states:

Then it was that Arthur was wont to fight against them in those days
along with the kings of the Britons, but he himself was dux bellorum,
leader of battles. *The first battle was at the mouth of the river, which*
is called Glein. The second, third, fourth, and fifth on another river,
which is called Dubglas and is in the region of Linnuis. The sixth battle
on the river, which is called Bassas. The seventh was a battle in the wood
of Celidon, that is Cat Coit Celidon. The eighth was the battle at
Castellum Guinnion, in which Arthur carried the image of saint Mary,
ever virgin, on his shoulders, and the pagans were put to flight on that
day and there was a great slaughter of them through the power of our
Lord Jesus Christ and through the power of saint Mary the Virgin, his
mother. The ninth battle was fought at the City of the Legion. The tenth
battle he fought on the shore of the river, which is called Tribruit. The
eleventh battle occurred on the mountain, which is called Agned. The
twelfth was the battle on Mount Badon, in which there fell together in one
day nine hundred and sixty men in one onset of Arthur, and no one laid
them low save himself alone. And in all the battles he remained victor.

History of the Britons, Wade-Evans, transl., p. 75

Suddenly we have the man, Arthur, plus glorious details of his deeds.
The similarities between this Arthur and Gildas' Ambrosius
Aurelianus are striking, and there can be no doubt they are – or
derive from – one and the same man. Both are brave war-leaders
rather than kings, both fight under the 'Christian flag' (though this
is implied in Ambrosius' case), both unite the Britons against the
invading Saxons, both fight a series of battles before the final victory
over the Saxons at the Battle of Badon Hill. The *History of the Britons*
makes two further references to Arthur:

When he hunted the boar Troynt, Cabal, who was the dog of Arthur the
soldier, impressed his footprint on the stone and Arthur afterwards
collected a pile of stones under the stone, whereon was the footprint of his
dog, and it is called Carn Cabal. And men come and carry the stone in
their hands for the space of a day and a night, and on the morrow it is
found upon its pile.

There is another marvel in the region which is called Ercing. There is to be found in that place a sepulchre by the well which is named Licat Anir, and the name of the man who is buried in the tumulus was called so, Anir. He was the son of Arthur the soldier, and he killed him in the same place and buried him. And men come to measure the tumulus, sometimes six feet in length, sometimes nine, sometimes twelve, sometimes fifteen. In what measure you should measure it in its turn, the second time you will not find it in the same measure, and I have tested it myself.

History of the Britons, Wade-Evans, transl., p. 120

The legend of Arthur has clearly been fleshed out by this point. No longer is the Arthur–Ambrosius figure a great war-leader, now there are magical aspects to his nature, and those of his dog and son (whom Arthur appears to have killed).

There is only one Dark Age chronicle reference remaining – the *Annales Cambriae*, dated to the later tenth century – and it makes two terse references to Arthur. The entry for 516 states that this was the year Arthur carried the Cross of our Lord Jesus Christ for three days and nights on his shield, defeating the Saxons at the Battle of Badon. The other entry, for 537, states that this year was the Battle of Camlann, in which both Arthur and Medraut fell.

There are other chronicle references to Arthur before Geoffrey of Monmouth, but they are generally based on one of the above examples. So what can we make of these three Dark Age historical accounts? Can we believe them?

We must be very careful to not take them at face value. Gildas, the nearest 'man on the scene', only refers to an Ambrosius Aurelianus, who may or may not be Arthur. Two hundred years later Bede, who follows Gildas exactly on this matter, also makes no reference to Arthur. Then, some *300 years* after Arthur would have lived, we suddenly have stunning new details of his life and adventures. The *History of the Britons* clearly relies on bardic lore to fill in these details (the description of twelve battles, most fought on rivers, are clearly from Celtic tradition), and its description of Cabal's foot-printed stone, as well as the amazing expanding and contracting tomb ('I've measured it myself!') can only be inserts from a highly magical and superstitious oral culture. Having decided that these new details are indicative of contemporary oral stories, and perhaps of the strength of the Arthurian tradition within popular culture, can we see them as indicative of historical fact?

Unfortunately, almost certainly not. We must even be careful of Gildas, whose work and description of Ambrosius Aurelianus provides the foundation for most later chronicles and legends (and, it must be said, for the belief that Arthur once existed). Gildas was no disinterested observer. He wrote his *Ruin of Britain* with a clear objective in mind: to contrast the corruption of contemporary kings and Church leaders with the heroes of the past. In other words, he had a point to prove, and he may very well have manipulated names and events in order to do so. Even if he had not consciously done this, Gildas' perception of past events would have been very different from ours. For instance, Gildas would have seen the hand of God (or of the Devil) in every event, and interpreted them in those terms. His interpretation of the past was a *Christian* interpretation, as are *all* the writings which have come down to us from the Church. An example of how this has altered their narration of the past is their accounts of the sixth-century Battle of Badon. It is more than likely that the Arthur-figure in this episode (if he or the event existed) was pagan, not Christian. This was an era of deep crisis for the Christian faith in the British isles – in fact, most people had forgotten the Christian god. But all the Dark Age chroniclers, as clerics of the Christian Church, could not possibly allow themselves to ascribe great victories to pagans (in all of these chronicles the villains are always pagan and the heroes always Christian). Thus the Arthur-figure is always Christian in the chronicles, and pagan in Welsh tradition. Which are we to believe?

The way in which medieval scribes or writers worked also affects our quest for the historical Arthur.[2] Evidence within historical documents –

2 I make a slight difference between a scribe and a writer in that a scribe copied out an existing manuscript for posterity (the printing press was not developed until the mid-fifteenth century) and a writer created a completely new work. The difference was so very slight as to be non-existent, as I explain further.

chronicles, annals and so forth – has been handed down through scores of generations of scribes. For example, Gildas wrote his *Ruin of Britain* in the mid-sixth century. It has not been printed until relatively recently. As far as I am aware, the original manuscript no longer exists (it would be an extraordinary historical achievement if it *had* survived 1,400 years of damp cellars and tinder-thatched attics). Thus Gildas' knowledge of Arthur (or of Ambrosius Aurelianus) has been preserved in generation after generation of carefully copied manuscripts. We owe medieval scribes a huge burden of debt for the preservation work they did, but it is very important to be aware that medieval scribes did not copy exactly in the way we understand it. A modern day transcriber would intend to copy out exactly the work before him or her. A medieval scribe made alterations as he saw fit. If there was an entry that the scribe did not entirely agree with, or something he thought was a mistake, then he would alter it. He would very often delete bits, and add lengthy interpolations of his own at another point.

There is one further point to be made about medieval writers and scribes. The medieval world was vastly different from ours, not so much in physical landscape and in the way people lived and looked, but in the landscape of the mind. The medieval mind understood the universe and humankind's place within it, as it understood the processes of daily life, in a very different way to us. Calendar time and dating was a very hazy process until the fourteenth or fifteenth century, and near enough was generally good enough. This was rather like their habit of using large numbers for effect (Arthur killed lots of men single-handedly) rather than as a literal truth (Arthur killed 960 men all by himself). Medieval people as a whole also had (in our way of understanding) an extraordinarily nebulous concept of the past. They had no concept of 'changing times', and believed they lived in precisely the same mental and physical world as Christ. A scribe (or even anyone listening to tales of Arthur) in the thirteenth century would not have been able to conceive of the almost 800 years that had elapsed from the time of a historical Arthur. One reason their minds could not have come to grips with such a massive amount of time was because they had no way of measuring such a long stretch of time. People referred to events in the past only by relating them to events in their own lifetimes ('my youngest child was born in the year the great storm came through and blew down the church steeple'). Thus the past was 'lost' to them . . . but only in our modern day concept of referring exactly to time past. For medieval people Arthur walked England's green hills in their grandfather's time, no earlier.

So the problem with trying to find the historical Arthur through Dark Age and medieval historical documents is that none of them were copied exactly, and the concepts of the past and of past events that they relate are very different to our current concept of time. If we know a certain event occurred in AD 865, then a medieval scribe would be happy enough with a general stab at using a calendar date (always awkward for them because they not only found the concept difficult, but they had few events in the past they could correctly identify with a date): we *need* to know it was AD 865; a medieval scribe – or an author writing an original document – would have been happy enough with 821, or 979, or whatever. Exactness was not a part of the medieval mind – rather, the perpetually battling and twisting shadows of good and evil were. Rather than presenting factual accounts of the past, medieval writers presented moralistic judgements through often imaginatively expanded tales.

In part, the same problems of concepts occur when trying to deal with the oral traditions of the European past. There is a rich tradition of Arthurian lore in Welsh or Celtic oral culture. Previous to the Christianised late medieval world, the vast numbers of people in European societies understood themselves and their past through an incredibly rich tapestry of oral culture and, to a remarkable degree, a very rich identification with the landscape. Oral culture – the Welsh myths that mention Arthur – does not provide our need for exact information for two reasons. First, the purpose of oral myth was not to preserve 'facts' 'exactly'. The tales were to delight and amuse, but they were also instructional and highly symbolic. The depth of symbolism used over 1,000 years ago we now find very difficult to understand (or even conceive of). So when we read ancient Welsh lore in translation – can we possibly understand what it is saying?

The second problem with ancient oral culture is that we are *reading* what is probably a much later version of the spoken language. At some point in the past these tales were written down (for example, medieval scribes wrote down most of the Welsh Arthurian tales in the late eleventh to thirteenth centuries) many hundreds of years after any historical Arthur, and *after the 'Monmouthian' Arthurian tradition had been established.* What do we have in our hands now? The original Welsh tales, or the medieval Christian scribes' interpretations of them? Were the scribes affected by the highly popular and influential Monmouthian tradition? It is relatively easy to redact, or sift out, later influences in medieval transcriptions of Welsh Dark Age material . . . but even *if* the scribes had written down exactly what they heard (and that is unlikely), then they wrote down a tale that had been through 500–700 years of oral reinterpretation according to the symbolism or moral needed: no human being (whatever their bardic training) ever hands down a piece of knowledge *exactly*. Thus oral culture, while useful in that it can be cross-checked against our meagre store of historical evidence, is not a reliable source of historical accuracy.

Having surveyed and, if not discarded, then at least grown uncomfortable, with two means of determining Arthur's historicity, then there remains one last way by which we might establish once and for all whether there was a real Arthur: archaeology. Alfred the Great left us his jewel-cum-bookmark inscribed with the words 'Alfred had me made'; what if we could find a wallet with the words 'Property of Arthur: please return to Post Box 322, Camelot'? Recently, archaeologists discovered a piece of slate, 35 centimetres by 20 centimetres, in the ruins of Tintagel Castle in Cornwall – a site closely associated with the legendary Arthur. The slate had been inscribed by knife in a sixth-century script: *Pater Coliavi ficit Artognov* ('Artognou, father of a descendent of Coll, has made this'). Amazingly, perhaps we *have* found the Arthurian equivalent of the Alfred jewel (although the striking similarities have occasioned some scepticism). Artognou was likely pronounced Arthnou, and so there is the possibility that the piece of slate refers to Arthur, but it would need far more corroborating evidence to establish its status as 'proof'. If Arthur did exist, and if he was as important as oral culture depicts, we need to discover that corroborating physical evidence.

Again, there are difficulties. Where to look? The English countryside is dotted with Arthur's Seats, Arthur's Walks and Arthur's tors, hills and so forth, but most of them date from well over 1,000 years after his supposed existence. So we must use the names provided by somewhat unreliable chronicles and embellished romances. First, Camelot *never* existed as a place. The name was a French romance import of the twelfth century and it has no historical basis (at least, not as a name; if Arthur did exist then naturally he would have had a seat of power somewhere). The English and Welsh traditions variously put Arthur's base at Caerlon-on-Usk, Celliwec in Cornwall, Carlisle, Winchester, Amesbury and more. Different scholars have located Arthur in Wales, Cornwall or the north of England.

However, some sites seem more likely to have been Arthur's haunt than others. In particular, there is Glastonbury Tor, once known as the Island of Avalon, and there is the site of South Cadbury Castle in Somerset, originally identified with Arthur by John Leland in the sixteenth century. Both these sites lie in close proximity to each other. The medieval Glastonbury Abbey, situated in the township of Glastonbury tucked underneath the tor, was the site of what might be called a medieval archaeological excavation, although 'staged recovery' would be a more appropriate term. In 1191 the monks of Glastonbury monastery happily proclaimed that they had dug up the remains of Arthur and Guenevere in their original burial place in Lady Chapel, a little south of the Abbey church. The exhumation was variably reported in several chronicles of the time. One monk, Giraldus Cambrensis, visited the Abbey about a year after the exhumation and examined the bones in detail. His report of the event bears relating in some detail:

In our own lifetime Arthur's body was discovered at Glastonbury, although the legends had always encouraged us to believe that there was something otherworldly about his ending . . . The body was hidden deep in the earth in a hollowed-out oak-bole and between two stone pyramids[3] which had been set up long ago in the churchyard there. They carried it into the church with every mark of honour and buried it decently there in a marble tomb. It had been provided with the most unusual indications which were, indeed, little short of miraculous, for beneath it – and not on top, as would be the custom nowadays – there was a stone slab, with a leaden cross attached to its under side. I have seen this cross myself and I have traced the lettering which was cut into it on the side turned towards the stone, instead of being the outer side and immediately visible. The inscription read as follows: HERE IN THE ISLE OF AVALON LIES BURIED THE RENOWNED KING ARTHUR, WITH GUINEVERE, HIS SECOND WIFE.

. . . . Her bones were found with those of her husband, but they were separate from his. Two thirds of the coffin, the part towards the top end, held the husband's bones, and the other section, at his feet, contained those of his wife. A tress of woman's hair, blond, and still fresh and bright in colour, was found in the coffin. One of the monks snatched it up and it immediately disintegrated into dust . . . .

You must know that the bones of Arthur's body which were discovered there were [extremely large]. The Abbot showed me one of the shin bones. He held it upright on the ground against the foot of the tallest man he could find, and it stretched a good three inches above the man's knee. The skull was so large and capacious that it seemed a veritable prodigy of nature, for the space between the eyebrows and the eye-sockets was as broad as the palm of a man's hand. Ten or more wounds could clearly be seen, but they had all mended except one. This was larger than the others and it had made an immense gash. Apparently it was this wound which had caused Arthur's death.

Gerald of Wales,
Journey Through Wales/Description of Wales, pp. 281–284

Unfortunately, not all this can be believed. This was, after all, an age when Moses' staff was fortuitously discovered buried in a French

3 Two standing crosses.

vegetable patch, two heads of Saint John the Baptist did the pilgrimage rounds, the blood of Jesus Christ was discovered in an English church together with a personally signed statement of authenticity, while there were enough of Christ's foreskins about for a veritable feast. Bodies, as body parts, were all the rage, and amazing discoveries were proclaimed every six months. It must also be said that Gerald was the *only* contemporary writer who put the words regarding Guenevere onto the cross, and he described the coffin as an oak-bole rather than the lead coffin of other reports.

That an exhumation took place is not doubted: archaeological excavations in the early 1960s revealed a large pit, traces of a pre-tenth-century mausoleum and, between mausoleum and pit, a large hole which had been excavated and then refilled in the 1180s or 1190s. There are two ways to view this early exhumation (the bones were reburied again in 1278, then dug up in the Reformation age and scattered): first as a complete fraud (the reasons for which I discuss in the next chapter); and secondly as an event which may have had a kernel of truth. Leslie Alcock puts forward a fascinating hypothesis in *Arthur's Britain* that the lead cross is of vital importance. Although there are no medieval drawings of the cross, it was traced and reproduced in William Camden's sixth edition of *Britannia* in 1607 (the cross vanished in the eighteenth century). The lettering on the cross is consistent with tenth-century writing. This can mean one of two things: either the Glastonbury monks, deep into fraud, knew that contemporary twelfth-century lettering would look wrong, and thus copied the lettering from one of their tenth-century monastic documents; or the cross is actually of tenth-century origin.

In the tenth century the Abbot of Glastonbury, Saint Dunstan, enclosed the ancient cemetery with a new wall. The archaeological excavations of the early 1960s show that the ancient mausoleum had been disturbed in the process. Had Saint Dunstan disturbed Arthur's grave? If there had been some kind of monument on top of the mausoleum, relating who lay within, then Saint Dunstan may well have wanted to preserve that knowledge, causing a new lead cross to be engraved to replace whatever had been destroyed during the tenth-century renovations.[4] Alcock freely admits this is only hypothesis, and without the actual cross no-one can be sure if it is a genuine tenth-century marker, or a twelfth-century forgery. That lost cross must surely become the Holy Grail in the contemporary hunt for Arthur.

SOUTH CADBURY CASTLE

Of modern archaeological excavations, only two stand out, and only one reveals anything that might be attributable to a historic Arthur. Just to the east of Glastonbury Tor is South Cadbury Castle, a smallish hill, or tor, 150 metres high. Its summit is a vague triangular shape enclosing some eight hectares. The steep sides of the hill are now heavily wooded (they were once clear, revealing extensive earthwork fortifications), the summit gently grassed, but even so showing the ridges and furrows of generations of ploughmen. The site has a commanding view over the Somerset basin and Glastonbury. In Dark Age and medieval times the area surrounding Glastonbury was marshland – lake country. Many factors make South Cadbury one of the best locations for Arthur's seat: its geographical placement; local landscape, particularly the lakes; the closeness to Glastonbury (Avalon); the knowledge that South Cadbury has been an important defence site for thousands of years (it is one of the largest hill forts in pre-medieval Britain); and the sheer convenience of the location – it is central to many of the sites associated with Arthur, ranging from Wales to Stonehenge to Tintagel to Winchester and Amesbury and particularly to the possible locations for the Battle of Badon Hill. These factors connect it to the Arthurian tradition (local opinion had it as the site of Camelot back in the early sixteenth century) so it is no surprise that extensive archaeological excavations have been carried out there.

4 Leslie Alcock, *Arthur's Britain* (Harmondsworth, Penguin, 1989 of 1971 edition), pp. 79–81.

There were several minor pre-twentieth-century excavations, and more this century, but none so important as that conducted by Leslie Alcock between 1966 and 1970.[5] He firmly established that there have been several major occupations of South Cadbury: during the Iron Age when the major earthworks were constructed; in the late Celtic period or early Roman occupation; during the fifth and sixth centuries; and finally during the Anglo-Saxon period, probably in the tenth and early eleventh century. For our purposes, as for Alcock's, it is the mid-Dark Age occupation that is of the most interest.

The entire hill site has never been excavated – only those areas most likely to contain evidence of significant buildings. The main areas excavated by Alcock were the south-west gateway, several trenches cut into the walled defences about the summit and two areas within the walls where the main buildings of the hill fort were likely to be found.

The Defences and the South-West Gateway

South Cadbury had walled defences constructed of timber and stonework that extended for over a kilometre. Because of the decay of the timber, it is impossible to know precisely how they were constructed, nor even how high they were. However, it appears likely that they consisted of a framework of timber beams some 16 centimetres square. Stonework was then laid against the external and internal walls, and the interior of the wall filled with rubble. The width of the wall varied between three to five metres. For the mid-Dark Ages, these defences represented a major construction project, and, from obvious repairs done at various times, indicate that the fort was occupied for several generations.

---

5 See Alcock's academic discussion of the excavations in *Cadbury Castle, Somerset: the Early Medieval Archaeology* (Cardiff, University of Wales Press, 1995). Alcock's earlier *'By South Cadbury is that Camelot . . .' The Excavation of Cadbury Castle 1966–70* (London, Thames & Hudson, 1972) is also very useful. My discussion of the excavations of South Cadbury is based largely on these two works.

The south-west corner of the summit contains the main gateway into the fort. In the fifth- and sixth-century occupation it was a relatively simple timber construction of four massive beams set in a square. These corner posts supported a 'roof' or walkway across the gate that linked the walls which were very likely balustraded with wickerwork. The interior walls of the gateway were made of timber planks, and there were undoubtedly timber gates at the front and rear (although no evidence for them has been found). There were no guard rooms. The road leading up to and through the gates was cobbled and deeply sunken. In the area immediately before the gateway were buried a large iron axe-hammer (some 1.5 metres in length and 40 millimetres thick) and a worn brooch made of bronze. Alcock, and other scholars, argue that these two artefacts were not 'lost', but deliberately deposited in front of the gate as protective devices. Iron has long been a symbol of power and protection (and such a large, expensive item as an axe-hammer could hardly have been 'misplaced'), while the brooch found is a style often associated with protective amulets. Whoever commanded the hill fort of South Cadbury during the mid-Dark Ages wished to give his power base very powerful supernatural protection.

The Interior

Excavation of two areas within the interior of the fort also reveals that South Cadbury was the site of a powerful warlord, or even king. The largest area commands the best view over the surrounding countryside. The archaeological team discovered a number of refuse pits (many of them undoubtedly dating from the Iron Age occupation), a circular house, a large hall (the only building which can be confidently dated to the fifth and sixth centuries), and deposits of pottery and glass.

The hall is a typical mid-Dark Age construction. Like the defences and the gateway, its framework was of timber posts set at about three metres apart supporting a roughly rectangular structure some nineteen metres long and ten metres wide. The walls of the structure were undoubtedly of wattle and daub supporting a steep thatched roof. Roughly a third of the way down the hall a wall trench suggests that a light screen (perhaps of wickerwork) divided the hall into two rooms. The larger room held a central open hearth. The type of flooring used is uncertain, as most evidence has been removed after centuries of ploughing, but it could have been one of two types: a packed dirt floor covered with straw or rushes, or a timber-planked construction. The proportions and construction of the hall, together with a comparison of similar British Dark Age halls, suggest that this was the feasting hall of a Dark Age king.

The fragments of pottery and glass recovered make this conjecture certain. Much of the pottery was imported and falls into three main types. The first is of fine red bowls, their rims decorated with rouletting; this type of ware generally originated in the eastern Mediterranean. The second type of pottery consists of a variety of large jars that were used to import wine and oil. The third class consists of a variety of grey bowls with a blue-black wash made in the Bordeaux region. The fragments of pottery, together with fine fragments of equally exotic glassware, were found in or close by the hall, indicating that this hall had witnessed many fine feasts where expensive imported wine (and probably local mead) was drunk from equally expensive and prestigious glassware. The alcohol would have been complimented by food served in fine red dishes. Thus, we know that the inhabitants of the South Cadbury hill fort, or its leading family, were wealthy enough to import pottery, wines and oils. Thus, our knowledge of the construction of the hall, together with the tableware and wine jars found in the area, indicate that South Cadbury was the base of a powerful warlord or king.

We know when the pottery was produced in the Mediterranean and the period when it was imported into Britain, enabling a relatively firm dating of the occupation of South Cadbury. Construction of the defences began no earlier than AD 450, but more probably from 475. The occupation did not last much longer that AD 550, but possibly held out until 600 (dating the end of the occupation is based on the lack of any shards of pottery known to have been imported extensively into Britain in the late sixth and early seventh centuries). The pottery imports most likely came into South Cadbury via the western Cornish port of Tintagel. The pottery would have been transported north along the west coast of Cornwall to Bridgewater Bay. There, a barge would have transported goods up the Parrat River, then the Yeo, and then overland by pack mule to South Cadbury.

Tintagel has played a major part in the post-Monmouth Arthurian legend. There Uther seduced Ygerna and conceived Arthur. While some twentieth-century archaeological work has been done at Tintagel, the results have not been as dramatic as at South Cadbury (apart from the recently discovered piece of slate). It is reasonably certain that Tintagel was a port during the fifth and sixth centuries (and probably an important one because of the value of the goods that passed through it). There is a sheltered harbour and an easily defensible headland. Not only was Tintagel responsible for the import of luxury goods, it also likely exported one of Dark Age Britain's major products – tin. Archaeological excavations have been carried out at Tintagel throughout this century, but although many later buildings and artefacts have been found, there is little to suggest what the port and headland contained during the fifth and sixth centuries. The only building contemporary to Arthur's lifetime is a Celtic monastery on the summit of the headland and, unfortunately, there is nothing about this monastery which can enlighten the Arthurian quest. Despite this lack of tangible evidence for Arthur (or at least, the existence of a duke or nobleman of Cornwall in the fifth century), it is nevertheless very likely that Tintagel was an important port during the Arthurian age, both for defence and for trade, and thus could well have been an appropriate location for a Cornish king.

Was South Cadbury Arthur's base? The simple answer is that no-one knows. First, unless something completely extraordinary comes to light, we will never be able to prove Arthur's existence or not. The most vocal of Arthurian apologists today base their 'proof' on extraordinarily poor understanding of the historical evidence – they read one chronicle, believe it implicitly, and – hey presto! – they have their 'evidence'. The excavations of South Cadbury have *not* proved Arthur's existence. All they have proved is that in the late fifth through to the mid-sixth centuries, South Cadbury was an important hill fort, the power base of an important war-leader or king. If Arthur had lived, then this could very likely have been his home base. His war-band would have been between 500 to 1,000 men (anything larger is improbable for this age) who drank and caroused in his hall, and who sallied forth to meet the Saxons through the imposing south-west gate. To theorise anything else is to sally forth ourselves into myth and imagination – King Arthur's true kingdom.

Arthur's historic existence must remain a mystery. No evidence we have today can prove his historicity. The lead cross has been lost, Arthur's bones have been scattered, Guenevere's golden hair turned to dust in the sweaty palm of a monk. We can hope, but we cannot prove.

14

ARTHUR'S JOURNEY THROUGH HISTORY

It is of this Arthur that the Britons fondly tell so many fables, even to the present day; a man worthy to be celebrated, not by idle fictions, but by authentic history.

WILLIAM OF MALMESBURY, *Chronicle of the Kings of England*, P. 11

Geoffrey of Monmouth began not only the Arthurian legend as we know it, but also the millennium of manipulation: today, Arthur is one of the most manipulated cultural icons in the English-speaking world, second only to Christ himself. Monmouth 'reinvented' Arthur from Welsh legend to English national hero as part of his own campaign for personal advancement. But whatever his personal motivations, Monmouth's greatest achievement was in giving form to the formless: he took a somewhat vague figure from Welsh tradition and made of him a chivalric hero to appeal to Normans and English alike. He gave the English a hero who rivalled – nay, bettered – the French Charlemagne in conquest, courtliness and courage. The Normans liked Monmouth's legend because it justified their own defeat of the Saxons (who had overrun the glorious realm of Arthur), and the common people adored the legend for the heroic aura it gave their past. Above all, Geoffrey gave the English nation, from monarch to villein, a national hero. Arthur quickly became a cultural and national icon for the English; in a sense, it is not going too far to say that the cult of Arthur provided one of the greatest impetuses for the foundation of English national identity. The glorious king of the past would one day return from the grave to lead England into future glory. Even in the darkest hour, there would always remain a hope.

Arthur – the man and the icon – has endured a bumpy ride through the past millennium. The medieval age idolised him (and sought to use him) as not only icon, but historical reality. Monarchs sought to justify their own power and glory by associating themselves with Arthur, abbots tried to increase pilgrimage traffic by their propitious 'discovery' of Arthur and Guenevere's bones, crusades were paid for through the sale of 'Arthur's weapons'. The early modern age (the sixteenth and seventeenth centuries), on the other hand, discarded him as both historical reality and as icon: he lived in a barbarous and barbarously immoral court and it was best to banish him to the fireside whispers of the common folk. Nineteenth-century Britain rediscovered (and sanitised) Arthur so his glory could reflect their own, while the twentieth-century western world uses him as a money-spinner and suitably non-religious Christ figure who may yet return to save us from ourselves.

Arthur has never been allowed to rest undisturbed in Avalon.

ARTHUR IN MEDIEVAL ENGLAND: A NATIONAL HERO

There is no doubt that Arthur was a popular figure among many of the ordinary people of medieval England before Geoffrey of Monmouth 'reinvented' him – William of Malmesbury had noted the profusion of 'fables' about Arthur within early twelfth-century popular culture. Monmouth's great accomplishment was to create a national hero who appealed to everyone, kings and bishops as well as peasants. Arthur rapidly became an icon for the English elite, particularly the

English medieval kings. The Norman dynasty ended in 1152 (shortly after Monmouth's work) to be replaced by the first of the Plantagenet kings, Henry II. The Plantagenets in turn were succeeded by the Tudor dynasty in 1485. While Arthur became extremely popular among the late Normans, it was the Plantagenets and the Tudors who took the cult of Arthur to its height. Led by the kings of England, this cult was almost entirely separate from the stories circulating among the common people (most of which we have lost entirely). Arthur as an icon and call to arms was so popular that many kings thought to ally themselves with him in order to increase their own aura of glory and to strengthen their grip over land and people. Arthur was a hero, but he was a hero who could be used.

The blatant attempts to manipulate Arthur's star for personal ends began in 1191 with the 'discovery' of his bones by the Glastonbury monks. Arthur was real after all (the debate over his actual existence, which eventually destroyed Arthur as a cultural icon in the sixteenth century, was brewing even in the twelfth century). The monks' search for Arthur's remains had been encouraged and funded by King Henry II:

> *when Henry II was reigning in England, strenuous efforts were made in Glastonbury Abbey to locate what must have once been the splendid tomb of Arthur. It was the King himself who put them on to this, and Abbot Henry, who was later elected Bishop of Worcester, gave them every encouragement.*

> Gerald of Wales,
> *Journey Through Wales/Description of Wales*, p. 284

There are several reasons why Henry (who unfortunately died in 1189, two years before Arthur's remains were found) sponsored this search. He might well have wanted to prove Arthur dead once and for all in order to destroy Welsh hopes that their hero might return and aid them in their fight against the English. Henry might also have hoped that finding Arthur's bones would reflect well on himself (and perhaps aid him in his continuing battle against his rebellious sons). Perhaps Henry may have planned to develop the grave site, when it was found, as a suitable place for English pilgrimage. This would not only have raised much needed revenue for both abbey and crown, it would also have deflected popular obsession with Thomas Becket's tomb in Canterbury.[1]

In the same year that the monks found what they said were Arthur's bones and Guenevere's hair, Richard I claimed to have the sword Excalibur in his possession. No-one knows the how and where of this splendid acquisition, but doubtless the king hoped that people would believe the sword had been found with Arthur's bones. Excalibur came in extremely useful. Richard was on crusade and in need of reinforcements and eventually swapped Excalibur with Tancred of Lecce, King of Sicily, for four large transport ships and fifteen galleys. Every national treasure has its price.

Having been discovered once, Arthur's and Guenevere's bones were not long left in peace. In 1278 Edward I arranged the exhumation of both sets of remains. He and his wife, Eleanor of Castile, were present when the grave was opened on the evening of 19th April. The next day Edward and Eleanor wrapped the bones in rich cloths, affixed their seals, and replaced them in a coffin. This was then eventually buried before the high altar of the Glastonbury Abbey church.[2] Why did Edward order the exhumation and reburial? Scholars have argued this case back and forth, but there is no doubt that for Edward and Eleanor this was a highly significant event. They were both present for the exhumation, and played a large and personal role in the wrapping and reburial of the bones. The occasion was obviously meant to be highly symbolic and meaningful. Edward could have been driven by one of Henry II's original motivations in sponsoring the search for Arthur's remains: showing the still rebellious Welsh that their hero was, indeed, so dead as to be utterly unable to effect a resurrection in time to aid them against the

1 Becket had been an enormously popular chancellor of England and archbishop of Canterbury, and his assassination at the hands of Henry's henchmen in 1170 made him a saint and object of popular veneration.

2 The bones were destroyed during the Reformation in the sixteenth century.

English. Edward had been involved in campaigns against the Welsh, and in 1277 (a year before the exhumation) he had initiated a major campaign against the charismatic Llywelyn ap Gruffydd, the Prince of Wales. It was not going well (Llywelyn completely evaded Edward's attempts to capture him), and Edward may have needed some symbolic gesture to convince the Welsh of the hopelessness of their campaign. A few years later, Edward confiscated from the Welsh what they claimed was Arthur's crown.

There is far more to Edward's exhumation and reburial of Arthur than an effort to cow the Welsh. Kingship in medieval England (and across Europe) was a highly symbolic affair. Much emphasis was placed on the regalia of state, as on a king's association with former kings and saints. By exhuming Arthur, and playing such a personal role in the proceedings, Edward was not only associating himself with Arthur, but also presenting himself as Arthur's successor. The exhumation can be viewed very much as the burial of a former king by his heir. It is as if Edward was saying, 'Here am I, present at the interring of the former king, and it is I who will protect and continue his works in this world.' It is worth noting also that the exhumation occurred two days after Easter – Edward cashed in heavily on the symbolism of resurrection.

Having discovered Arthur's grave, handed his sword over to the King of Sicily, and dug up, rewrapped and then reburied Arthur's remains, the English kings appeared content with the physical aspects of their manipulation of the Arthurian cult. The symbolism, however, continued. Edward III directly appealed to the popular cult of Arthur when he swore to re-establish Arthur's order of knights at a 'Round Table' tournament in 1344, and he worked over the next four years to finally establish the Order of the Garter in 1348. He caused Saint George's Chapel to be built in Windsor to house the new order, complete with ecclesiastical fittings, stalls in the chapel, chapter meetings and a college of knights.

No-one, however, planned to use the Arthurian connection more than Henry VII, the first of the Tudor kings. Henry was always sensitive to the fact that his claim to the throne was highly tenuous (he had defeated Richard III at the battle of Bosworth in 1485, but even that could not wipe out the stain of being bastard-bred). So Henry spent a great deal of time and effort legitimising his claim to the English throne. He took as his wife Elizabeth, daughter of Edward IV, and when she bore him a son, Henry named him Arthur. Distant and base royal blood was going to be reinforced by association with past heroes. The naming was a deliberate attempt to make use of King Arthur's popular appeal: Prince Arthur Tudor was to be the new Arthur of England's dawning golden age. Unfortunately, Prince Arthur was unable to live up to anyone's expectations, dying of consumption in his mid-teens.

Medieval kings were not the only ones with a vested interest in Arthur's image. The Glastonbury monks' search for Arthur's remains may have been sponsored and encouraged by Henry II during the 1180s, but the monks nonetheless had their own reasons for wanting to find Arthur's corpse. This was an era where every church, cathedral and religious sanctuary needed to have its own saintly relic or else miss out on the lucrative pilgrimage trade. Churches and religious orders competed fiercely with each other to acquire the most prestigious of relics. It was not unknown for a band of monks to sally forth in the dark of a moonless night and steal the envied relic of a neighbouring church. They justified this by arguing that if the saint allowed his or her relic to be carried out of its current resting place, then very obviously the saint had wanted the relic moved in the first instance. Had anyone been struck to stone when the relic was shifted? No? Then the saint obviously approved, and the new custodians took careful security measures to ensure that their recent acquisition might not be 'reacquired' by some other band of envious monks.

There could be no better 'saint' than Arthur for the Glastonbury monks. Geoffrey of Monmouth had popularised the area as intimately associated with Arthur. In the legends the body of Arthur had been taken to Avalon (Glastonbury Tor), so no-one would doubt the authenticity of any bones found at the abbey. Arthur meant pilgrims, pilgrims meant cash, and that meant the Glastonbury monks would prosper. It also meant they would be able to raise the funds needed for badly needed restoration work: a massive fire had caused profound damage to the Abbey church in 1184. Henry II had previously funded restoration work, but when he died in 1189 funds were not forthcoming from either of his surviving sons, Richard or John. A new source had to be found.

If the discovery *was* a deliberate fraud, then the entire event would have been carefully planned and stage-managed. Bones were obtained from somewhere (some historians have suggested that the monks robbed the burial site of an ancient Saxon chieftain and his wife, but this is an unlikely scenario), buried, then 'discovered'. The discovery of the lock of Guenevere's hair, which fortuitously turned to dust when handled, must also have been carefully staged. The anxious monk who leaped down into the grave and grabbed the lock was the only one who actually saw the hair, and any dust he then produced in his clenched fist could have come from anywhere. The witnesses present were either in on the fraud, or desperate to believe in the authenticity of the grave's remains. The bones were not reburied until 1193, providing the abbot of Glastonbury with plenty of opportunities to drag out Arthur's shinbone and dazzle the impressionable with its size.

Was this event a carefully staged fraud, or simply the discovery of an old grave with enough ancient symbols attached to convince the monks they'd found Arthur's remains? No-one knows, although it is more likely fraud than anything else (it is a wonder the monks didn't find a portion of the True Cross gripped in Arthur's hand as well). Whatever the truth surrounding the actual discovery in 1191, the Glastonbury monks knew a winning attraction when they found one. Arthur's and Guenevere's bones attracted not only pilgrims, but kings as well.

Not content with having just the remains of the great king and his wife, within fifty years of the graves discovery by the Glastonbury monks combined ancient beliefs, vaguenesses and legends and further stated that their monastery had been founded by Joseph of Arimathea (the man who obtained the body of Christ from Pilate and placed it in his own tomb). Joseph, they claimed, had fled the Holy

Land after Christ's death and resurrection, and travelled to Britain where he founded the church at Glastonbury about the year AD 63.[3] There were several fourteenth-century attempts made to discover Joseph's body at Glastonbury, but none were successful. Later generations of monks grew tired of digging, and made no further attempts at archaeological discoveries.

The rumours and beliefs survived, however, particularly in regard to a thorn tree believed to have sprung from Joseph of Arimathea's staff. This thorn tree has had a chequered history: it has been repeatedly demolished by pilgrims' and tourists' knives in the eternal quest for a genuine souvenir to take home to impress the neighbours, as well as being chopped down by Puritans during England's seventeenth-century civil war. The tree that stands there now is not the original (and even the 'original' was late medieval at best). Even less likely to have originated in medieval times is the legend that Joseph of Arimathea brought the chalice from the Last Supper to Glastonbury and secreted it in the bottom of a well. The story is fairly recent, possibly even as recent as the Victorian Age; medieval monks did not allude to it at all.

The Arthurian legend served Glastonbury Abbey well, and continues to serve the town and local region well to this day. Pilgrims may have been replaced by tourists, but the pull of the Abbey and the legends created by the monks and their successors have not diminished.

There can be no question that Arthur was a real person for the medieval English (and the Welsh and Cornish). Although some scholars question some of the more enchanted aspects of his life (for example, his 'undead' existence on the Island of Avalon), there was never any serious doubt in medieval minds that Arthur had been a real king of the past. Indeed, kings and Church alike depended on the reality of Arthur, and were hardly likely to foster any rumour that he may have been a myth or mere fabrication of Geoffrey of Monmouth's ambition. For the ordinary folk, Arthur must have been

3 A Celtic church existed in Glastonbury in the mid-Dark Ages, and a monastery was founded there in the seventh century.

close to a god. The fables and stories that circulated among the ordinary labourers of England have mostly been lost to us, but they are referred to time and time again. Where nobles and Church scholars may have regarded the more magical aspects of the Arthurian tale with some suspicion, the ordinary people would have believed in them implicitly. Magic played a large part in their daily lives, and they would not have doubted for an instant the enchantments that surrounded the Arthur they knew and loved.

Because medieval people had such a poor concept of the past, or of the progression of ages, their Arthur was the epitome of chivalric knighthood. They had no idea that had Arthur truly existed, he would not have lived amid the stunning spires of Camelot, nor commanded an army of tens of thousands of shining knights. Arthur was to them everything their local lord may not have been: magnanimous, protective, stern, loving, splendid. Nobles also recreated Arthur in their own image. Tournaments were held in his honour, and reflected what the nobles felt were the same standards and ideals of Arthur's court. King Arthur was, for all medieval people, a chivalric knight, not a Dark Age warrior-chieftain or warlord.

Medieval chroniclers and historians tried their best to separate fact from fiction. Two chroniclers who wrote just prior to Geoffrey of Monmouth, William of Malmesbury and Henry of Huntingdon, followed the ninth-century *History of the Britons*, giving a brief but flatteringly heroic portrait of King Arthur. Malmesbury also mentioned the many 'idle fictions' circulating among the common people concerning King Arthur: Malmesbury must have been aghast at what Monmouth came out with some ten years later.

Geoffrey of Monmouth's imaginative expansion of what had been known about Arthur to 1136 became an instant hit, and it influenced many chronicles to come – Layamon and Robert Mannyng of Brunne, for example. Medieval histories generally tried to eschew the influence of romantic literature as much as they could, but for several hundred years they were led astray by Monmouth's version. However, by the early fourteenth century chroniclers were starting to become a little wary of Monmouth. The belief in Arthur's existence was still rock solid, but more and more scholars were starting to separate fact from romantic fiction . . . and an increasing number of them were starting to think that maybe Monmouth had taken poetic licence a little too far.

By the fifteenth century Monmouth's star was on the wane, and as his reputation fell, so also did Arthur's. The revision of the king had begun – and eventually it would all but destroy Arthur and his household.

ARTHUR IN EARLY MODERN ENGLAND: THE DESCENT INTO OBLIVION

Historiographers do contend . . . at what time Arthure *florished. And this contention hath so encreased, and gathered force, that doubts . . . as yet sticke to the feeble conceipts of the Readers.*

Leland, *The Assertion of King Arthure*, p. 78

In the first half of the fourteenth century a Chester Abbey monk named Ranulph Higden compiled the *Polychronicon*, a universal history that covered everything from the beginning of the world until 1327. Fifty years later Higden's Latin chronicle was translated into English by John Trevisa. Trevisa added lengthy commentaries on whatever he felt needed it during the process of his translation (an excellent example of the typical intervention of medieval scribes). The result are dual dialogues in the *Polychronicon*: Higden, and Trevisa's numerous (and often indignant) insertions. On the matter of Arthur, both Higden and Trevisa acknowledge his existence and his importance in English history, but they both attacked Geoffrey of Monmouth's interpretation of Arthur's life. Higden commented that it was to be marvelled that Monmouth had so expanded the Arthurian story when there was no evidence for his interpretation in Dark Age authors. Trevisa spoke of how many men had over-fancified Arthur's life, and how some 'mad men' actually believed in the magical tale that Arthur would one day come back. Higden and Trevisa both attempted to strip away the detritus of Monmouth's imagination. Arthur had lived, he had been a great king, but Geoffrey of Monmouth's version of his life, as so many tales spread about in popular culture, were complete fabrications.

The *Polychronicon* was enormously influential within scholarly circles (although it was probably not widely read among the general populace), and it marked a slow turning point in the manner that Arthur was depicted in the increasing number of histories being produced. Imaginative literature flourished, as best exampled by Malory's *Morte Darthur*, but more scholars and historians were making the point that such tales *were* imagination, and that the life of Arthur, though deserving of high praise, should not be understood in such magical or imaginative terms. By the end of the fifteenth century there was a growing disquiet within many circles. Scholarly and public opinion was becoming more and more polarised: which version to believe? Monmouth's wonderful and glorious history, or the soberer offerings of more temperate historians?

In the first half of the sixteenth century the issue reached the heights of public debate. The cult of Arthur had not diminished one iota since the twelfth century, and yet it appeared – to general public confusion – that some men were determined to push Arthur back into the ranks of mere mortals. One man who caused a storm of protest was Polydore Vergil, an Italian commissioned by Henry VII in 1505 to write a history of England. Vergil not only stripped Arthur of his mythical and demi-godlike status, he vehemently attacked Monmouth's version of Arthur's life. Vergil noted dryly that Monmouth had 'somewhat augmented' the ancient histories of Arthur. Monmouth had couched his tale in Latin and given it the 'colour' of a history. Moreover, Monmouth had also published the prophecies of Merlin as the 'most assured and approved truth', but always adding 'somewhat of his own'. Vergil was having none of it. His purpose was to present as factual a history as he could, and he threw Monmouth out the window with a tight-lipped sneer. Vergil's own treatment of Arthur is terse and more than a little cynical. He related some of the fables surrounding Arthur (for example, Arthur's extensive conquests), and commented on the common people's 'wondrous admiration' of Arthur but his treatment gave the entire Arthurian tale (reduced in his history to one paragraph) a disagreeable veneer, and he ended his discourse on Arthur with a brief comment on the discovery of Arthur's bones at Glastonbury Abbey, 'whereas in the days of Arthur this abbey was not built'. A fraud then, by implication if not accusation: as far as Vergil was concerned, not even Arthur's bones remained authentic.

Thus Vergil washed his hands of Arthur and hoped to wash English history of Arthur's myth. Arthur had, for the first time in easily available print, been publicly and devastatingly stripped of his mythical demi-god status to a man who, 'if he had lived long', may have been able to accomplish something worthwhile. One can almost see the dismissive Italianate shrug of indifference.

Vergil was enormously influential.[4] However, not surprisingly, his book caused a storm. The fact that he was an Italian (a *foreigner*!) did not help. Numerous denunciations of Vergil appeared in print, but none were more indignant nor more patriotically defensive than John Leland's *Assertion of King Arthure*, published some few years after Vergil was finally published in 1534 (Leland was also the first man to publicly identify South Cadbury with Camelot). Leland defended Arthur against every public accusation thrown against him. To begin with, Geoffrey of Monmouth was a man highly learned, whatever 'persons ignorant of antiquitie' might say, and Monmouth's account of Arthur must be trusted before the 'fond fables or base stuffe of forraine writers'.

> *[Vergil] handleth* Arthures *cause in deed, but by the way, he yet is so faint harted, luke warme & so negligent that he makes me not onely to laugh, but also to be angry (as while he is contrary to truth, and filled with* Italian *bitternesse) I know not whether he smile or be angry.*
>
> Leland, *The Assertion of King Arthure*, p. 53

4 Many subsequent sixteenth-century English historians based their own work on Vergil.

Having insulted Vergil as much as he dared, Leland then got down to a serious defence of Arthur's historicity. Gildas may not have mentioned Arthur, but then Gildas did not mention many a famous man, thus it was only 'Italian reason' to assume that because Gildas made no mention of Arthur, then the king had not existed. Many works of Gildas may have been lost, and Gildas may well have written of Arthur in these. As for Bede, the other eminent Dark Age historian, well, doubtless this particular holy man refused to mention Arthur because the king had been born in adultery; Bede could also have been alienated by the prophecies that clung to the story of Arthur. The Romans made no mention of him, but neither is that surprising for they preferred to make the European world their bond-slaves, and certainly would not have praised any of their heroes (and, Leland insinuates, Romans were *Italians*, and what can you expect from *that* race?). The Saxon writers were also hardly likely to make any mention of the hero who had so valiantly denied them Britain while he lived. Leland also countered Vergil's assertion that the Abbey of Glastonbury had not existed at the presumed time of Arthur's death. Leland used two charters, one from the second century (which has subsequently been shown to be a forgery) and one from the time of Henry II (sadly misleading) to try to prove the existence of a Glastonbury Abbey in the sixth century. Thus, Leland concluded, did he 'shutte up the mouthes of brabling backbyters' who denied Arthur's existence.

Leland also felt the need to defend the characters of Arthur and other key members of his family against some of the more indecent slurs that had become attached to the story of Arthur. Thus Ygerna was a wonderful woman who simply let lust get the better of her; Arthur's subsequent bastardy did nothing to tarnish his valiant courage and honesty. Arthur was also a sincere Christian who even undertook a pilgrimage to Jerusalem. Arthur did nothing wrong in trusting Mordred when anyone would have been deceived by him (here a nephew rather than incestuous son; Leland was having none of French romance interpolations). Morgan le Fay was demoted from evil enchantress to a woman of incomparable goodliness who undertook to bury Arthur in Avalon (Glastonbury). Leland was willing to admit that certain obscure and absurd reports had crept into some histories of Arthur, but this in itself was no reason to deny Arthur's existence, or the magnificence of his deeds. Having dismissed the fables, Leland then embraced them, arguing for Lancelot's existence, although carefully pointing out that Lancelot was a careful and faithful friend of Arthur's (and remarking that the tale of an adulterous affair with Guenevere was false). Leland also gave, word for word, Arthur's stirring speech to his troops before the final battle against Mordred; this Leland almost certainly made up. It did not help his cause, and when push came to shove, Leland's defence of Arthur failed to convince an increasingly sceptical public (even Leland's early modern publisher and editor commented that his poetical wit generally won out against his 'right discerning').[5]

John Foxe, who wrote a massive book entitled *Acts and Monuments*, published in the 1560s, also defended Arthur against Vergil. Vergil, Foxe mooted, may well have destroyed evidence proving Arthur's existence for his own sinister Italianate purposes.[6] In an age where many English believed most Italians had a leaning towards Machiavellian machination, the depiction of Vergil as consummate rogue was not unpopular.

Polydore Vergilius – *that most rascall dogge knave in the worlde, an Englyshman by byrth, but he had Italian parents: he had the randsackings of all the Englishe lybraryes, and when he had extracted what he pleased he burnt those famouse velome manuscripts, and made himself father to other mens workes – felony in the highest degree; he deserved not heaven, for that was too good for him, neither will I be so*

5 Albert C. Baugh, ed., *A Literary History of England* (London, 1967), p. 335, n.
6 Cited in James P. Carley, 'Polydore Vergil and John Leland on King Arthur: The Battle of the Books', in Kennedy, ed., *King Arthur: A Casebook* (Garland, 1996), p. 193.

uncharitable to judge him to hell, yet I thinke that he deserved to be hanged between both.[7]

But whatever the invective and the cries of 'Foul!', little could save Arthur from drifting into another long sleep. Arthurian apologists could not stem the rising anti-Arthur sentiment in England.

The common people might still love Arthur, and Arthur might still appear in several major Elizabethan pieces of literature,[8] but publicly two movements were pushing Arthur's reputation deeper and deeper into his ancient grave. The moral and intellectual rigours of the Protestant Reformation and Renaissance humanism hit English intellectual life during the sixteenth century, and Arthur survived neither movement. Renaissance humanism, originally a product of fifteenth-century Italy, stressed the need for careful re-examination of original sources to weed out fanciful medieval interpolations: humanism witnessed the rise of history as a science rather than as a branch of imaginative literature. Sixteenth- and seventeenth-century historians, intent on researching England's past, became more interested in the meticulous checking of records and the verification of facts than the unquestioning acceptance of poetic – but suspect – medieval chronicles.

What was the actual historical evidence for Arthur? Very little, whispered the new breed of English historians, turning their backs to their French colleagues' triumphant waving of their weighty documentary evidence for Charlemagne's majesty and achievements. Early modern English scholars stripped Arthur of his grand deeds, his enchantment, and the majority of his knights, and thrust him back into what the early modern age thought should be his true place: a competent war-captain who aided Ambrosius Aurelianus and

7 A sixteenth-century margin comment in Bale, *Scriptorum Illustrium Maioris Brytanniae Catalogus*, cited in James P. Carley, 'Polydore Vergil and John Leland on King Arthur: The Battle of the Books', in Kennedy, ed., *King Arthur: A Casebook* (Garland, 1996), p. 193.

8 For example, Edmund Spenser's *Faerie Queene* and Michael Drayton's *Poly-Obion*.

who may have done something worthwhile at some place which perhaps could have been called Badon. John Clapham's cautious handling of Arthur in 1606 is typical of many of his contemporaries:

> *Divers strange and incredible things to the prejudice of posteritie, have been written of this Prince, of Queen* Guinever *his wife, of* Gawen *his sisters sonne, and of* Merlin, *a phantastical Prophet, with others, commonly called,* Wandering Knights: *matters indeede more fit for feined Legends, and poeticall fictions, then for a Historie, which ought to be a Register of things, either truely done, or at least, warrantable by probabilitie.*
>
> Clapham, The Historie of Great Britannie, p. 200

Some historians continued to (more than carefully) mention Arthur, but many others preferred to ignore him completely. English history before the Norman conquest was too lost in the mists of time for accurate rendering, and the Arthurian myth (as it was now perceived) was far too inaccurate to speculate about. Scholars preferred to,

> *passe over the severall peoples that have inhabited this Island, and the times of their continuance, as Britans, Romans, Danes and Saxons, and to come to times more nere unto us, for that my purpose is not to wade into uncertaine waters.*
>
> Boemus, Manners, Laws, Customs, p. 392

For late-sixteenth- and seventeenth-century English historians Arthur had become a historical embarrassment. The only 'evidence', such as it was, for his existence was mainly mere myth, and mere myth counted for nothing in this newly scientific world. Loudly, rather than quietly, historian after historian dropped Arthur from their works. 'And as for [Arthur's] Round Table,' wrote Thomas Fuller in the mid-seventeenth century, 'with his knights about it, the tale whereof hath trundled so smoothly along for many ages, it never met with much belief among the judicious'.[9]

9 Thomas Fuller, *The History of the Worthies of England* (London, 1840), vol. I, p. 312.

Moreover, by the later sixteenth century Arthur had also become a moral embarrassment. The sober county gentleman class was quietly becoming a powerful force in English politics and culture – and this rank was increasingly influenced by a religious and moral conservatism later dubbed Puritanism. Not only was Arthur historically unverifiable, the tales that surrounded his household and court were morally outrageous. The sexual licence! The lustful depravity! No wonder Arthur failed, no wonder his realm collapsed. He should stand as a perfect example of a king 'gone wrong', his court so corrupted with sexual depravity that the entire kingdom eventually succumbed. The perfect example of this growing moral distaste for Arthur is shown in Richard Lloyd's book *The Nine Worthies* and Thomas Hughes' drama, *The Misfortunes of Arthur*, both published in the late sixteenth century. Both Lloyd and Hughes pointed out the sexual depravity inherent in the Arthurian myth and both used it to depict what could happen once the godly laws of chastity were flouted. But there was worse. Not only did the Arthurian stories promote sexual licence, they also promoted murderous mayhem. Malory, according to the indignant Roger Ascham, a scholar of the mid- to late-sixteenth century, should be discarded, together with all other manuscripts of idle monks and wanton canons:

> As for . . . Morte Arthur; *the whole pleasure of which book standeth in two special points, in open manslaughter and bold bawdry. In which book those he counted the noblest knights, that do kill most men without any quarrel, and commit foulest adulteries by subtlest shifts: as Sir Launcelot, with the wife of King Arthur his master; Sir Lamerock, with the wife of King Lote, that was his own aunt . . . I know, when God's Bible was banished the court, and* Morte Arthur *received into the prince's chamber.*
>
> *What toys the daily reading of such a book may work in the will of a young gentleman, or a young maid, that liveth wealthily and idly, wise man can judge, and honest men do pity.*
>
> Ascham, *The Scholemaster*, p. 159

Ascham's *Scholemaster* was a highly influential work in late-sixteenth-century England; concerned parents all over the country moved in the dead of night to quietly remove Malory and any other Arthurian tale from the bookcases of their impressionable children. The county gentry cast nervous eyes towards the excesses of the Stuart court of the early to mid-seventeenth century and vowed never to let their own children be corrupted. As Arthur did, so too would the Stuart kings fall: and the gentry made sure of this by lopping off the head of Charles I in 1649 and abolishing the corrupt contagion of court life completely. Arthur's star, as well as his believability, fell alongside that of the English monarchy.

THE LONG DARK, AND THE EVENTUAL RESURRECTION

By the mid-seventeenth century only the occasional history made mention of Arthur – generally apologetically and in the profoundest of whispers lest anyone should notice – and he made the odd (in both senses of that word) appearance in stage drama, but as a cultural icon Arthur – like the English monarchy – had retreated into the mists until he would be again called forth. The common English man and woman almost certainly continued to enjoy tales of their hero, but few examples of their ballads and popular tales remain. The ballads that do survive are largely 'fragments', telling of only one episode or one character. It is possible that the 'entire' legend was largely lost during the seventeenth and early eighteenth centuries. Thomas Deloney's late-sixteenth-century ballad *The Noble Acts of Arthur of the Round Table* has very little in it about Arthur, and nothing of the core legend. Instead, the ballad sings the praises of Lancelot, and relates a joust with a knight called Tarquin.

Arthur, his household and his deeds, sank quietly into the swamp of localised legend. For some 150 years printed, elite and even popular culture abandoned him. And then . . . Bishop Thomas Percy. Percy was an antiquarian and writer of some note during the mid-eighteenth century. Both his own enthusiasm and that of his friends encouraged him to publish a three volume set of *Reliques of Ancient English Poetry* in 1765. This contained six Arthurian ballads, dating from the sixteenth and early seventeenth centuries: *King Arthur's Death*, *King Ryence's Challenge*, *The Legend of King Arthur*, *The Marriage of Sir Gawaine*, *Sir Lancelot du Lake*, and *The Boy and the Mantle*. The collection marked the beginning of an amazing resurgence in Arthuriana in the late eighteenth and early nineteenth centuries: Malory was reprinted, mythologies were concocted, Arthurian-inspired verse was churned out and Arthurian paintings dotted the walls of the well off. Arthur the king was reborn: hail the king.

The nineteenth-century age did not so much believe in Arthur as a historical figure as an icon. All things medieval had never been so popular: castles were built, battles and tournaments re-enacted. Yet the legend was sanitised: bowdlerised chivalry for a dark and industrial age. Malory was all very well, but often the story was genteelly reworked to suit a culture which looked backwards to find a golden age in which it could reflect its own glory. Thus the Victorians gleefully seized upon the Arthurian legend: it appealed to the Janus-faced Victorian morality which, on the one hand, corseted its women in rigid decorum and stiff drawing rooms while on the other its men engaged in rampant sexual licentiousness and the subjection of the masses in smoky and poisonous hells called factories. Tennyson's Arthur is stainless and blameless; he is also a cold-hearted prig. Arthur had been remade into the Victorian ideal.

Arthur has undergone a thorough revision and has enjoyed a spectacular resurgence in fame in the mid to late twentieth century. He is more popular than ever, although few understand his tale, or the lesson it is supposed to teach (the fact that the Arthurian story *is* a moral tragedy makes most modern people uncomfortable). No age has been able to manipulate the Arthurian icon quite like the late twentieth century. There are films, novels, and sundry calls to arms:

the western world is disintegrating, England is under attack from the European Union, the stresses of the modern life are too much.

And here is Arthur, re-packaged and re-modelled: or is he? The modern western world has come full circle in its attitude to Arthur. No longer is he a disreputable, immoral and utterly unhistoric figure. Arthur is again our hero and saviour. We have returned to the medieval belief in Arthur, we conduct archaeological searches as desperate as that of the Glastonbury monks, we associate ourselves with, and make use of, Arthur's name as assiduously as did the medieval monarchs. Arthur's name is used as a rallying cry for all manner of modern crusades.

Arthur the king is reborn into splendour, but it is a misguided and misunderstood splendour. Arthur the king is as flawed and fragile as ever he was: we simply refuse to believe it.

15

THE ONCE AND FUTURE KING:
Arthur as Saviour

The Britons . . . refuse to believe in the king's death, saying it will happen only at the end of the world on Doomsday . . . The Britons believe that he will come, and they look to when he will return to this land as he promised before going hence.

LAYAMON, *Brut*, BZDYL, TRANSL., P. 215

The belief in Arthur has gone through three distinct stages: from the late Dark Ages until the sixteenth century the mass of the British believed implicitly in Arthur's existence. From the sixteenth century until the nineteenth century the intellectual and cultural elite denied Arthur's existence, and even within popular culture it is likely Arthur survived only as an agreeable myth rather than a once-living, breathing hero. Now, particularly since World War II, there has been a resurgence not only in the popularity, but in the belief in the historicity, of King Arthur. But for our 'scientific' and 'fact-obsessed' belief systems, we have necessarily had to reinvent our Arthur. We prefer to believe in Arthur as the valiant war-captain, the *dux bellorum*, rather than the chivalric hero. As a major concession to the need to scientifically explain

Arthur, we can even come to terms with the fact that Arthur may not even have been a 'king' as we understand the concept. In this way we rationalise Arthur (and we rationalise our belief in him) into a plausible historic context.

Medieval Europe believed in the chivalric Arthur, but they were misguided. The early modern age forgot Arthur, but they were too doubting. We now have an Arthur back, but even amid our rational, plausible reinvention of the man, we still yearn for a saviour. The growing certainty among many people that Arthur's return is imminent is not only an indication of his appeal – he is a suitably Christ-like redeemer for our secular world – but also an indication of our need for salvation in a society which some feel is careening further and further out of control. Modern society has failed us, we need a hero to emerge from the past.

The current belief in Arthur takes two forms: the belief that he did exist; and the belief in Arthur as secular Christ, the resurrection man or saviour who will one day return to 'save' the English (or Welsh or British or western society as a whole). The former belief is the most widespread, but the latter is becoming more popular, especially among the disenfranchised and the neo-pagans.

Now, scholars are prepared to admit that there might be some historical viability to the Arthurian legend: in a sense, the 'where there's smoke, there's fire' theory. Oral culture is no longer discarded as being totally unreliable; carefully used, it can reveal 'facts' about the past. Coupled with archaeological work – particularly the excavations at South Cadbury – the knowledge gained from redacting oral culture has moved Arthur from legend to possible (and probable, many argue) historic identity. What the twentieth century has done is reinvent Arthur without the medieval hype and uncomfortable morals. We have created a 'new' Arthur: what I call the 'new witch' syndrome.

From the late Dark Ages, the Catholic Church went on an offensive against what it perceived to be pagan hangovers in European society. As part of this offensive, it announced that witches had never existed, and could not exist. People who believed in witches were either drunkards or heretics, and possibly both. This official stand on witches became part of Church law. This was all very well, except that it tied the Church's hands when it came to trying to ferret out whatever witches were left over from pagan days. The problem became acute when fourteenth-century Dominican inquisitors began to mumble about the enclaves of witches they'd found in the Pyrenees and the southern Alps. The Church could do nothing – witches officially did not exist. Dominican inquisitors, however, always found it hard to keep calm when they'd discovered something that needed to be tied to a stake and set alight. For some hundred years prior to the late fifteenth century they agitated to be allowed to initiate a witch hunt. For 100 years the Vatican sent word back that, sorry, they weren't allowed to do a thing because canon law quite categorically stated that witches didn't exist and it would be very embarrassing if the Church had to admit that it had made a mistake. Then, in the 1480s, the Dominicans had a brainwave. They had not found the old sort of witch – which everyone agreed legally did not exist – they had found a *new* sort! Vatican officials almost wept with collective relief, and sent out the word that Europeans everywhere were to hunt down the 'new sort' of witch as if their souls depended on it. The era of the witch hunts had begun.

The resurgence and renewal in our belief in Arthur has followed much the same pattern. To our relief, we have found a 'new sort' of Arthur, one that we are allowed to believe in (and one we don't have to learn uncomfortable moral lessons from). The major obstacle in our quest to believe in Arthur has been that we know that the Arthur of medieval romance, chronicle and legend is a historical impossibility. Imagine the excitement, then, when word went out that a 'new sort' of Arthur had been theorised. This Arthur lived in the late fifth or early sixth century, and was no heroic king (although he was patently a courageous leader), but a *dux bellorum*, a leader of battles. He probably had a fellowship of warriors, but not of the glorious (and now rather silly) Round Table collection of knights. His influence extended over much of Britain (or at least of the south, or perhaps the north), but he was not a European conqueror. He was a man who briefly united British resistance against the Saxons, who sallied forth from wooden-walled hill forts instead of a pinnacled Camelot, who undoubtedly belched, dressed in furs and leather wraps, and used no more enchantment than today's bus drivers. Suitably revised, Arthur has become a man we can believe in. With relief we can now see that medieval people had it all wrong. Somehow the *real* Arthur had been warped by medieval romance and ambitious chroniclers, and it is no wonder that sixteenth-century scholars rejected that version. It has been left to modern scientific and historical inquiry to establish the real Arthur.

This Dark Age leader of battles has been suitably popularised through fiction, particularly fantasy fiction. Writers like Rosemary Sutcliff, Mary Stewart and, to a lesser extent, Marion Zimmer Bradley, have constructed fictional Arthurs. Gone (or partly gone) are the romantic imports. Gone are the world-conquering campaigns (politically sensitive in this most politically sensitive of ages). Gone is the overt magic (although there are still prophesying and visionary dreams aplenty). Ostensibly having thrown out all the medieval trash, writers can now reinsert paganism into what was once an entirely Christian legend: our new Arthur is more often than not a pagan or a luke-warm Christian at best. Attacks on the missionary Dark Age Christian Church are also 'in': today's novels are as likely to portray the major conflict of the Arthurian story as that between a malicious and invasive Christian Church and the more passive and nature-worshipping pagan faiths.

The fantasy genre's treatment of Arthur has proved enormously influential: even though what they offer is fiction, people somehow believe them to be presenting a truth. It is a false perception and a worse hope. These novels have little historical plausibility because none of these authors can drag themselves away from the French romance tradition. Any one of Sutcliff, Stewart or Bradley can argue that they have stuck to ancient chronicle (or even Welsh oral) tradition, but all three nevertheless use hefty doses of French romance imports, thoroughly confusing the issue. Particularly, none of them can resist using the Guenevere/Lancelot affair, or the

Lancelot character which occurs nowhere in Arthurian literature before the twelfth century – roughly 600 years after the existence of a historical Arthur. No reader should believe fantasy presents a believable historical reality: for example, as magical and as romantic as Bradley's *The Mists of Avalon* is, it is nevertheless an amazing and often unworkable hotchpotch of late medieval constructs that simply cannot be squashed back into a Dark Age setting. Nevertheless, many people choose to believe it. This is, after all, the 'new' Arthur (however, with all the attributes of the 'old Arthur'). *The Mists of Avalon* has become a cult book, and to some degree, the 'cult bible' of many neo-pagan groups. Unfortunately, much of the modern belief in Arthur is as based on as much misapprehension and misinformation as the medieval cult was.

It is perfectly plausible that an historic figure called Arthur may have once existed, but *nothing* of the legends can be attributed to him. Even though people want to believe in a historic Dark Age warlord, we cannot attribute to him the glory and charisma and enchantment of popular legend. It simply doesn't work, and it cannot work. And yet we insist on doing it: Arthur the warlord must be, in his own way, as splendid and as mighty as the legendary chivalric king. Whatever we mouth about historical realities, we still need Arthur the saviour, Arthur the secular Christ, Arthur the resurrection man. We are still held in the grip of a thousand years of legend.

THE ARTHURIAN CULT: ARTHUR AS RESURRECTION MAN

The twentieth-century world has changed remarkably from the sometimes naive, but always self-confident Victorian age. Since 1914 the western world has suffered several blows to its self-confidence: world wars, recessions and the sense that societies everywhere are running out of control. Technology and businessmen are taking over, and the individual has become a mere pawn in a cruel game. At the same time that people feel society is hurtling out of their control, new scholarship has suggested that perhaps Arthur had existed after all. Once people have been allowed to believe in Arthur as a plausible historic figure, then myth has sidled in the open window, and the hope has begun to build that maybe, *maybe*, Arthur might also exist as saviour. After all, what do we know of Celtic mysticism? Celtic magic? As the millennium approaches, there is a small, but growing, sentiment among many people that Arthur is about to make a return. Arthur the saviour enjoys more popularity now than he has done since the medieval era.

Most societies in the world have at least one un-dead figure; western society has a plethora of them. Jesus Christ is the prime heroic figure – crucified, resurrected and with an agenda that includes an eventual return to this world. The Arthurian myth has two un-dead-and-bound-to-return-soon figures: Merlin and Arthur. Both almost but not quite died. Merlin had his power stolen by Nimue, and was subsequently trapped in a crystal cave where he sleeps to this day. Arthur, mortally wounded by Mordred, was carried off by between one to four enchantresses to Avalon to be lost in the mists of time and legend.

The belief that Arthur lies in undead sleep and will one day return appears fairly early in medieval belief. If we assume for the moment that there was a historic Arthur, then the legend about his eventual return could well have been started by the British, who hid his grave from the Saxons. The British would, firstly, not have wanted the Saxons to desecrate his grave (as Henry II and Edward I were later to do), and, secondly, they would have wanted the Saxons to remain unsure enough about Arthur's death to plan for his possible reappearance. Welsh traditional culture does not exactly have a strong 'undead' component as far as Arthur is concerned, but there is some ambiguity about his grave: the thirteenth-century *Black Book of Carmarthen* notes that the grave of Arthur was a mystery (or a wonder) to the world.[1] In

1 There is no obvious Monmouth influence in this manuscript, but it may have been affected by contemporary Welsh belief in Arthur's imminent return.

the twelfth and thirteenth centuries the Welsh believed very strongly that Arthur would come back to lead them to victory against the English; many of them believed that Arthur had been reborn as Arthur, son of Geoffrey of Anjou and Constance of Brittany (this Arthur was a grandson of Henry II who sponsored the late-twelfth-century search for Arthur's grave in order to prove him dead once and for all). In the first decades of the 1100s William of Malmesbury noted that Arthur's grave had never been found, while a man called Hermann de Tournai, passing through England, wrote in his itinerary that in 1113 he'd seen Cornishmen fighting over whether or not Arthur was dead, and added that Bretons fought with the French over the same issue.[2] Geoffrey of Monmouth left the matter of Arthur's death open: he ended merely by describing Arthur being carried off to Avalon 'so that his wounds might be attended to'. It might not be explicit, but Monmouth implicitly states that Arthur did not die.

There was no holding back popular belief at this point, although several medieval chroniclers tried their best to dispel it. Henry of Huntingdon, who completed a chronicle history of England that just pre-dated Monmouth, subsequently supplemented his work in 1139 by adding a very convincing description of Arthur's certain death to try and counter his countrymen's cherished conviction that Arthur did not die and would one day return. At the close of the twelfth century William of Newburgh criticised Geoffrey of Monmouth for yielding to the popular belief that Arthur had been carried off to Avalon to heal his wounds:

> *It is clear that everything which that man [Geoffrey] took care to write about Arthur . . . was invented in part by himself, in part by others, either because of an unbridled love of lying or even a desire to please the Britons, most of whom are reputed to be so stupid that even now they are said to be awaiting Arthur's return and will not bear to hear that he is dead.*

Newburgh, cited in Lappert ,

'Malory's Treatment of the Legend of Arthur's Survival', pp. 357–358

---

2 Peter Korrel, *An Arthurian Triangle* (E.J. Brill, 1984), p. 70.

Further, Newburgh wrote,

> *And it is to be noted that he relates that afterward Arthur, who was mortally wounded in the battle, having settled the succession, departed for the healing of his wounds to that island called Avalon which the British tales invent. Because of his fear of the Britons he does not dare say that he [Arthur] is dead whom the truly stupid Britons expect to return.*
>
> Newburgh, in Lappert, p. 358

In the early thirteenth century Layamon mentioned on several occasions the Britons' belief that Arthur would return one day: 'The Britons believe that he will come, and they look to when he will return to this land as he promised before going hence.'[3] The suggestion here is that people now believed Arthur promised to return. No longer *might* he return, Arthur said he would come back, and so he shall. At some points Layamon obviously tried to distance himself from commonly held beliefs, but at the end of his Arthurian section he wrote: 'No man nor woman can say truly more of Arthur except what the prophet Merlin himself once said – and his words are true: an Arthur will yet come to help the English.'[4] *An* Arthur: a small distinction, but an important one. For whatever reason, whether the Church wanted all popular belief in Arthur quashed (as they wanted all popular belief in witches quashed), or because all these (clerical) chroniclers were serious scholars who could not believe in the fabulous tales circulating in contemporary society, medieval chronicle after medieval chronicle tried to set the record straight and negate Monmouth's influence. Arthur had died on the battlefield of his wounds, he hadn't been carried off to any mythical island, he lay in the care of no elf queen, and he most definitely wasn't coming back. None of their appeals to sense made any difference at all. The common crowd continued to hanker after their hero. Malory's mid-fifteenth-century treatment of the legend continues the belief in

3 Layamon, p. 215.
4 Layamon, p. 254.

Arthur's return, although he was (perhaps deliberately) mildly ambiguous: the four queens who pick up the dying Arthur in their barge subsequently transport him to his grave. Nevertheless, Malory continues,

> *some men say in many parts of England that King Arthur is not dead,*
> *but had by the will of Our Lord Jesu into another place; and men say he*
> *shall come again, and he shall win the holy cross. I will not say it shall*
> *be so, but rather I will say, here in this world he changed his life. But*
> *many men say that there is written upon his tomb this verse: HIC JACET*
> *ARTHURUS, REX QUONDAM REXQUE FUTURIS.[5]*

> Malory, *Morte Darthur*, Vol. 2, Book XXI, Chap. 7

The popular medieval belief in Arthur's (imminent) return is obvious in the grave hunts of the period. Both Henry II and Edward I hoped to dispel popular Welsh hopes that an undead Arthur would return by digging up and displaying his bones. As attached to the Arthurian myth as the English kings were, doubtless they all hoped fervently that Arthur was not going to return during *their* reign (imagine the chaos). The first of the Tudor monarchs, Henry VII, tried to manipulate the timing of Arthur's return by naming his first-born son after the legendary hero: *Arthur is reborn, and he is my son.* Unfortunately – and ironically – Prince Arthur died in his mid-teens, the same age that the legendary Arthur assumed the throne. Legend will not be outsmarted.

But it can be discredited. From the sixteenth century the popularity of the myth, as well as any widespread belief in Arthur's imminent return, faded until it was almost non-existent. The nineteenth-century Arthuriana mania likewise did not include any sustained belief that Arthur was likely to stage a return from the grave. But attitudes are quietly changing. Today, a literal belief in Arthur's resurrection is rare, but it does occur. One group in Britain believes strongly that Arthur's return is imminent. It claims to know

---

5 Here lies Arthur, the once and future king.

the site of his grave (but conveniently refuses to tell where it is). The fact that the group is currently fighting tooth and nail to stop the building of a particular motorway strongly suggests the road works are scheduled to plough right through Arthur's interment site. The hero's return from his un-dead existence could prove worse than futile if he was splattered across an English motorway by a furniture removal truck the instant he stepped forth. Others have already claimed Arthur's identity for their own. 'Arthur Pendragon' has made an appearance in the British courts in recent times, petitioning for the return of his sword Excalibur (seized by the police). For the curious, there is a current web site for the reborn Arthur Pendragon at http://arthurpendragon.ukonline.co.uk. The reborn Guenevere currently lives in Vancouver, Canada, another in Montana, and several others are located at discrete intervals along the eastern seaboard of the United States (should the reborn Arthur wish it, he could summon quite a harem); Arthur's war-band thunders forth at a score of medieval recreations about the world each year; while there are so many stern-visaged Merlins about, waving their magical staves, that any hope for world peace is under dismal threat from the inept wizard. Arthur reborn is a growth industry for today's mass market.

While relatively few people believe literally in Arthur's return (or believe that they are the reborn Arthur), a sense that *an* Arthur might return (to use Layamon's phrase) is quite strong. More people are embracing paganism, variant forms of witchcraft,[6] and investigating a variety of spiritual paths than ever before. This is surely a sign of hope that people are prepared to investigate different paths and values. But a belief in the return of *an* Arthur is – if we construct the who and the what of Arthur from medieval legend (as most people do) – a sad delusion.

---

6 Those groups basing themselves on the witchcraft the Dominican inquisitors dreamed up over a flagon of Rhenish Red are doing nothing but promoting a desperate medieval clerical fantasy.

The Arthur we want to believe in is a fabrication of the medieval mind, even though the legend has its roots in Celtic oral culture. The legend was designed by its medieval authors not only as an entertaining tale, but also as a moral parable to demonstrate what can happen to even the greatest when they become corrupted with sin and pride. Arthur has never been an unstained hero, and he must always bear the larger proportion of the blame for his betrayal and fall. In medieval legend, Arthur was a European conqueror and the builder of the most magnificent court in Christendom, but he was also a cuckolded husband, an indecisive man and a cruelly proud and ambitious monarch. Even in Welsh tales Arthur makes appearances as a ravager and a hopeful rapist. Yet, despite the way Arthur has been depicted, popular culture has always demanded he be a hero. For 1,000 years folk belief and need have portrayed Arthur as a saviour, a secular Christ, but the legends from which he strides portray him as a human being, as flawed as any one of us, and an example of what can occur to man, family and realm when sin and pride consume common sense and virtue. Arthur as saviour has never been more than an intangible dream, a hope for the directionless and an icon to be manipulated for the gain of the powerful. The historic man was lost 1,500 years ago and will never again be found. Arthur the man lies forgotten within the damp earth of Britain, the reality of his mouldering bones of little use to a society requiring a hero and a saviour.

Appendix A

GEOFFREY OF MONMOUTH'S STORY OF ARTHUR

Monmouth begins his *History of the Kings of Britain* with the settlement of the island of Albion (Britain) by Trojans led by Brutus, the great-grandson of Aeneas; until this time only a few giants had populated the island. Brutus' successors continue to rule the island, among them Leir, who attempts to divide his kingdom among his three daughters (Goneril, Regan and Cordelia) according to how much they profess to love him.[1] Kings come and go until the Romans invade Britain. The Romans pull out of Britain in the early fifth century as the Roman Empire comes under increasing attack from Germanic tribes, and the British are left to fend for themselves. The island is invaded by many tribes, among them the savage Picts. In an attempt to cope with these invasions, the British (and Christian) King Vortigern invites in pagan Saxon mercenaries. (Vortigern had seized the throne by arranging the murder of the previous king, Constans.)

It is a mistake. The Saxons come in ever-increasing numbers, settling large areas of Britain. Eventually, Vortigern tries to repel the Saxons, but fails. Driven down into Wales, the king asks his magicians what he can do. They advise him to build a large tower to act as a final fortress if the rest of Britain falls to the Saxons. However, whenever

1 The story formed the basis for Shakespeare's drama *King Lear*.

stonemasons and engineers try to construct this tower, it keeps collapsing. Again summoning his magicians, Vortigern is told he must find a boy without a father, kill him, and sprinkle his blood over the foundation stones of the tower.

Thus enters the magician Merlin into the tale. Born of a mother who claimed she had been impregnated by a spirit lover, Merlin is disinclined to be butchered, and tells Vortigern that under the foundations of the tower, deep in the earth, he will find a pool, at the bottom of which rest two large stones in which two dragons sleep. The stones having been exposed, Merlin begins to prophesy, detailing the fortunes of Britain to the end of time, and in the process describing the rise of Arthur, the 'Boar of Cornwall'. He also tells Vortigern that the younger brothers of Constans, Aurelius Ambrosius and Uther Pendragon, currently in exile overseas, will return, burn Vortigern for his sins, and seize the nation. Aurelius will take the throne, Uther will succeed him, and finally Uther's son, Arthur, the Boar of Cornwall, will take the throne.

As foretold, Aurelius invades and seizes the throne. During Aurelius' reign, Merlin persuads him to bring the Giants' Ring from Mt Killaraus in Ireland and to set it up in Britain as Aurelius' memorial (Stonehenge). When Uther succeeds as king, he holds a council in London at Eastertide one year. Gorlois, the duke of Cornwall attends, with his beautiful wife, Ygerna. Uther is filled with lust for Ygerna. This causes bad blood, and eventual war, between Uther and Gorlois. Ygerna is barricaded in the duke's castle at Tintagel, and, desperate, Uther summons Merlin for aid. With the aid of strange drugs, Merlin changes Uther into the likeness of Gorlois, by which device Uther is able to make his way into Tintagel and bed Ygerna. Meanwhile, Gorlois is killed in battle. Uther marries Ygerna, and they have a son named Arthur and a girl named Anna.

The Saxons, who had been driven out by Aurelius, now re-invade. Uther keeps them at bay, but is killed by poison. Arthur succeeds to the throne of Britain at the age of fifteen.

Arthur might only be young, but he is so courageous and

generous, and filled with such innate goodness, he is immediately loved by all. Arthur decides to drive back the Saxons (led by Colgrin), so that with the wealth he would acquire from his victory over the enemy, he might reward his own retainers. Allied with King Hoel of Brittany, who brings 15,000 men to Arthur's aid, and Duke Cador of Cornwall, Arthur decimates the Saxons at Lincoln and then drives them to Caledon Wood. The Saxons, starving, bargain with Arthur for their release. They agree to leave behind all their gold and silver, and to take a boat for Germany in exchange for their lives.

The deal is made, hostages are taken (to ensure the Saxons keep their side of the bargain) and the Saxons set sail. Treacherously, however, they repent of their bargain and instead turn back for Britain, landing on the coast near Totnes where they commence to ravage the countryside and lay siege to the town of Bath. Furious, Arthur slaughters the hostages and then, armed with his sword Caliburn, which had been crafted on the Island of Avalon, Arthur leads his force into desperate battle with the Saxons. Many die. Arthur fights with splendid courage, personally killing 470 men.

The Saxons flee. Arthur sends Duke Cador after them with 15,000 men, while he takes the remainder of his force back to relieve King Hoel, who has been besieged by Picts and Scots. Eventually Cador reunites with Arthur and Hoel, and they chase the Scots and Picts into Moray, to Loch Lomond, where the Scots and Picts seek refuge on sixty islands in the centre of the lake. Arthur lays siege to them by boat, reducing them to starvation. Then the King of Ireland invades with his force, hoping to relieve the Scots and Picts. Arthur cuts them to pieces and forces them to return home. Turning his attention back to the Scots and Picts, he eventually gives way to their pleas for mercy and pardons them.

As Britain is in a state of some disorder after the recent wars, Arthur sets about rebuilding churches and restoring various minor kings to their heritages. Finally, when he has restored the island to its dignity he marries a woman called Guenevere, descended of a noble Roman family and the most beautiful woman in Britain.

The next summer, Arthur sails to Ireland and conquers it in short order. Then he sails to Iceland, and defeats that realm. At this point, the kings of Gotland and the Orkneys give Arthur their homage and fealty of their own free will rather than suffer invasion themselves.

Arthur returns to Britain and reigns there in peace and goodwill for twelve years. He establishes a splendid court and a code of courtliness. His fame spreads, and kings of far countries tremble at the thought that they might be invaded and subdued by Arthur. This fact is reported to Arthur. Instantly he conceives of the idea to conquer all of Europe. He sails to Norway, and subdues that country, as well as Denmark. This conquest is accomplished through acts of unparalleled savagery: most towns are burned, the population decimated. Arthur then sails to Gaul (France), which is under the jurisdiction of Tribune Frollo, ruling in the name of the Emperor Leo. Again, Arthur proceeds to lay waste to the countryside. Frollo cannot defeat him, so he flees to Paris. Arthur lays siege to the city, and Frollo suggests they settle the matter through single combat. Arthur and Frollo meet outside the city gates, and after a dreadful battle, Arthur finally slays Frollo with Caliburn.

Arthur sends King Hoel on a campaign of further terror through the remaining hostile provinces of Gaul and, once they have been subdued, Arthur rules in Gaul for nine years. He gives Normandy to his cup-bearer, Bedevere, and the province of Anjou to his seneschal, Kay. Finally he returns to Britain.

There he takes up residence in the City of Legions, on the River Usk in Glamorganshire,[2] near the Severn Sea. At Whitsun he holds a magnificent feast to which many kings, ecclesiastics and noble men and women come. There is a ceremony at which Arthur is again crowned as king, Guenevere by his side. Afterwards there is music and entertainment and feasting and games held in the meadows beyond the city. On the fourth day of celebrations, Arthur rewards all his retainers with rich gifts and posts.

While he is so employed, twelve men come as envoys, bearing a letter from Lucius, Procurator of the Republic [of Rome]. This letter berates Arthur for not paying Britain's tribute to Rome, and for seizing Gaul

2 Now Monmouthshire.

and various other territories, and it orders Arthur to appear in Rome. If he fails to do so, the letter says, then Rome would again invade Britain. Arthur withdraws to a high tower with sundry of his nobles to consider what has to be done. Cador, Duke of Cornwall, makes a speech urging Arthur to war against Rome, his reason being that his knights are now more used to dicing than warring and they need some battle experience. Many other nobles back him: war with Rome, they cry!

Arthur then speaks, saying that nothing that was acquired by force and violence could be held legally by anyone (this is in reference to Rome's initial invasion of Britain hundreds of years previously). In fact, Arthur believes that Rome owes Britain tribute (a reference to the fact that, in Geoffrey's version of history, the Britons had invaded and captured Rome in the very distant past). Arthur is backed by several kings present, and the meeting decides to make war on Rome. All the nobles and kings send Arthur men (the total strength of Arthur's eventual force was 273,000, although Monmouth only adds it up to 180,000).

News of preparations spread, and Rome builds up its own army from men from the Orient to a total of 400,000, and they march towards Britain.

Arthur sails for Europe, leaving Britain in the hands of his nephew, Mordred and wife Queen Guenevere. While on ship, Arthur dreams of a battle between a bear and a dragon, the dragon finally victorious. He lands his fleet at Barfleur and, while waiting for his army to establish itself, hears of a giant that has snatched the niece of King Hoel and fled with her to the top of Mont-Saint-Michel. Arthur, accompanied by Bedevere and Kay, sets out to rescue her. Bedevere climbs the hill first, where he finds the girl's old nurse, who informs him that the girl has died (a virtuous self-sacrifice to avoid rape) and that the giant has raped her (the nurse). Bedevere creeps back down the hill and tells Arthur what has happened. Arthur climbs the hill and in a fearful battle, slays the giant (Arthur then, in triumph, recounts the story of another giant, Retho, he had slain some years previously).

Having defeated the giant, Arthur then turns his attention to the Romans. There follows a series of confrontations, in which Arthur's nephew, Gawain, and Bedevere feature. Eventually the Britons win a decisive battle, although it is with much loss of life (Bedevere and Kay being the worst casualties).

Arthur winters in Gaul, and the following summer makes preparations to march on Rome itself when news comes that Mordred and Guenevere are living adulterously, and Mordred has placed the crown on his own head and has allied himself with the Saxons, Scots, Picts and Irish. Forced to abandon his attack on Rome, Arthur sails for Britain and meets Mordred and his army at Richborough. There ensues great slaughter. Mordred is driven from the battlefield and seeks shelter in Winchester. Guenevere, hearing of this news, weeps and flees home to the City of Legions where she joins a nunnery and takes vows of celibacy.

Arthur lays siege to the city of Winchester, and defeats Mordred in battle again. Again Mordred escapes, fleeing to Cornwall, Arthur in close pursuit. The two meet again in battle at the River Camblam.[3] Many thousands die, along with Mordred himself. Although the victor, Arthur is mortally wounded and is carried off to the Isle of Avalon so that his wounds might be attended to. He hands over the crown of Britain to his cousin Constantine, the son of Cador, Duke of Cornwall. It is the year 542.

---

3 Camelford on the River Camel. Local legend has it that Arthur met Mordred in a meadow by the aptly named Slaughter Bridge.

Appendix B
KEY TEXTS

Geoffrey of Monmouth's History of the Kings of Britain (1136)

See Appendix A and Chapter 2. His influence has been dramatic, shaping the core legend which Malory so successfully married with elements of the French romance tradition.

Layamon's Brut (1250s to 1280s)

As with all 'sober medieval chronicles', Layamon's *Brut* is as much lively poem as it is hard history. No medieval chronicler felt burdened by the modern historian's curse of footnotes, bibliography, and stolid but workmanlike prose designed to bore first year university students; their aim was rather to excite the imagination of the reader or listener. Layamon was possibly rather more poet than chronicler, but that simply makes his chronicle treatment of Monmouth's Arthurian story the more joyous to read. He stuck fairly consistently to Monmouth's version of events, although he did alter or add some things (for example, the brief passage on the Round Table which he probably got from Wace – a poet who translated Monmouth from Latin to French). Like Malmesbury in the decade before Monmouth, Layamon mentioned the contemporary popularity of King Arthur. The Britons 'boast' of the Round Table, they tell many 'falsehoods' about Arthur in order to glorify his memory, and bards sing Arthur's praises throughout the country. Clearly Arthurian enthusiasm was still in full flight in thirteenth-century England. More interestingly, Layamon also stated that the Britons fervently believe that Arthur did not die, and would one day return to once more lead his country to glory. Layamon furthered whatever superstition the common folk appended to Arthur's death by couching it in supernatural terms himself:

> [Arthur speaks on his death bed] 'I will go to Avalon, to the fairest of maidens, the beautiful elf Queen Argante. She will make my wounds whole, heal me completely with a potion to drink, and afterwards I will return to my kingdom to dwell in joy with the Britons.'
>
> Even with these words, two beautiful women approached in a small boat floating on the waves. They took Arthur, placed him gently in the boat, and went forth. Thus was Merlin's prophecy that there would be countless sorrow at Arthur's going forth fulfilled. The Britons believe that Arthur is still alive and dwells in Avalon with the fairest of all elves. They still look to when Arthur will return. No man nor woman can say truly more of Arthur except what the prophet Merlin himself once said – and his words are true: an Arthur will yet come to help the English.
>
> Layamon, *Brut*, Bzdyl, transl., p. 254

Available in modern translation by Donald G. Bzdyl, Layamon's chronicle is the best of all the medieval Arthurian chronicles, certainly surpassing Monmouth's in the musicality of language and beauty of imagery.

The Stanzaic Le Morte Arthur (1350s)

The two poems – the stanzaic *Le Morte Arthur* and the alliterative *Morte Arthure* – have similar names, but little else in common.[1] Separated by

---

1 Stanzaic and alliterative refer to the different styles of verse. The alliterative style, common to Old English, underwent a revival in the north-west of England in the fourteenth century.

some 100 years, they represent the differing traditions of the Arthurian legend. The *Le Morte Arthur* closely follows the French romance tradition, and in fact is a condensed version of the French prose *Mort Artu*. Like many other medieval works, *Le Morte Arthur* concentrates on the final part of Arthur's reign when the Arthur/Mordred and Guenevere/Lancelot tragedies approach their zenith. Again, like most French, or French-inspired romances, Arthur is presented as a somewhat impotent (in the sense of strength of character) and weak-willed king, particularly as regards the affair between his wife and Lancelot: Arthur never quite seems to know how to cope with it, and listens to all the wrong advice. How many times does Arthur sentence Guenevere to 'bale-fire' burning, and how many times must Lancelot ride in at the last moment to save her? The poem continues past the death of Arthur to conclude with the eventual deaths of Guenevere and Lancelot. While both love each other, and on the death of Arthur are free to marry, Guenevere is appalled at the loss of life that she and Lancelot have indirectly caused. She spurns her lover and takes a nun's veil. Lancelot, too, seeks consolation in religion, spending seven years as a priest before he dies. A fortnight later Guenevere also dies and is buried at Arthur's side: the final tragedy is that Guenevere is laid to rest with Arthur, not Lancelot, the man she really loved.

The *Alliterative* Morte Arthure (*1440s*)

The alliterative *Morte Arthure* hails from mid-fifteenth century northern England and is based very much on the English chronicle tradition (Monmouth, Wace, Layamon and Mannyng), although it has also been influenced by the French romances. Again, like the stanzaic *Le Morte Arthur*, the poem concentrates on the final years of Arthur's reign: his fateful European expedition of conquest, during which time Mordred launches his treachery at home, seizes the throne and takes Guenevere as a defacto wife (with the additional detail of two children being produced of this union). Arthur hurries home, meets Mordred in battle, Mordred is killed and Arthur receives his mortal wound. Although the Mordred/Guenevere theme differs slightly from usual (specifically in their two children, who Arthur orders killed when he is on his death bed), the alliterative *Morte Arthure* follows the usual chronicle tradition in having Mordred as Arthur's nephew, not his son by incest. The poem also contains another unusual point: in several versions of the Arthur legend, generally those influenced by the French romances, Arthur's sister, Morgan le Fay, steals his sword, Excalibur, to give to her lover, Accolon. In the alliterative *Morte Arthure* Guenevere is the one who apparently (although this is not explicitly stated) presents Mordred with Arthur's ceremonial sword, Clarent (this is used to dub earls and dukes, while Arthur uses Excalibur in battle): only she knows where Arthur had hidden Clarent in the armoury. As with Layamon (and with Wace), in this version Guenevere and Mordred are lovers before Arthur leaves the country, his departure presenting them with the perfect opportunity for the ultimate treason.

Rather like Monmouth, the *Morte Arthure* largely lays the blame for Arthur's fall on the king himself: vaunting pride and ambition are seen to be his undoing. Mordred is merely the instrument for Arthur's demise, rather than the actual cause. Arthur has destroyed too many sinless men and ravaged too many lands, delighting in vainglory: 'Take shrift for your shame and shape up for death!' advises a sage when interpreting Arthur's dream in which Fortune attacks and mutilates him.

Sir Thomas Malory's Morte Darthur (1450s to 1480s)

Very little is known about Sir Thomas Malory. He was born some time in the early fifteenth century, succeeding to his ancestral estates in 1433 or 1435. His younger life was marked with violence and lawlessness; various reports have charged him with robbery, attempted murder, rape and extortion. Whatever the case, Malory appears to have spent a fair part of his life in and out of prison (in itself not unusual in such politically turbulent times; Malory's various incarcerations may not have been for criminal behaviour). Malory apparently wrote *Morte Darthur* while imprisoned in Newgate where he would have had ample time to read the French romances and English chronicles from which he composed his version of the Arthurian tale.

William Caxton ensured *Morte Darthur*'s popularity. He took the manuscript, thoroughly re-edited it (taking Malory's eight separate romances and collating them as one work of twenty-one books) and printed it in 1485. The original Malory romances, collated eventually as the one work, were: *The Tale of King Arthur, The Tale of King Arthur and the Emperor Lucius, The Tale of Sir Lancelot du Lake, The Tale of Sir Gareth of Orkney, The Book of Sir Tristram de Lyones, The Tale of the Sangreal, The Book of Sir Launcelot and Queen Guinevere* and *The Most Piteous Tale of the Morte Arthur Saunz Guerdon.*

Malory's Arthur is continually praised as the best king in the world, yet his actions belie the praise. Arthur is often unseated in tournaments or jousts, he is a little too eager to slaughter his foes, Merlin and Nimue constantly have to save him, in a fit of cruelty Arthur condemns many children to death in his efforts to kill Mordred (reminiscent of Herod's actions in trying to kill Christ and yet even less justifiable, for Arthur well knows where to look for his newborn nemesis), he is just a little petulant when confronted with Lancelot's undoubted superiority on the field of war (and in the king's bed, come to that), and, finally, Arthur is downright stupid to leave Mordred in charge of the realm when he's been warned time and time again that Mordred will prove his downfall. Guenevere is treated reasonably sympathetically. If she is disloyal to her somewhat dim-witted and cool husband, well, who can blame her? Lancelot also comes out of the *Morte Darthur* well, being portrayed not only as an excellent knight, but also as a deeply spiritual man (if a little too given to fits of madness) and one committed to Guenevere.

In the final analysis, Malory left no lack of causes for Arthur's downfall: Guenevere and Lancelot blame themselves, the Orkney boys have their part to play, Arthur's sin in begetting Mordred obviously cannot be overlooked (although Malory does not make much of it), Arthur must shoulder some of the blame himself, and his sister Morgan le Fay's constant attempts to destabilise Arthur's grip on power also contribute. Even the entire English people have to bow their heads in guilt. If they hadn't been so obsessed with 'new-fangleness' in backing Mordred, then Arthur might yet have lived out his life in something faintly resembling glory and peace.

Thomas Hughes' The Misfortunes of Arthur (*1588*)

The temptation to use Spencer's *Fairy Queen* as a representative text for the Elizabethan age proved, in the end, no great temptation at all. The *Fairy Queen*, although considered one of the great Elizabethan works, does not fulfil one of the prime criteria of a key text for this study: it does not retell the core legend. Instead, it is a mass of often confusing allegory, and would serve no purpose here. However, the obscure drama, *The Misfortunes of Arthur*, is ideal. It was probably performed only once, on 28th February 1588, by the Gray's Inn Gentlemen before Queen Elizabeth herself, before sinking into obscurity. There are two likely reasons for such obscurity – one, the drama is generally a dreadful piece of writing,[2] and, two, its political sensitiveness. The play claims that Arthur failed because of his father's adultery with Ygerna: Ygerna's husband, Gorlois, curses the Pendragon dynasty in the opening prologue. Uther's sexual sin is repeated in Arthur, who sleeps with his twin sister, Anne, begetting Mordred, his usurper and murderer. The shame of Uther's lusts is visited on the entire dynasty, resulting in its extinction.

2 'My heart doth throb, my liver boils,' Guenevere exclaims when she hears of
   Arthur's imminent return from the continent to discover her treachery with
   Mordred, 'somewhat my mind portends, uncertain what, but whatsoever, it's
   huge.' Act I, sc. ii.

This was an extraordinary scenario to present before the aging Elizabeth (in her mid-fifties), the last of the Tudor dynasty. The entire plot must have vividly recalled in everyone's minds the sexual exploits (doubtless no-one's mind dared embrace the word 'sin') of Elizabeth's father, Henry VIII, who begat her on his first wife's lady-in-waiting. Could Elizabeth's childlessness and the inevitable extinction of her dynasty be seen as the result of the sin of her father? No-one in the audience on that cold February night could have missed the allusion, and to my mind it is remarkable the play was presented in the first instance.

The Misfortunes of Arthur is a basic re-telling of the core legend, in sometimes execrable verse, concentrating on the theme of sexual sin rebounding on later ages. Here, Uther's sexual misconduct is made as much of as Arthur's. Lancelot is entirely absent, and Guenevere sins only with Mordred.

Alfred Lord Tennyson's Idylls of the Kings (1859–85)

Tennyson wrote two versions of the *Idylls*. The first effort, published in 1859, contained only four idylls, or books: *Enid, Vivien, Elaine* and *Guinevere*. All four appeared in 1857 in a private edition, and appended to each of the titles were the words *The True* or *The False*. These first *Idylls* were very much a contrast between the true and false woman: Enid and Elaine the true, Vivien and Guinevere the false. As 'false' women, Vivien and Guinevere excel: the nasty, wily harlot Vivien deceives Merlin, the 'womanly weak' Guinevere deceives (and destroys) a nation. Through all four idylls, Arthur remains the 'blameless king'. As in the later, expanded idylls, Tennyson's strident morality sometimes overwhelms.

Over the next decade and more Tennyson revised these four idylls into twelve: *The Coming of Arthur, Gareth and Lynette, The Marriage of Geraint* (1872) (part of the old 1859 *Enid*); *Geraint and Enid* (1872) (also part of the old 1859 *Enid*); *Balin and Balan* (written about 1870 and published in 1885); *Merlin and Vivien; Lancelot and Elaine; The Holy Grail; Pelleas and Ettare; The Last Tournament* (1872); *Guinevere* (1859); and *The Passing of Arthur* (1869), which was a revision of an early poem, *Morte d'Arthure*, written partly to work through his grief for, and immortalise, his friend Arthur Hallam. Only a few of the idylls which directly deal with Arthur and his household will concern us here.

Tennyson generally depicts Arthur as totally blameless, or 'stainless', as he sometimes calls him. Even the manner of Arthur's conception is carefully rearranged so that the lustful Uther marries a 'stainless' Ygerna before bedding her. Mordred no longer is Arthur's son, but his nephew by his sister, Bellicent, and King Lot. Thus all sexual sin (save on the part of the 'false' and 'stained' women) is removed from Arthur's immediate vicinity. Again and again Tennyson drives home his contention that Arthur is blameless – Arthur even manages a magnanimous forgiveness of Guenevere as she grovels at his feet in the nunnery (only Tennyson could have rearranged events so that Arthur manages to stop off and confront Guenevere on his way to the Final Battle) which increases Guenevere's sin and brightens yet further Arthur's 'stainlessness'.

Reaction against Tennyson's depiction of the Arthurian legend, particularly of the female characters in it, occurred during his own lifetime, but none of this affected the huge popularity and influence of his *Idylls*.

T.H. White's The Once and Future King (*late 1930s to mid-1940s*)

Terence Hanbury White wrote the five books that comprise *The Once and Future King* between the late 1930s and the mid-1940s and the influence of World War Two is readily apparent in the books' strong anti-war message. To class the five books – *The Sword in the Stone, The*

Witch in the Wood, The Ill-Made Knight, The Candle in the Wind and *The Book of Merlyn* – as children's literature is too simplistic. Unfortunately, many people never get past the first book, *The Sword in the Stone*, which has a rather typical 1930's '*Boys Own* adventure' feel to it, and perseverance is needed to get through some of the passages (which could possibly be criticised as a trifle self-indulgent). This initial reaction to the cycle is a shame, because the following books are well worth the read. Perhaps because of the approaching European war, or perhaps because of his own fascination with Malory and the inevitability of Arthur's betrayal and death, White imbues the final four books with a sense of approaching doom that never becomes overwhelming, or overly tragic (a considerable achievement), but rather unites the books.

White generally sticks to the core legend, although there are a few variations. *The Sword in the Stone* relates the childhood of Arthur (or Wart, as he is called here). Merlin guides Arthur through an education that includes his transformation into various beasts of the land, sea and air so that he might the better learn the important lessons of life. *The Witch in the Wood* begins just as Arthur has ascended the throne and largely concerns itself, as the title suggests, with Morgause, Queen of Lothian and Orkney, Arthur's incestuous begetting upon her of Mordred, and the sense of wrong-doing that binds Morgause's four sons. *The Ill-Made Knight* concerns itself with the introduction of the Guenevere and Lancelot theme. It is a large book, often told from Lancelot's perspective, and it covers the greater part of Arthur's reign. It also clearly defines the elements of the looming tragedy, Lancelot's internal turmoil reflecting the inner turmoil of the kingdom. *The Candle in the Wind* propels all the characters towards the final doom which White has introduced in the previous two books. Guenevere and Lancelot's love, Mordred's treachery, Morgause's four boys and Arthur's inability to cope with everything at once inevitably have their tragic way. It ends with a wretched Arthur awaiting the last battle. The final *Book of Merlyn* encapsulates the lessons taught in the first four books. Arthur sits alone in his tent. Merlin appears to him again, and Arthur is magicked underground to re-meet many of the animals he knew in his childhood, and to relearn many of the same lessons. This book does not so much contribute to, or retell, the core Arthurian legend, as provide the author with a chance to drive home his anti-war message.

Throughout the books, Arthur struggles to promote the idea that Might is not Right. He endeavours to build a kingdom on the principle that Might should only be used for Right: that bad must be turned into good for the benefit of all. Of course, Arthur's attempts fail, doomed by the flawed nature of humankind and the very court of Camelot itself. Worse, in his attempts to build the perfect state and to deny the principle that Might is Right, Arthur inevitably finds himself immersed in war and blood. Was it better to die for the most golden of principles, or to live under a tyrant? Arthur touches the precious, but he can never grasp it.

The Once and Future King, strongly influenced by Malory, uses all the key ingredients of the French romance tradition. Arthur is undone from the start, he begets his own doom and the tragedy is compounded (and driven forward) by the poignant love between Guenevere and Lancelot. Of all key texts, this is the most moralistic. White had a message and he wasted no opportunity to make it patently clear – to the point of adding an entire fifth book to make sure everyone understood what he was trying to say in the first four.

The Once and Future King was one of the last of the Malory-inspired chivalric romances (although the authors I discuss below have also obviously been influenced by Malory) to appear as a modern novel. Within only a few years of *The Once and Future King*'s publication as a complete work (1958), the Arthurian legend had been reinterpreted to present Arthur and his troubles as an 'almost' genuinely historical figure.

Rosemary Sutcliff's Sword at Sunset (*1963*)

Sutcliff's *Sword at Sunset* was one of the first, and for many years, one of the most successful, attempts to reinterpret Arthur as a possible

Dark Age historical figure. Gone are the knights in shining armour, gone is the world conqueror, gone is the entire Round Table and bevy of knights chasing dragon and skirt in equal amounts. This is the *real* Arthur (according to the blurb on the back cover), called here Artos, son of Uther from a servant girl, nephew of Ambrosius, war-leader and reluctant king trying to save a Dark Age Britain from the incursions of sundry invaders. Like White, the sense of doom in this book is its unifying theme, but Sutcliff's work has none of White's humour, and is oppressive in its joylessness. The background research is excellent – the detail of Dark Age life impressive – and the attempt clearly is to create a historic Arthur. Yet the widely accepted 'Malory-version' of the Arthurian legend forces all authors who attempt to put Arthur back into a genuine historical setting as a genuine historical figure to include the two French romance-inspired themes critical to Arthurian tragedy: the love affair between Guenevere and Lancelot and the incestuous conception of Mordred which results in tragedy. Ultimately, this destroys any historical credibility of the novel, but the current market demands both ingredients and no novelist can afford to leave them out. Sutcliff is no exception. The Guenevere/Lancelot love affair appears, although Sutcliff has changed the characters' names to the suitably British Guenhumara and Bedwyr respectively, while Mordred is back to the Medraut of the tenth-century *Annales Cambriae*. Again, following the French tradition, Arthur is eventually undone by the incestuous conception of Mordred on his own sister. While *Sword at Sunset* does not allow Arthur to succeed to the throne until he is in mid-life, it follows the core legend relatively closely.

Mary Stewart's The Crystal Cave, The Hollow Hills, The Last Enchantment, The Wicked Day (*1970–83*)

Of all the modern 'historically-orientated' Arthurian novels, Stewart's are probably the best. The trilogy of *The Crystal Cave, The Hollow Hills* and *The Last Enchantment* is written from Merlin's perspective. These are 'gentle' novels, both in the sense of the time taken to move action forward (while never allowing the pace to lag) and in the treatment of the 'inevitable doom because of incest' theme. Inevitable doom there must be, but Stewart still allows her characters joy and beauty and laughter. As with Sutcliff, the setting is a Dark Age Britain struggling to cope with the withdrawal of the Romans and sundry invasions. Also like Sutcliff's version, the Lancelot role is taken by Bedwyr. Likewise, Stewart's tale follows the core legend closely although the trilogy ends when Merlin withdraws from an active role at Arthur's court, at the same time as Morgause brings the youth Mordred to Camelot.

In *The Wicked Day* Stewart dares to write a novel from Mordred's point of view. I say 'dares', because of all the main characters in the Arthurian legend, Mordred is surely the most difficult to deal with sympathetically. Born in incest (admittedly not his fault, although he can never escape being 'a child of sin'), Mordred has striven in treachery for 1,000 years, sometimes in willing collusion with Guenevere, sometimes involving her against her will. Stewart's is one of the only works I am aware of which tries to deal sympathetically with Mordred. She does not excuse his treachery, but she does (not entirely successfully) try to put it in context: according to her interpretation, Mordred was Arthur's heir, Arthur had left Mordred in charge of the realm when he went fighting on the continent, Mordred heard false reports of Arthur's death and naturally (for any medieval prince) seized the throne to ensure his own succession.

Marion Zimmer Bradley's The Mists of Avalon (*1983*)

Bradley's *The Mists of Avalon* must surely be the most influential Arthurian novel of our time. First published in 1983, it remains at the top of the best-seller lists. Again, like the previous two authors,

Bradley puts her cast of characters back into a Dark Age setting in order to give them some historical believability, but she adds something a little different. An undercurrent to Sutcliff's and Stewart's work was the clash of pagan and Christian values. In Bradley's book this becomes one of the prime themes: if Avalon has been lost to us now, she suggests, it is partly the fault of the Christian Church. If Arthur fell, then that too was partly as a result of the Christian influence exerted on him by Guenevere (even though so much of the story is seen through the female characters' eyes, it is difficult to think of Bradley's work as feminist given her appalling depiction of Guenevere) and his own inability to counter it.

Bradley packs virtually every plot line and every character ever associated with the Arthurian legend into her massive book: she even manages to incorporate the Grail mystery, no small feat for a Dark Age setting. This is probably the major failing of the book: every French romance element imaginable has been stuffed back into a 'chronicle tradition' Dark Age Britain, and at times it grates.

Glossary

ACCOLON: son of King Uriens and lover of Morgan le Fay. He makes an ill-fated attempt on Arthur's life.

AGRAVAIN: son of Morgause and King Lot of Orkney. He actively plots against Lancelot and Guenevere.

ANNE: occasionally named as Arthur's sister, instead of Morgan le Fay or Morgause.

ARTHUR: High King of Britain, son of Uther Pendragon and Ygerna of Cornwall.

AUREALIS AMBROSIUS: High King of Britain, brother to Uther Pendragon and uncle of Arthur.

AVALON: an enchanted island where Morgan le Fay takes Arthur to be healed of the injuries sustained in his deadly combat with Mordred. Closely identified with Glastonbury Tor which in medieval times was surrounded by marsh.

BEDWYR: a knight of Arthur's court and one of Arthur's closest friends.

BELLICENT: Arthur's sister in Tennyson's *Idylls*.

BORS: a knight of the Round Table

CADOR: usually a Duke of Cornwall during Arthur's reign, sometimes a son of Gorlois from an earlier marriage. Occasionally Cador is named as Arthur's successor.

CALIBURN: Arthur's sword; also known in the French romance tradition as Excalibur.

CAMELOT: the legendary site of Arthur's court.

CLARENT: sometimes Arthur's ceremonial sword in medieval English literature.

COLGRIN: a Saxon chief in Monmouth's version of the legend.

CONSTANTINE: High King of Britain, father of Aurealis Ambrosius and Uther, and grandfather of Arthur.

ECTOR: foster father of Arthur, raising him from babyhood to the age of fifteen when Merlin takes Arthur to court to claim his heritage.

ELAINE: sometimes the daughter of King Pelles, sometimes from Ascalot, she is the seducer (and sometimes wife) of Lancelot, and mother of his son, Galahad.

EXCALIBUR: Arthur's sword in the French romance tradition; also known as Caliburn in the English chronicles.

FROLLO: tribune of Gaul (France) in Monmouth's story of Arthur.

GAHERIS: son of Queen Morgause and King Lot of Orkney and one of the knights of Arthur's court.

GALAHAD: son of Lancelot and the Lady Elaine. Because of his chastity Galahad is the purest knight in the world and is thus the only one to attain and experience the Holy Grail during the great Quest.

GARETH: the youngest son of Queen Morgause and King Lot of Orkney, and one of the favourite knights of Arthur's court. He is killed by Lancelot.

GAUL: a Dark Age name for France.

GAWAIN: eldest son of Queen Morgause and King Lot of Orkney, and one of the principal knights at Arthur's court. He is one of Arthur's closest friends.

GORLOIS: Duke of Cornwall, husband of Ygerna.

GRAIL, HOLY: originally an enchanted vessel that, via the French romance tradition, came to be identified with the cup from the Last Supper. The Quest for the Holy Grail takes the knights of the Round Table on many an adventure.

GUENEVERE: Queen of Britain. In the English tradition she comes of Roman stock and is bred in the Duke of Cornwall's court, in the French tradition she is the daughter of King Leodegan and brings the Round Table to Arthur as her dowry when she becomes his wife. Lover of Mordred in the English tradition, and of Lancelot in the French tradition.

HEMISON: a lover of Morgan le Fay.

HOEL: a British king, and ally of King Arthur.

HYLIN: Arthur's (or Artos') daughter in Sutcliff's *Sword at Sunset*.

JOYOUS GARDE: Lancelot's castle.

KAY: son of Sir Ector and foster brother to Arthur. Kay is Arthur's seneschal and one of his closest friends.

KEVIN: holder of the office of Merlin in Bradley's *The Mists of Avalon*.

LANCELOT: the 'best knight in the world' and Queen Guenevere's lover in the French romance tradition.

LAMORAK: knight, and lover of Queen Morgause of Orkney. He is eventually murdered by one or more of her sons.

LEODEGAN: King. Father of Guenevere.

LLACHEU: a son of Arthur in Welsh legend.

LOT: King of Orkney. Sometime political foe of Arthur, and husband to his sister, Morgause.

MADOR: a knight of the Round Table. Mador's brother was poisoned at a banquet hosted by Guenevere.

MELIAGAUNT: (or MELIAGAUNCE): a king who kidnaps Guenevere.

MELWAS: King of the Summer Country; kidnapper and ravisher of Guenevere.

MERLIN: wizard and prophet, protector of Arthur during the earlier part of the king's reign.

MORDRED: incestuous son of Arthur by one of his sisters (often Morgan le Fay).

MORGAN LE FAY: daughter of Ygerna and Gorlois of Cornwall, older half sister of Arthur, wife to King Uriens. In medieval French romances Morgan le Fay is often the mother of his son, Mordred. She is also the queen who carries Arthur off to Avalon to be healed of his wounds.

MORGAUSE: Queen of Orkney. Daughter of Ygerna, sister to Arthur and the mother of Arthur's son, Mordred, in many modern versions of the Arthurian legend. Morgause is wife to Lot of Orkney, and is mother of his four sons: Gawain, Gaheris, Agravain and Gareth. Morgause is murdered by one or more of her sons.

NIMUE: (or VIVIEN): Lady of the Lake. Enchantress and protector of Arthur, she trains with Merlin before seducing him and absorbing all his power.

PATRISE: a knight of the Round Table who died after eating poisoned fruit at a banquet hosted by Guenevere.

PINEL: a knight of the Round Table, and true murderer of Patrise.

TINTAGEL: Duke Gorlois' castle stronghold in Cornwall. Tintagel was an important port on the northern coastline of Cornwall.

TRISTRAM: knight of Arthur's court, and lover of Queen Isolte of Cornwall.

ULFIN: a man-servant to King Uther.

URIENS: King of North Wales, or sometimes of Rheged in northern Britain. Husband of Morgan le Fay, father of Uwain and Accolon.

UTHER PENDRAGON: High King of Britain after Aurealis Ambrosius, and father of Arthur.

UWAIN: son of King Uriens.

VORTIGERN: High King of Britain.

YGERNA: wife to Gorlois, Duke of Cornwall, then to Uther Pendragon. Mother of Morgan le Fay, Morgause and Arthur.

Bibliography
PRIMARY SOURCES[1]

Ascham, Roger, *The Scholemaster* (1570), in Dr Giles, ed. and transl., *The Whole Works of Roger Ascham* (London, 1864–65), III.

Aston, Ed., transl., *Manners, Laws, Customs* (London, 1611).

Bannerman, Anne, *The Prophecy of Merlin* (1802), The Camelot Project, University of Rochester.

Bede, *A History of the English Church and People* (731), Leo Sherley-Price, transl. (Penguin, 1982).

Boemus, J., *Manners, Laws, Customs* (London, 1611).

Bradley, Marion Zimmer, *The Mists of Avalon* (Sphere, 1983).

Brereton, Jane [Melissa], *Merlin: A Poem* (1735), The Camelot Project, University of Rochester.

Brut, or The Chronicles of England (a fifteenth-century translation of a French copy), Friedrich W.D. Brie, ed. (Early English Text Society, 1906), Part I.

Camden, William, *Remains Concerning Britain* (1605), (University of Toronto Press, 1984), R.D. Dunn, ed.

Carew, Richard, *The Survey of Cornwall* (London, 1602).

Cawein, Madison, *A Guinevere* (1907), The Camelot Project, University of Rochester.

Chretien de Troyes, *Cliges* (Online Medieval and Classical Library Release # 21).

———, *Erec et Enide* (Online Medieval and Classical Library Release # 21).

---

1 All the Camelot Project documents are available at http://www.lib.rochester.edu/camelot/mainmenu.htm, all Online Medieval and Classical Library documents at http://sunsite.berkeley.edu/OMACL/

_____, *Lancelot, or The Knight of the Cart* (Online Medieval and Classical Library Release # 21).

_____, *Yvain, or The Knight with the Lion* (Online Medieval and Classical Library Release # 21).

Clapham, John, *The Historie of Great Britannie* (London, 1606).

The Cokwolds Dance (c. 1600), in W. Carew Hazlitt, ed., *Remains of the Early Popular Poetry of England* (London, 1864), vol. I.

The Death of King Arthur (La Mort le Roi Artu) (1230–35) (Penguin, 1971), James Cable, transl.

Drayton, Michael, *The Poly-Obion A Chorographicall Description of Great Britain* (London, 1622), Part I.

Field, Eugene, *The Vision of the Holy Grail* (1905), The Camelot Project, University of Rochester.

Fuller, Thomas, *The History of the Worthies of England* (London, 1840), vol. I, P. Austin Nuttall, ed.

Geoffrey of Monmouth, *The History of the Kings of Britain* (1136) (Penguin, 1966), Lewis Thorpe, transl.

Gerald of Wales, *The Journey Through Wales & The Description of Wales* (Penguin, 1978).

Gildas, *The Ruin of Britain* (c. 540), Michael Winterbottom, transl. and ed. (Phillimore, 1978).

The Greene Knight (c. 1650), The Camelot Project, University of Rochester, Thomas Hahn, ed., originally published in *Sir Gawain: Eleven Romances and Tales*, Kalamazoo, Michigan: Western Michigan University for TEAMS (1995).

H.C.C., *Guinevere to Lancelot* (1869), The Camelot Project, University of Rochester.

Hardyng, John, *The Chronicle* (London, 1543).

Hawker, Robert S., *The Doom-Well of St. Madon* (1869), The Camelot Project, University of Rochester.

_____, *The Quest of the Sangraal* (1864), The Camelot Project, University of Rochester.

_____, *Queen Guennivar's Round* (1869), The Camelot Project, University of Rochester.

Higden, Ranulph, *Polychronicon, with the English Translations of John*

Trevisa and of an Unknown Writer of the Fifteenth Century (c. 1250) (Longman, 1874), vol. V, Rev. Joseph Rawson Lumby, ed.

High History of the Holy Graal (c. 1500–1525), The Camelot Project, University of Rochester.

Hovey, Richard, *The Last Love of Gawaine* (1898), The Camelot Project, University of Rochester.

_____, *The Quest of Merlin, A Prelude* (1891), The Camelot Project, University of Rochester.

Hughes, Thomas et al, *The Misfortunes of Arthur* (1588).

Huntingdon, Henry of, *The Chronicle of Henry of Huntingdon* (London, 1853), Thomas Forester, transl. and ed.

Jewett, Sophie, *The Dwarf's Quest: A Ballad* (1905), The Camelot Project, University of Rochester.

Jonson, Ben, *The Speeches at Prince Henries Barriers* (1610), The Camelot Project, University of Rochester.

The Knightly Tale of Gologras and Gawain (1508), The Camelot Project, University of Rochester, Thomas Hahn, ed., originally published in *Sir Gawain: Eleven Romances and Tales*, Kalamazoo, Michigan: Western Michigan University for TEAMS (1995).

Lancelot of the Laik (c. 1450–1500), The Camelot Project, University of Rochester, Alan Lupack, ed., originally published in *Lancelot of the Laik and Sir Tristrem*, Kalamazoo, Michigan: Western Michigan University for TEAMS (1994).

Langtoft, Pierre de, *The Chronicle* (c. 1275–1300) (Longmans, 1866), Thomas Wright, ed.

Layamon, *Brut: A History of the Britons* (c. 1205) (Medieval and Renaissance Texts, vol. 65, 1989), Donald G. Bzdyl, transl.

Leigh, Joseph, *Illustrations of the Fulfilment of the Prediction of Merlin Occasioned by the Late Outrageous Attack of the British Ship of War The Leopard, on the American Frigate Chesapeake, and the Measures Taken by the President, Supported by the Citizens Theron* (1807), The Camelot Project, University of Rochester.

Leland, John, *The Assertion of King Arthure* (1544), in Christopher Middleton, *The Famous Historie of Chinon of England* (Early English Text Society, 1925).

Lewis, Charlton Miner, *Gawayne and the Green Knight: A Fairy Tale* (1903), The Camelot Project, University of Rochester.

Lloyd, Richard, *A Brief Discourse of the Most Renowned Actes and Right Valiant Conquests of those Puisant Princes called the Nine Worthies* (London, 1584).

Lowell, James Russell, *The Vision of Sir Launfal* (1848), The Camelot Project, University of Rochester.

The Mabinogion (Everyman, 1991), Gwyn Jones and Thomas Jones, transl.

Malory, Sir Thomas, *Morte Darthur* (1485), Electronic Text Centre, University of Virginia, http://etext.lib.virginia.edu/

Mannyng, Robert, of Brunne, *The Chronicle* (c. 1338) (Medieval and Renaissance Texts, vol. 153, 1996), Idelle Sullens, ed. Translations used in this book are my own.

Morris, William, *The Chapel in Lyoness* (1858), The Camelot Project, University of Rochester.

———, *The Defence of Guenevere* (1858), The Camelot Project, University of Rochester.

———, *King Arthur's Tomb* (1858), The Camelot Project, University of Rochester.

———, *Near Avalon* (1858), The Camelot Project, University of Rochester.

———, *Sir Galahad, a Christmas Mystery* (1858), The Camelot Project, University of Rochester.

Morte Arthure, Le Morte Arthur (Stanzaic 1350s, Alliterative 1440s) (Penguin, 1988), Brian Stone, transl.

Nennius, *History of the Britons* (c. 796–801) (London, 1938), A.W. Wade-Evans, ed.

Newbolt, Henry, *Mordred, a Tragedy* (1895), The Camelot Project, University of Rochester.

Percy, Bishop Thomas, *Reliques of Ancient English Poetry, Consisting of Old Heroic Ballads, Songs and Other Pieces of Our Earlier Poets, Together With Some Few of Later Date* (1765). The Arthurian poems are available at The Camelot Project, University of Rochester.

The Prophesy of Merlin (c. 1300s) (Bodley manuscript), The Camelot Project, University of Rochester, James M. Dean, ed., originally published in *Medieval English Political Writings*, Kalamazoo, Michigan: Western Michigan University for TEAMS (1996).

The Prophesy of Merlin (c. 1300s) (Dublin manuscript), The Camelot Project, University of Rochester, James M. Dean, ed., originally published in *Medieval English Political Writings*, Kalamazoo, Michigan: Western Michigan University for TEAMS (1996).

The Prophesy of Merlin (c. 1300s) (Magdalene College manuscript), The Camelot Project, University of Rochester, James M. Dean, ed., originally published in *Medieval English Political Writings*, Kalamazoo, Michigan: Western Michigan University for TEAMS (1996).

Risdon, Tristram, *The Chorographical Description or Survey of the County of Devon* (London, 1811).

Robinson, Edwin Arlington, *Merlin* (1917), The Camelot Project, University of Rochester.

Rossetti, Dante Gabriel, *God's Graal* (1848), The Camelot Project, University of Rochester.

Seeger, Alan, *Vivien* (1916), The Camelot Project, University of Rochester.

Simcox, George Augustus, *The Farewell of Ganore* (1869), The Camelot Project, University of Rochester.

Sir Gawain and the Carle of Carlisle (c. 1400), The Camelot Project, University of Rochester, Thomas Hahn, ed., originally published in *Sir Gawain: Eleven Romances and Tales*, Kalamazoo, Michigan: Western Michigan University for TEAMS (1995).

Sneyd, Ralph de Tunstall, *Vivian and Merlin* (1929), The Camelot Project, University of Rochester.

The Song of Courtesy (1859), The Camelot Project, University of Rochester.

Spenser, Edmund, *The Fairy Queen* (1590), Douglas Brooks-Davies, ed. (Everyman, 1996).

Stewart, Mary, *The Crystal Cave* (Heinemann & Octopus, 1978).

———, *The Hollow Hills* (Heinemann & Octopus, 1978).

———, *The Last Enchantment* (Coronet, 1980).

———, *The Wicked Day* (Hodder & Stoughton, 1983).

Saint Louis' Advice to his Son (Internet Medieval Source Book).[2]

---

2 Found at http://www.fordham.edu/halsall/sbook.html

Sutcliff, Rosemary, *Sword at Sunset* (1963) (Tor, 1987).

Swift, Jonathan, *A Famous Prediction of Merlin, The British Wizard, Written Above a Thousand Years Ago, And Relating to the Year 1709 With Explanatory Notes By T.N. Philomath, Written in the Year 1709*, The Camelot Project, University of Rochester.

Teasdale, Sara, *Guenevere* (1911), The Camelot Project, University of Rochester.

Tennyson, Alfred Lord, first edition of *The Idylls of the King (The True or The False)*, first printed 1859, in *Poems of Tennyson* (Oxford University Press, 1913).

————, *The Idylls of the King in Twelve Books*, in *The Complete Works of Alfred Lord Tennyson* (Macmillan, 1898).

————, *Sir Launcelot and Queen Guinevere, a Fragment* (1842), The Camelot Project, University of Rochester.

Trask, Katrine, *Kathanal* (1892), The Camelot Project, University of Rochester.

The Turke and Sir Gawain (c. 1500), The Camelot Project, University of Rochester, Thomas Hahn, ed., originally published in *Sir Gawain: Eleven Romances and Tales*, Kalamazoo, Michigan: Western Michigan University for TEAMS (1995).

Vergil, Polydore, *The English History* (1534), (Camden Society, 1846), vol. I, Sir Henry Ellis, ed.

The Wedding of Sir Gawain and Dame Ragnelle (c. 1500s), The Camelot Project, University of Rochester, Thomas Hahn, ed., originally published in *Sir Gawain: Eleven Romances and Tales*, Kalamazoo, Michigan: Western Michigan University for TEAMS (1995).

White, T.H., *The Once and Future King* (1958) (Voyager, 1977).

William of Malmesbury, *Chronicle of the Kings of England* (London, 1847), J.A. Giles, ed.

Wilmer, Lambert A., *Merlin, A Drama in Three Acts* (1827), The Camelot Project, University of Rochester.

Yeats, W.B., *Time and the Witch Vivien* (1889), The Camelot Project, University of Rochester.

Ywain and Gawain (c. 1400), The Camelot Project, University of Rochester, Mary Flowers Braswell, ed., originally published in *Sir*

Perceval of Galles and Ywain and Gawain, Kalamazoo, Michigan: Western Michigan University for TEAMS (1995).

SECONDARY SOURCES

Adams, Alison, Armel H. Diverres, Karen Stern, Kenneth Varty, eds, *The Changing Face of Arthurian Romance*, Arthurian Studies XVI (Boydell, 1986).

Alcock, Leslie, *Arthur's Britain* (Penguin, 1990).

———, 'By South Cadbury is that Camelot,' *Antiquity*, XLI (1967), pp. 50–53.

———, *'By South Cadbury is that Camelot . . .' The Excavation of Cadbury Castle 1966–70* (Thames & Hudson, 1972).

———, *Cadbury Castle, Somerset. The Early Medieval Archaeology* (University of Wales Press, 1995).

———, 'Excavations at South Cadbury Castle, 1967. A Summary Report', *The Antiquities Journal*, vol. XLVIII, part I (1968), pp. 6–17.

———, 'A Reconnaissance Excavation at South Cadbury Castle, Somerset, 1966', *The Antiquities Journal*, vol. XLVII, part I (1967), pp. 70–76.

App, August J., A.M., *Lancelot in English Literature, His Rôle and Character*, PhD Thesis, Catholic University of America (1929).

Ashe, Geoffrey and Norris J. Lacy, eds, *The Arthurian Handbook*, second edition (Garland, 1997).

Bogdanow, Fanni, 'The Evolution of the Theme of the Fall of Arthur's Kingdom,' in Edward Donald Kennedy, ed., *King Arthur, A Casebook* (Garland, 1996), pp. 91–103.

Brewer, Derek, 'The Presentation of the Character of Lancelot', in Lori J. Walters, ed., *Lancelot and Guinevere, A Casebook* (Garland, 1996), pp. 3–27.

Brewer, Elisabeth, 'The Figure of Guenevere in Modern Drama and Fiction', in Thelma S. Fenster, ed., *Arthurian Women, A Casebook* (Garland, 1996), pp. 307–18.

Brown, Arthur C.L., 'Arthur's Loss of Queen and Kingdom', *Speculum*, vol. XV, no. 1 (January, 1940), pp. 3–11.

Carley, James P., 'Polydore Vergil and John Leland on King Arthur: The Battle of the Books', in Edward Donald Kennedy, ed., *King Arthur, A Casebook* (Garland, 1996), pp. 185–204.

Darrah, John, *Paganism in Arthurian Romance* (Brewer, 1994).

Ellis, Deborah S., 'Balin, Mordred and Malory's Idea of Treachery', *English Studies*, vol. 68 (1987), pp. 66–74.

Fries, Maureen, 'Female Heroes, Heroines, and Counter-Heroes', in Thelma S. Fenster, ed., *Arthurian Women, A Casebook* (Garland, 1996), pp. 59–73.

Fry, Carrol L., 'The Goddess Ascending: Feminist Neo-Pagan Witchcraft in Marian Zimmer Bradley's Novels', *Journal of Popular Culture*, vol. 27 (1993), pp. 67–80.

Gilbert, Elliot L., 'The Female King: Tennyson's Arthurian Apocalypse', *Publications of the Modern Language Association*, vol. 98 (1983), pp. 863–878.

Gladwin, Frances, *The Depiction of King Arthur in the Historia Regnum Britanniae by Geoffrey of Monmouth*, Honours thesis, LaTrobe University of Northern Victoria (1992).

Guerin, M. Victoria, *The Fall of Kings and Princes, Structure and Destruction in Arthurian Tragedy* (Stanford University Press, 1995).

Harty, Kevin J., 'Film Treatments of the Legend of King Arthur', in Valerie M. Lagorio and Mildred Leake Day, eds, *King Arthur Through the Ages* (New York, 1990), vol. II, pp. 278–90.

Hill, Susan, 'Recovering Malory's Guenevere', in Lori J. Walters, ed., *Lancelot and Guinevere: A Casebook* (Garland, 1996), pp. 267–77.

Holbrook, Sue Ellen, 'Nymue, The Chief Lady of the Lake, in Malory's *Morte Darthur*', in Thelma S. Fenster, ed., *Arthurian Women, A Casebook* (Garland, 1996), pp. 171–190.

Kennedy, Elspeth, 'Failure in Arthurian Romance', *Medium Aevum*, vol. 60, no. 1 (1991), pp. 16–32.

Korrel, Peter, *An Arthurian Triangle. A Study of the Origin, Development and Characterization of Arthur, Guinevere and Mordred* (E.J. Brill, 1984).

Lappert, Stephen F., 'Malory's Treatment of the Legend of Arthur's Survival', *Modern Language Quarterly*, vol. 36, no. 4 (December, 1975), pp. 354–68.

Loomis, Roger Sherman, ed., *Arthurian Literature in the Middle Ages* (Clarendon, 1959).

_____, *The Grail, From Celtic Myth to Christian Symbol* (University of Wales Press, 1963).

_____, 'Morgain la Fée in Oral Tradition', *Studies in Medieval Literature* (Burt Franklin, 1970), pp. 3–33.

MacBain, Danielle Morgan, 'The Tristramization of Malory's Lancelot', *English Studies*, vol. 74 (1993), pp. 57–65.

Matthews, Caitlín, *Arthur and the Sovereignty of Britain: King and Goddess in the Mabinogion* (Arkana, 1989).

Matthews, John, 'Merlin in Modern Fiction', in R.J. Stewart, *The Book of Merlin* (Blanford Press, 1987), pp. 87–106.

Morris, Rosemary, *The Character of King Arthur in Medieval Literature*, Arthurian Studies IV (Brewer, 1982).

Parsons, John Carmi, 'The Second Exhumation of King Arthur's Remains at Glastonbury, 19 April 1278', in James P. Carley and Felicity Riddy, eds, *Arthurian Literature XII* (Brewer, 1993), pp. 173–77.

Radford, C.A. Ralegh, 'Tintagel: The Castle and Celtic Monastery Interim Report', *The Antiquities Journal*, XV, no. 4 (1935), pp. 401–19.

Rider, Jeff, 'The Fictional Margin: The Merlin of the *Brut*', *Modern Philology*, vol. 87 (1989), pp. 1–12.

Rosenberg, John D., 'Tennyson and the Passing of Arthur', in Christopher Baswell and William Sharper, eds, *The Passing of Arthur, New Essays in Arthurian Tradition* (Garland, 1988), pp. 221–34.

Samples, Susan, 'Guinevere, A Re-Appraisal', in Lori J. Walters, ed., *Lancelot and Guinevere, A Casebook* (Garland, 1996), pp. 219–228.

Staines, David, *Tennyson's Camelot. The Idylls of the King and its Medieval Sources* (Wilfrid Laurier University Press, 1982).

Starr, Nathan Comfort, *King Arthur Today. The Arthurian Legend in English and American Literature 1901–1953* (University of Florida Press, 1954).

Thomas, Charles, 'Are These Walls Camelot?', *Antiquity*, XLIII, no. 169 (March 1969), pp. 27–30.

Thompson, Raymond H., 'Conceptions of King Arthur in the Twentieth Century', in Edward Donald Kennedy, ed., *King Arthur, A Casebook* (Garland, 1996), pp. 299–311.

_____, *The Return From Avalon. A Study of the Arthurian Legend in Modern Fiction* (Greenwood Press, 1985).

Whitehouse, Ken, 'Stand Up For England', *This England* (Spring, 1998), p. 41.

Juliet Marillier
Daughter of the Forest

BOOK ONE OF THE SEVENWATERS TRILOGY

The seven of us are as the parts of one body. If we are torn asunder, it may seem as if there is no tomorrow for us. But like pools in the same stream, we must meet and part and meet again. We belong to the flow of the lake and to the deep beating heart of the forest.

Lord Colum of Sevenwaters is blessed with seven children: Liam, a natural leader; Diarmid with his passion for adventure; twins Cormack and Conor each with a different calling; rebellious Finbar grown old before his time by his gift of Sight; and the young compassionate Padriac.

But it is Sorcha, the seventh child and only daughter, too young to have known her mother, who alone is destined to defend her family and protect her land from the Britons and the clan known as Northwoods. For her father has been bewitched by Lady Oonagh and her brothers bound by a spell that only Sorcha can lift.

Exiled from Sevenwaters and cast out into the forest and beyond, Sorcha falls into the hands of the enemy. Now she is torn between the life she has always known and a love that only comes once.

Catherine Jinks
The Notary

*'I told you,' said Gaillard, upon being pressed once more for information,
'all I know is that he was slain and found by his scribe. And that his
genitals were gone.'*
'Gone!' I exclaimed.
'Not there. Vanished.'
'Somebody stole them?'
'A nun,' Othon remarked, unleashing a shout of laughter.

Raymond Maillot is a lustful young notary who prefers wine, women and
song to the pursuit of professional renown. But when he's employed by
Father Amiel, a sober Dominican monk charged with investigating a
particularly shocking murder, his life begins to change.

Now Raymond is torn between his taste for irresponsible pleasures and
his desire to find refuge in the church. His journey of self-discovery,
however, begins with a severed penis.

The Notary by award-winning writer Catherine Jinks is a tantalisingly
cryptic tale of dismemberment, debauchery and demonic visitation in
fourteenth-century France.

Praise for Catherine Jinks

'. . . queen of narrative drive'
THE SUNDAY AGE

'Jinks . . . deserves cult status'
VOGUE

Jack Whyte
The Skystone

THE CAMULOD CHRONICLES

We all know the story – how Arthur pulled the sword from the stone, how Camelot came to be, and the power struggles that ultimately destroyed Arthur's dreams. But what of the time before Arthur? What were the forces that helped create him?

And how did the legend really come to pass?

Before the time of Arthur and Camelot, Britain had become a dark and deadly place, savaged by warring factions of Picts, Celts, and invading Saxons. The Roman citizens who had lived there for generations were suddenly faced with a deadly choice. Should they leave and take up residence in a Roman world that was corrupt and utterly foreign? Or stay and face the madness that would surely ensue when the Roman legions – Britain's last bastion of safety for the civilised – leave? For two Romans, Publius Varrus and his friend Caius Britannicus, there can be only one answer. They will stay, try to preserve what is best of Roman life, and create a new culture out of the wreckage. In doing so, they will plant the seeds of the legend.

'An extraordinary story, totally original, and clearly there is a lot more excitement to come in the upcoming volumes.'
ROSAMUNDE PILCHER

'Jack Whyte is a master storyteller . . . Whyte breathes life into the Arthurian myths by weaving the reality of history into them.'
TONY HILLERMAN

'From the building blocks of history and the mortar of reality, Jack Whyte has built Arthur's world and showed us the bone beneath the flesh of the legend.'
DIANA GABALDON

Jack Whyte
The Singing Sword

THE CAMULOD CHRONICLES

The legions have departed. The last vestiges of Roman authority are gone and a thriving colony that has lasted for more than four hundred years is poised on the brink of destruction.

Publius Varrus and Caius Britannicus are two Romans who choose to stay, choose to fight for their adopted land. They will build a hill-top fort that will withstand the onslaughts of the barbarians who seek to plunder Britain's wealth.

Out of their struggles a new Britain and a new people will emerge – Britons who are a carefully crafted alloy, a tempered fusion of Roman and Celtic greatness.

And one thing more . . .

These two men are great-grandfathers to the man known as Arthur, King of the Britons, and their actions will help shape a nation . . . and forge the sword known as Excalibur.

'Whyte breathes life into the Arthurian myths by weaving the reality of history into them. The first volume has left me eagerly awaiting the forthcoming sequels.'
TONY HILLERMAN

'Perhaps not since the early 1970s, with Mary Stewart's *The Crystal Cave* and *The Hollow Hills*, have the Roman Empire and the Arthurian legends been intertwined with as much skill and authenticity.'
PUBLISHERS WEEKLY